Motherhood and Disability

Motherhood and Disability

Children and Choices

Ora Prilleltensky
Peabody College
Vanderbilt University, USA

First published 2004 by
PALGRAVE MACMILLAN
Houndmills, Basingstoke, Hampshire RG21 6XS and
175 Fifth Avenue, New York, N. Y. 10010
Companies and representatives throughout the world

PALGRAVE MACMILLAN is the global academic imprint of the Palgrave
Macmillan division of St. Martin's Press, LLC and of Palgrave Macmillan Ltd.
Macmillan® is a registered trademark in the United States, United Kingdom
and other countries. Palgrave is a registered trademark in the European
Union and other countries.

ISBN 1–4039–0495–2 hardback

This book is printed on paper suitable for recycling and made from fully
managed and sustained forest sources.

A catalogue record for this book is available from the British Library.

Library of Congress Cataloging-in-Publication Data
Prilleltensky, Ora, 1959–
    Motherhood and disabillity : children and choices / Ora Prilleltensky.
        p. cm.
    Includes bibliographical references and index.
    ISBN 1–4039–0495–2 (cloth)
        1. Parents with disabilities. 2. Motherhood. 3. Women with disabilities.
I. Title.

HQ759.912.P75 2004
306.874′3′087–dc22   2004043875

10   9   8   7   6   5   4   3   2   1
13   12   11   10   09   08   07   06   05   04

Printed and bound in Great Britain by
Antony Rowe Ltd, Chippenham and Eastbourne

To Isaac and Matan,
The loves of my life

Contents

List of Tables

Acknowledgements

My husband Isaac Prilleltensky provided invaluable assistance and immeasurable support throughout the research and the book writing process. He actively encouraged me to embark on the book writing journey, participated in stimulating discussions, and provided insightful feedback on the many drafts he has read. In addition to his intellectual contribution to the book, Isaac kept me on track and kept things running at home. His love, patience and unwavering support are an ongoing source of strength. My son, Matan Prilleltensky, provided the inspiration for the book. Being Matan's mother is an important part of my identity and parenting him has been a continual source of joy and fulfillment. Matan's sharp intellect and spirited nature have made for some challenging parental moments, while his caring personality and passion for social justice make it all worthwhile. Also noteworthy are the contributions of my parents Rachel Rapoport and Nathan Rapoport. They are committed parents and grandparents who have contributed to our lives in multiple ways.

I am indebted to my study participants who shared personal life stories and thoughtful insights in focus groups and interviews. I was touched by their positive response to the study and by the generosity and openness that marked our interactions. I am also indebted to my editor Briar Towers and her assistant Jen Nelson of Palgrave Macmillan as well as to Shirley Tan and her staff at Expo Holdings. This study was supported by a scholarship from the Social Sciences and Humanities Research Council of Canada. Portions of two of my previous publications have been reproduced with permission from the following sources:

1. Prilleltensky, O. (2003). A ramp to motherhood: The experiences of mothers with physical disabilities. *Sexuality and Disability*, 21(1), 21–47.
2. Prilleltensky, O. (2004b). My child is not my carer: Mothers with physical disabilities and the well-being of children. *Disability and Society* (May 2004), http://www.tandf.co.uk.

Introduction

It was a bitterly cold winter morning in Winnipeg, the sort of morning you want to stay in a nice cosy bed. Of all days, my husband Isaac had an early morning meeting at work and could not take three-and-a-half year old Matan to pre-school. I would have to take him on my way to work. There was only one child to be dropped off and the pre-school was immediately next to our home. However, this seemingly simple task was not easy for me as a disabled mother. There was no parking right next to the building so I decided to walk Matan to pre-school and then come back for my car.

Matan was somewhat fussy that morning; young children have a special talent for taking their time when they sense parental pressure to hurry. We left later than we should have, I walked faster than I should have and promptly found myself on a cold, snow-covered ground. For a moment, I felt a mixture of irritation and concern. I was irritated with my husband who had to leave early, and with my young son who took his time. Befittingly, my knee-jerk reaction was: "We should have left earlier". However, Matan's question of "Is it my fault, mommy?" quickly dissipated my irritation. I assured him that he was in no way responsible and that we would find a solution. I was still on the ground, however, unable to get up unassisted. Concern took over. It was –25°C and there was no one in sight. Several cars past by; however, I doubted that they could see us behind the colossal snow banks that separated the sidewalk from the road. Matan extended his little arm: "I'll help you get up, mommy". I explained as best I could under the circumstances, that he is not strong enough to lift me up; only an adult can do that. I felt the chilling wind and noticed that Matan's face was getting red from the cold. Doing my best to stay calm, I told him to walk to the building and ask someone to come and help me. He took several steps forward and then backtracked. "But the door is too heavy for me, I won't be able to get it open". He was on the verge of tears; I did my best to reassure him as I considered my next step.

Another few cars passed by and the two of us waived at them frantically. I breathed a big sigh of relief when I noticed a car slowing down. I was further relieved when I saw a woman getting out; I always feel more comfortable getting this type of assistance from women. I still remember the petite and cheerful teacher who lifted me to my feet. I was impressed that a woman so small could be so powerful. We thanked her and ever so carefully, walked to the school. We came in, got Matan out of his boots and snowsuit and into the class. His teacher was very sympathetic and helped me comfort my clearly distressed child.

Along with my concern for Matan, I started to think about the meeting at work that I would undoubtedly be late for. I was a clinician in the school system and on that morning, had arranged to meet with a parent and with the school. The mother was highly reluctant to come to the school. It took some convincing on my part to get her to agree to the meeting. I had assured her that I would be there. I phoned the school to inform them that I would be late and slowly, carefully, walked to my car. Luckily, I had an extra set of car keys in my wallet, as my key holder was buried somewhere under a pile of snow. When I arrived at work, I was relieved to hear that the mother called to say that she would be late. After phoning the preschool to hear how Matan was doing, I sat down in the staff room for a cup of coffee. Finally, I had a few moments to think about the impact that this experience had on me. I could not deny that it had left me shaken.

Safely at home at the end of the day, Matan and I told dad what had happened. The distress no longer there, Matan was nonetheless bothered by the incident. "But I didn't help you up," he kept repeating. I sat him on my lap and explained that he did the best he could. Following my instructions as well as he did was the best help he could have provided. A little later, Matan came up to me with some of his little toy cars. He wanted to play what had happened. "One car goes by, and doesn't stop. Another car goes by and doesn't stop. Another car goes by and stops". He demonstrated with his cars as he spoke. Going along with his game, I said: "This must be the nice lady who came to help us". Matan raised his head from his cars and looked up at me with his big brown eyes. "No mommy, this is me when I'm big. I get out of the car and help you up".

This is a cherished story in our family, one that continues to move us despite the 13 years since the incident has taken place. Much has happened in our lives since that cold wintery day some 13 years ago. Matan is now 16 years old and taller than both his parents. He has since had many opportunities to fulfill his childhood dream of helping mommy up. In fact, I now fall rather frequently at home where I do not use my power wheelchair, and Matan lifts me to my feet gently and with ease. My husband Isaac has published a number of books and his academic positions have taken us to different places; I've completed a doctorate in counselling psychology and have worked as a practitioner and an academic; there have been changes in jobs, schools, even continents.

In addition to typical transitions that families go through, we are also responding to the progressive nature of my disability and to the need to continuously modify certain tasks and routines. Life isn't always easy and some days the disability is more of an issue for me than other days. Notwithstanding these challenges, I continuously strive for meaning, fulfilment, and a sense of well-being. For the most part, I am successful. I have a loving family, meaningful friendships and a fulfilling career that enables me to integrate my knowledge and experience of disability into my teaching and writing. I live in a disability-friendly house a block from Campus and am able to zoom with my power wheelchair from home to office to class. The combination of fulfilling relationships, meaningful work and near-optimal living and working conditions allow me to have a life that is deeply satisfying despite its hardships. I am aware that many of my disabled brothers and sisters face greater challenges in their quest for self-determination and control over their lives.

Being a mother is an important part of my identity and I'm forever grateful that I was able, together with my husband, to exercise the choice to have a child. It is not a decision that we made lightly; raising a child is a challenge for all parents and mothering with a disability has its added complexities. Nonetheless, raising Matan continues to enrich our lives even as we are less than two years away from the transition to College. The caring and compassion he demonstrated in early childhood has been a defining feature of who Matan is as a person.

This book is about the intersection of motherhood and physical disability. It is based on a study that explored the lived experience of women with physical disabilities, those who are mothers as well as those who are not mothers. It is couched within a social model understanding of disability that increasingly emphasizes the social, cultural, political, and economic determinants of lived experience (Gill, Kewman & Brannon, 2003). The study attempts to answer some of the following questions: What meaning does motherhood have for women who have physical disabilities? What is it like for them? What messages do they receive about themselves as women, with or without children? What barriers do they foresee and/or come across? How do they see their future in relation to motherhood? Utilizing a combination of in-depth interviews and focus groups, I explored these and other mothering-related issues from the vantage point of disabled women with and without children.

As I indicated above, this research stems from my own lived experience, and as such, it is personally meaningful and significant. However, choosing it as my area of inquiry goes beyond a personal interest and a search for meaning. It is based on my belief that it can contribute to women participating in the research, to other women with physical disabilities, and to knowledge in the areas of disability and motherhood. The intersection of these two entities, motherhood and disability, has received little attention from the academic community. Despite technological advancements and an ethos of diversity, disabled women are rarely thought of as mothers or in conjunction with motherhood. The rich discourse on motherhood, including that which is explicitly feminist, has not traditionally included women with disabilities. It is this space that is created between motherhood and disability that I wished to explore; it is the invisibility of these women that I wished to examine and interrupt; it is their (our) stories and dreams that I wished to present. My decision to include women with and without children in the study emanated from my belief that women who do not have children also have issues regarding motherhood, issues that need to be heard and explored. I see this as fundamentally important for women with physical disabilities who live in a society that often regards motherhood as synonymous with womanhood and counter-indicated with disability.

Although I included women with and without children in the study, I chose to be specific about the types of disabilities that would be represented. The study is thus limited to women with physical disabilities who have varying levels of mobility/limb impairment. Most of the participants are wheelchair users. At least seven different types of disabilities are represented in the study. Among them are Muscular Dystrophy, Cerebral Palsy, Spinal Cord Injury, Spina Bifida and Multiple Sclerosis. My reason for limiting the sample to women with physical disabilities is based on my belief that the particular issues and barriers they face in relation to motherhood may be inherently differ-ent from those faced by women with developmental or psychiatric disabilities. Whereas individuals with intellectual and physical impair-ments share some common experiences of discrimination, this should not obscure important distinctions that may be of relevance to policy and practice.

The book specifically explores the intersection of motherhood and physical disability and reviews literature that is specific to physical impairment. The importance of researching the lives of differently dis-abled women notwithstanding, I believe that lumping them together in one research study cannot do justice to either group. Nonetheless, I acknowledge that the book can be criticized for its focus on women with physical disabilities, women that typically participate in this type of research. As Carole Gill has noted, "a lot of research has relied on samples of those of us who are most visible: white heterosexual women with physical disabilities who are functioning in the world and who can speak or write without difficulty" (Gill, 1996a, p. 14). I admit that this description applies to my group of participants. It is my hope that future studies will focus on women with other types of disabilities and on the braiding of gender with other constructs of identity.

1
Disability: A Sociopolitical Construct

When I was diagnosed with Muscular Dystrophy at age 18, I struggled with how to incorporate the construct of disability into my sense of self. Initially, the slowly progressive adult-onset type of my impairment made it easy to conceal from others and minimize for myself. I couldn't run as fast as some of my peers and soon lost the ability to run altogether. However, as a young woman looking at herself through the male gaze, I took comfort in my "normal" appearance. It didn't occur to me then, or for years to come, that my disability was anything more than a personal problem, something to be accepted, reckoned with, and surmounted.

The disability as tragedy model was well entrenched in my psyche. If anything, my undergraduate training in Special Education only reinforced the stereotypical equation of disability with passivity, vulnerability and lack of agency. The prominent role that social barriers, marginalization and systematic exclusion play in the experience of disability came at a much later stage, as I began to engage with critical literature written from a disability rights perspective. Like many other disabled people around the world, this conceptualization of disability was meaningful and empowering. It has caused me to question the direct causal link between my deteriorating muscles and the barriers I was facing. As a white, middle class, well-educated woman with a non-disabled, well-educated spouse, it also accentuated the role of privilege in circumventing certain barriers and hence minimizing disability.

In this chapter I present a brief overview of some of the prevailing models of disability that have influenced my thinking. In the functional limitation model (also referred to as the medical model, the individual model and the personal tragedy model), disability is perceived as an attribute of individuals and thus requiring person-based solutions. Conversely, the British social model, the American minority model and other recent perspectives highlight social-structural barriers rooted in prejudice and discrimination. Notwithstanding some variability in their perception of disability and specific roadmap for change, they share a fundamental belief and adherence to societal transformation. These models build on the groundbreaking work of earlier disabled activists primarily in Britain and in the US. Improvement in the quality of life of millions of people with disabilities is largely due to these activists' tireless pursuit to shift the collective focus from impaired bodies and minds to societal failure to accommodate differences.

Critiques and debates from within and without the disability rights movement and the various feminist perspectives that have emerged in the past decade are challenging the field to move forward and are contributing to a richer discourse. This diverse body of literature provides the context for my research on motherhood and disability. It has further facilitated my attempts to identify and articulate a position on disability that is consistent with my own lived experience.

The functional limitation model of disability

We all stood around and watched her. She was sitting on a mat on the floor, clad in shorts and an undershirt, struggling to put a top on. Time and time again, she attempted, unsuccessfully, to pull the top over her head. In the fourth or fifth trial, she finally succeeded. Her treating therapist provided warm words of praise, and we all smiled. We were a group of first year Education students who were on a field visit to a school for children with Cerebral Palsy. She was a seven or eight year old girl in the midst of an occupational therapy session. We were many, she was one; we were standing, she was sitting on the floor; we were professionally dressed, she was in an undershirt. She was disabled; we were not.

This scenario took place some 25 years ago when I was a young Special Education student. I remember the distinct yet unarticulated discomfort I felt at that moment. No one asked this little girl if she consents to some twenty young students walking in on a dressing session. Similar such experiences of professional control and lack of autonomy can be found in various autobiographical accounts of people with disabilities. Such experiences are heavily entrenched in a view of disability as a personal tragedy, and in affected individuals as the inevitable victims of organic pathology. Historically, this was the operating model that framed the perceptions of professionals and the experiences of those they were entrusted to treat.

Also referred to as the medical model, it gained momentum in the 1800s and replaced an earlier view of disability as emanating from a moral transgression (Olkin, 1999). The equation of disability with organic pathology translated into a narrow focus on cure, remediation and rehabilitation. The focus on bodily abnormality meant that medically driven solutions were called for. Treatment was designed, implemented and evaluated by a host of professionals, with disabled individuals having little input regarding the process (Barnes, Mercer & Shakespeare, 1999; Oliver, 1996). What could not be cured had to be rehabilitated, and what could not be rehabilitated had to be accepted. People with disabilities were regarded as helpless, dependent victims who are in need of professional assistance and care. More often than not, they spent their lives in institutions with limited contact with the wider community. Their daily routine was primarily determined by professional attempts to maximize institutional efficiency. The very identity of people with disabilities became inextricably bound with their perceived incapacity (Barton, 1998; Brisenden, 1998).

The personal tragedy model has also been pervasive in psychological research and practice. The following quote attests to the traditional perception of impairment within the mental health field, as an inevitable cause of distress and probable cause of psychological maladjustment:

> Patients must be allowed to come to terms, they must grieve and mourn for their lost limbs, lost abilities, or lost looks and be helped to adjust to their lost body image. Personally, I doubt if anyone who has not experienced the onset of irreversible disability can fully understand the horror of the situation.   (Dickinson, 1977, p. 2, in Abberly, 1993, p. 108)

The above quote is particularly extreme in its depiction of disability as a tragedy of immeasurable proportions. However, helping people with disabilities "adjust" and "come to terms" with their impairments was, and often continues to be regarded as an important function of mental health professionals (Livneh, 2001; Livneh & Wilson, 2003; Livneh & Antonak, 1997; Oliver, 1996; Thomas, 1999). The "adjustment literature" (Linton, 1998, p. 98) in psychology postulates the presence of stages that individuals go through in coming to terms with their impairment. Shock followed by denial, anger, and depression, are believed, according to one such model (Miller, 1977, in Barnes, Mercer

& Shakespeare, 1999), to be important precursors to ultimate adjustment or acceptance. More current phase models (Livneh, 2001; Livneh & Wilson, 2003; Livneh & Antonak, 1997) continue to support the notion of an orderly process of adaptation to chronic illness and disability, while acknowledging that contingent upon a host of contextual factors, phases may reverse, overlap, or be omitted altogether.

Notwithstanding the acknowledgement of the mitigating role that external factors play in psychosocial adaptation, there is a strong focus in this literature on person-centered attributes such as problem solving skills, sense of efficacy, and ability to regulate emotions, along with a disregard to issues of power, oppression and discrimination. For example, Livneh and Antonak (1997) in their summary of the phases of adaptation literature, describe "external hostility" as a phase that follows "internalized anger" and precedes "acknowledgment" and "adaptation":

> Externalized hostility, viewed as an attempt at retaliation against imposed functional limitations, is hostility directed at other persons, objects, or aspects of the environment believed to be associated with the onset of the disease or the disability or with obstacles encountered during the rehabilitation process. Aggressive acts, other-blaming verbalizations and behaviors, feelings of antagonism, demanding and critical attitudes, abusive accusations, and passive-aggressive modes of obstructing treatment are usually manifest during this phase. (pp. 21–22)

Nowhere do these authors indicate that "externalized anger" may also be a legitimate reaction to condescending and paternalistic attitudes, preventable barriers to needed resources, and systemic exclusion from full participation in society.

In concert with the World Health Organization's (1980) distinction between impairment, disability and handicap, Livneh and Antonak (1997) define the latter as the "sociocultural, economic, and environmental consequences (i.e. exterior self-system) that results from impairment or disability" (pp. 5–6). Such handicaps, according to the authors, are "generally irreversible conditions of prolonged duration because of well-entrenched societal belief and value systems" (p. 6). While the well-entrenched nature of societal beliefs and value systems is irrefutable, referring to such barriers as "generally irreversible" is inaccurate and counter-productive. From a professional point of view, it runs the risk of legitimizing the almost exclusive focus not only on individual client attributes associated with positive outcomes, but on such person-centered interventions as teaching adaptive coping skills, working through perceptions of loss, and modification (by the client) of environmental barriers (Livneh, 2001). Unless such person-centered interventions are supplemented by attempts to expose and rectify systemic barriers and exclusionary practices, they can be experienced as disempowering and iatrogenic to people with disabilities.

Naming and resisting oppression: the emergence of the social model

Empowerment for groups that have been marginalized and denied opportunities does not happen as a result of spontaneous enlightenment by the majority group. It was women, rather than men, who brought to the forefront the oppressive factors that constricted their lives; just as leaders from within disadvantaged minority groups challenged white privilege. In the same vein, it was the bold and tireless work of disabled activists that began to challenge public perspectives on disability. The work of these activists, most notably in Britain and the US, illuminated the magnitude of marginalization and oppression suffered by disabled individuals. Written accounts of their work is inspirational in its portrayal of people with disabilities as active agents of change rather than passive and submissive subjects of oppression.

In the US, the formation of the Independent Living Movement in the 1960s and 1970s resulted in greater individual autonomy, while the work of grassroots coalitions and organizations contributed to important legal gains. For example, political action by disabled activists is credited with bringing into fruition the signing of the Rehabilitation Act, passed in Congress in 1973 but still awaiting signature four years later. The Act was signed following protests around the country by "persons in wheelchairs, with ventilators, signing and with canes or guide dogs" (Olkin, 1999, p. 27). The minority group model became the dominant paradigm in the US with its emphasis on discrimination as the primary barrier for people with disabilities. Undoubtedly, the signing in 1990 of the Americans with Disabilities Act is largely due to the work of disabled activists and their supporters. In a push to hasten Congress's approval of the bill, "thousands of Americans with disabilities lobbied their federal representatives, and many engaged in pro-ADA civil disobedience" (Francis & Silvers, 2000, xix).

In Britain, The Union of the Physically Impaired Against Segregation (UPIAS) was one of a number of groups formed by disabled activists in the early 1970s. The following quote attests to the outrage and militancy that was spawned from years of powerlessness and subjugation:

> We reject the whole idea of "experts" and professionals holding forth on how we should accept our disabilities, or giving learned lectures about the psychology of impairment. We already know what it feels like to be poor, isolated, segregated, done good to, stared at, and talked down to – far better than any able-bodied expert. We as a union are not interested in descriptions of how awful it is to be disabled. What we are interested in is the ways of changing the conditions of life, and thus overcoming the disabilities which are imposed on top of our physical impairments by the way this society is organized to exclude us...We look forward to the day when the army of "experts" on our social and psychological problems can find more productive work to do. (UPIAS, 1976, pp. 4–5, as cited in Barnes, 1998, p. 68)

Along with an adamant rejection of the disability as tragedy paradigm and professional control over disabled people's lives, these activists highlighted the poverty, lack of affordable and accessible housing, low employment rates and poor education that characterized the lives of those identified as disabled. They argued that these conditions do not emanate from biology and cannot be attributed to physical or intellectual impairment. Rather, they are the result of socially constructed factors that systematically exclude people with disabilities from active participation in society (Barton, 1996; Oliver & Barnes, 1998).

The assertion of the UPIAS that "...it is society which disabled physically impaired people" (UPIAS, 1976, p. 14, in Barnes, Mercer & Shakespeare, 1999, p. 28) set the stage for the development of the social model of disability (Oliver, 1990). According to this model, the very meaning of the word disability is the social oppression that constricts the lives of individuals with impairments. Proponents of the social model have argued for a conceptual separation of impairment, the biological disorder, from disability, the social barriers to participation. The removal of disability is therefore contingent upon the eradication of societal barriers rather than the cure and rehabilitation of disorders (Barton, 1998; Barnes, 1998; Morris, 2001).

British disabled activists and academics have produced a rich and diverse body of literature on the social model of disability (Morris, 2001; Oliver, 1990; Barnes, Mercer & Shakespeare, 1999; Thomas,

1999). Surprisingly, this body of work has received relatively little attention in American critical conceptualizations of disability. I was surprised, for example, that in a series of articles about the new paradigm of disability in the American Psychologist (2003), this work is marginally referred to in two publications and altogether ignored in others. Despite diverse points of view and published debates about different aspects of the model, the commonality amongst British social modelists lie in their definition of disability as social oppression: "Disability is the disadvantage or restriction of activity caused by a society which takes little or no account of people who have impairments and thus excludes them from mainstream activity. (Therefore, disability, like racism or sexism, is discrimination and social oppression)." (The British Council of Disabled people, as cited in Morris, 2001, p. 2).

Disabling barriers and the social construction of disability

Defining disability as social oppression is the hallmark of the British social model of disability and has been recently adopted by some critical theorists in North America (Linton, 1998; Silvers, 1998). Others who present critical perspectives on disability (Asch, 2000; Olkin, 1999; Pledger, 2003; Wendell, 1996) do not define it in strictly social terms. However, the differences in defining disability should not obscure a shared belief that many of the barriers associated with it are socially constructed.

Critical theorists have argued that the historical segregation of people with disabilities had more to do with meeting the needs of the non-disabled majority than with protecting vulnerable individuals. For example, the need for workers during WWII led to the "release" into the work force of many institutionalized adults (Silvers, 1998). Like women who were needed to fill positions of men who had gone to war, these individuals were let go when the war ended (Linton, 1998).

Whereas the existence of ramps allow physical access and laws protect from outright discrimination, more subtle barriers continue to hinder full social and economic participation. People who receive government assistance in the form of disability pensions often forgo employment for fear of losing the benefits they require to meet their basic needs. In the US, the assumption that people with significant disabilities are unemployable underlies such programs as Social Security Disability Insurance (SSDI) and Social Security Income (SSI). Beyond the cash payment of these programs, they are used in determining eligibility for Medicare and Medicaid. Those who leave the program through gainful employment face the prospect of losing access to health care coverage (Batavia, 2000).

Given the higher medical costs associated with some impairments, this policy creates a clear disincentive to work (Batavia, 2000). At the time of their creation, these programs were closely associated with the medical model and gained public acceptance "as long as individuals with disabilities were perceived as ill, not at fault, and incapable of independence" (Illingworth & Parmet, 2000, p. 8). Although these underlying assumptions are clearly erroneous and incompatible with the spirit of the ADA, they negatively impinge the lives of millions of people.

Indeed, wide gaps between those with and without disabilities persist. There is a 70% unemployment rate amongst Americans with disabilities with 33% living in household incomes below 15,000 (Batavia, 2000). Silvers (1998) reports that a mere 26% of working-age Americans with disabilities are in the work force compared with 82% of non-disabled people. In Britain, disabled people of working age are twice as likely as their non-disabled counterparts to be living at or below the poverty line (Fawcett, 2000). And despite some safeguards against employment discrimination and an emphasis on gainful employment, this does not clearly translate into the availability of support mechanisms that would facilitate job entry, sustainability, and advancement (Fawcett, 2000). Increased access to higher education and greater physical accessibility has certainly improved the lives of many people with disabilities, especially those with sensory and mobility impairments. However, as a group, people with disabilities continue to be the most socially disadvantaged (Batavia, 2000).

Wendell (1996) discusses the relationship between an increased pace of life and the construction of disability. In modern society, the increased pace of the world of work has elevated the bar of what is considered "normal" performance, excluding more and more people who are unable to reach it. The slower pace that is often needed for people with disabilities to operate is not accommodated in a society obsessed with efficiency and productivity. Inflexible work schedules do not lend themselves to incorporating one's impairment into one's working life. Neither do insurance policies that classify individuals as either capable of holding a full time job or totally incapacitated and incapable of gainful employment. Those who are no longer able to meet the former criteria, typically have to make a case that they meet the latter, in order to claim insurance benefits.

Notwithstanding the legislation of ramps, the public world continues to be largely organized according to a narrow range of functioning. "For instance, where would you rest for a few minutes in a supermarket if you needed to?" (Wendell, 1996, p. 39). Just as women were once relegated to the private world of home and children, so are people with disabilities:

> The public world is a world of strength, the positive (valued) body, performance and production...weakness, illness, rest and recovery, pain, death and the negative (devalued) body are private, generally hidden, and often neglected. Coming into the public world with illness, pain, or a devalued body, people encounter resistance to mixing the two worlds; the split is vividly revealed. (Wendell, 1996, p. 40)

I would add that the dictate to separate the private and public worlds is often well internalized by people with disabilities. I always took it as a given that I take extra work home when needed to compensate for my daytime fatigue that can at times result in lowered productivity. I am not suggesting that this is necessarily a problem; in fact, I prefer to have the flexibility to do so. The point is that disallowing private bodily struggles to interfere in any way with productivity can sometimes come at a price. For example, it can deplete energy from other valued domains such as family life and leisure activities. My own desire to work and "measure up" to non-disabled norms usually renders me unable to participate, at the end of the day, in any of the mundane household chores that are part of running a family. My husband's willingness to shoulder those responsibilities means that our home is still able to function while I conserve energy for more fulfilling and desirable activities.

Historically, the ethos in special education and in medical rehabilitation was to "normalize" people with disabilities and thus help them "blend in". Deaf children were prohibited from signing in attempts to normalize them by insisting that they speak. Consequently, they only had access to limited language during crucial years of language development, leaving a legacy of reduced literacy in the deaf community (Silvers, 1998). Likewise, "cosmetic normality at the cost of functional performance has been the acknowledged goals of many rehabilitation programs" (Amundson, 2000, p. 107).

Tracy Odell writes the following about growing up in an institution in Canada in the mid 1960s to mid 1970s:

> My life in the institution revolved around rejecting the disabled part of myself by "improving" it through therapy. All of us were taught

it was better to use crutches than a wheelchair, better to limp along off balance than use crutches. The goal was to look as normal as possible. Many of us learned later that function was better than appearance. The nurses snubbed my pleas for a motorized wheelchair that would give me effortless mobility, saying it was better to use my arms. Pushing a chair wore me out so much I was good for little else halfway through the day.   (Odell, 1993, p. 56)

Not only was this youngster's functional mobility sacrificed for the sake of a less stigmatized appearance, her ability to invest energy in academic and social pursuits was undoubtedly compromised, given that most of it was spent on pushing her chair.

Remnants of this approach can be detected in scales that purport to assess quality of life for people with disabilities. In one such scale, the Health Status Index (HIS), four points are given for walking freely, three for walking with limitations, and two for ambulating independently in a wheelchair. Furthermore, despite the freedom that wheelchairs accord many people, we continuously hear of individuals who are "wheelchair bound" or "confined to a wheelchair". It is little wonder that some people continue to struggle without mobility aides rather than use devices that would enhance their functioning yet make their impairment more visible (Amundson, 2000).

This issue was brought close to home for me in my recent decision to switch from a scooter to a motorized wheelchair. My reluctance to do so, though couched in supposedly functional considerations (I can carry more books on the scooter), is clearly related to a "cosmetic" preference rooted in social prejudice. I am happy to say that although I am not immune from internalization of societal norms, logic prevailed and I chose the smaller, more compact power chair that I can use indoors as well as out. My supportive family and the empowering nature of this literature have undoubtedly contributed to my ability to choose the more functional yet more stigmatized (and stigmatizing) wheelchair.

My past professional experience as a psychologist in a rehabilitation setting has advanced my understanding of the social construction of disability. The overarching goal of rehabilitation is to enable individuals to return to previous levels of functioning, resume roles, and re-integrate into society with as little disruption as possible. This is a desired outcome for most patients and serves as a major motivating factor for the hard work they invest in their various therapies. The difficulty arises when the importance attributed to certain functions (such as independence in self-care) is regarded as a truism, devoid of social meaning.

I worked with physical and occupational therapists that cared about their patients and were committed to their well-being. However, none of them questioned or critically reflected on the elevated value attributed to physical independence. If a person does not find meaning in preparing breakfast for herself, a task that may take her 45 minutes and drain her of energy that may already be in short supply, perhaps another person could do it for her in five minutes. One patient jokingly told me of the routines he goes through in order to appease his treating therapists who decided that he should participate in "breakfast group". A stroke had left this man with significant physical impairments, while his cognitive functioning remained intact. It was very clear to him that he would not be attending to his own breakfast at home given the time and energy that this required of him. However, he preferred to be a "good patient" and avoid conflict that may be more trouble than it is worth. Besides, he was truly appreciative of his therapists' hard work and did not want to disappoint them.

Disability rights activists and academics have deconstructed the terms dependence and independence, pointing to ableist notions that impregnate them with meaning. They have argued that the need for assistance in self-care, even with the most intimate tasks of daily living, is not tantamount to losing autonomy and control (Brisenden, 1998; Morris, 1991, 1996, 2001; Shakespeare, 1996). Independence is more about the freedom to make important life decisions and have control over daily routines. It is also about the right to decide what assistance is needed, how and when it will be delivered and by whom. Making decisions on behalf of others is what truly robs people of dignity and control over their lives.

Disability in the arts, the media and in daily life: the images that surround me

An understanding of the social factors that construct disability cannot be divorced from its cultural representation. "From Victorian times, Western fiction and drama have portrayed tarnished images of people with disabilities which mirror and magnify prevalent societal perceptions. Prominent among these tarnished images are characterizations of disabled people as helpless, useless, pitiable, undesirable. They are dependent, incomplete in body and basic expressions of personhood" (Peters, 1996, p. 216). This cannot simply be dismissed as belonging to an archaic prejudicial past. In films, television and printed media, disabled people are rarely depicted as active and in control of their lives (Linton, 1998). And whilst disability is often featured in documentaries and movies, rarely is it presented as an incidental or minor characteristic "which has no more significance to character and storyline than hair or eye color" (Marks, 1999, p. 159). When disability is portrayed it tends to be centered to the point of subsuming and rendering irrelevant all other characteristics of identity.

Working on this book has caused me to reflect on the disability-related images that I have recently come across. I am reminded of a television commercial of a young man with Down syndrome eating breakfast with his sister. The commercial is rather sweet and shows the brother and sister engaging in playful behavior. However, it is a commercial for an investment plan that encourages the young woman to invest wisely so that her brother is provided for, even if she is gone. In the local paper I read a sensational story about a young pregnant woman with a profound intellectual impairment and the state's failure to protect her. In the very same edition there is a picture of a slender 40-year old mother of nine doing her daily exercise routine. The caption under the picture reads something like: "Mother of nine, and look at her body!" In *Time* magazine I come across a picture of a man sitting in a motorized wheelchair. "A Malpractice Victim: How the System Failed One Sufferer" reads the title of this piece.

These pieces are unrelated and the stories they refer to are not presented here nor critiqued. However, the association of disability with tragedy, suffering and dependency is unmistakable. Given the wide consumption of mass media and its impact on the formation of attitudes and beliefs (Milligan & Neufeldt, 2001), exposure to such images runs the risk of reinforcing stereotypes. I am not advocating for a moratorium on media reporting; nor am I suggesting that references to suffering have no room in disability discourse. I am suggesting that such images can have a virulent effect when they are not balanced with depictions of people with disabilities leading ordinary lives. It is worth considering when we last saw a disabled child on a cereal box, a disabled parent picking up food on the way home from work, or a disabled man (or woman) in an intimate encounter with a partner. My guess is that most would say never. For me, a noteworthy exception to this is a television commercial I saw a few years ago. It was a Royal Bank commercial in Canada where the client is a working mother who is utilizing the services of the bank. Only toward the end of the commercial do we learn that she is also a blind woman who reads her bank statements in Braille. I remember thinking at the time that more such images can contribute to a healthier, more realistic portrayal of people with disabilities.

Amongst the disability-related books that presently crowd my desk there is a current book on adult development (Lemme, 2003). I have been asked to team-teach a human development course to incoming freshmen and this is the core textbook that is used. Since I have to read it in preparation for teaching, I thought it might also be useful for this book. After all, the subject of human development is clearly pertinent to any discussion on girlhood, womanhood and motherhood, the subject of this book.

Among the various chapters on human development covering self concept and self esteem; sexuality and intimacy; social development and family ties; career development and the world of work, I could find no mention of disability. The exception to this is in a section on family care giving where the focus is on the providers of care who look after elderly family members. Any reference to illness, impairment or disability is relegated to chapters dealing with illness prevention, aging, bereavement and death.

In the subject index under "disability" I found "aids for"; "fear of"; and "trends in", the latter referring to incidence of disease and impairment. Among the chapters that cover developmental issues most relevant to young adults (friendships, sexuality, intimacy, partnering and parenting, working), disability is conspicuous in its absence. Any mention of diversity is limited to ethnicity and sexual orientation. This reinforces a claim by some disability activists that society's acknowledgement of discrimination based on disability status lags behind its acknowledgment of discrimination based on gender and race. As Davis (2000) has claimed, "while we may acknowledge we are racist, we barely know we are ableist" (p. 232).

In the absence of realistic cultural representations of the experience of disability it is not altogether surprising that many non-disabled people cannot conceive of life with a disability. Statements like "I'd rather be dead than disabled" (or be unable to walk, take care of my own needs, be a burden on others, etc.) testify to the uncritical equation of disability with suffering in the minds of many people. Such assumptions are typically born from lack of exposure to people with disabilities. When non-disabled individuals are asked to speculate on some of the major difficulties encountered by people with disabilities they tend to focus on the actual impairment. In contrast, people with disabilities tend to point to social barriers and others' negative attitude as the main impediments to well-being (Olkin, 1999). I tested this with my own students prior to a presentation I made on women with disabilities. Although someone did ultimately mention structural and attitudinal barriers as a main source of difficulty, it followed speculations about feelings of loss, bitterness, and even envy of non-disabled people.

A number of disability theorists have suggested that stereotypical and unrealistic cultural representations of disability can be attributed to non-disabled people's anxiety about their own body and its vulnerability. This fear is projected onto disabled individuals who then become the "other" (Marks, 1999; Morris, 1991; Shakespeare, 1994). Silvers (1998) believes that rather than fear being the motivating factor, non-disabled people fail to identify with people with disabilities in the first place and it is thus impossible for them to envision what life with a disability would be like. It seems to me that while the former (fear-based) explanation is more consistent with errors of commission (i.e. portrayal of disability as pathetic and pitiable), the latter (inability to identify), is more consistent with errors of omission (failing to include people with disabilities in a shared cultural understanding of human experience). Irrespective of the forces that promote it, the result is the same. The association of disability with dependency and neediness is often so ingrained that those who defy such images may meet with resistance. Linton (1998) asserts that people with disabilities "...confound expectations when we have the temerity to emerge as forthright and resourceful people, nothing like the self-loathing, docile, bitter and insentient fictional versions of ourselves the public is more used to" (p. 3).

The problem is self-perpetuating in that it reduces the likelihood of social interaction between people with and without disabilities. The less exposure there is to "real" disabled people and their shared human experiences (studying, working, falling in love, having children), the more will people resort to fictional representations and stereotypes when they come across disability. Furthermore, cultural representations (or lack thereof) interact with material disadvantage and barriers to social participation. The disproportionately high levels of poverty and low levels of employment amongst people with disabilities reduce the possibilities for social encounters between people with and without disabilities. In such interactions based on shared interests, expertise and experiences, the disability status can recede to the background rather than being front and center in the human encounter. I am in no way suggesting that people hide, ignore or undermine their experience of disability. However, incorporating disability into one's sense of self does not compel it to become the dominant feature of one's identity (Thomas, 1999). The feminist notion of multiple identities or one that is comprised of multiple components is more consistent with the goals and experiences of people with disabilities.

Whilst we know that contact between non-disabled and disabled individuals influence the former's attitude toward the latter, research clearly indicates that the nature of the contact is crucial to the outcome. When the contact is between people who are of equal status (co-workers) or when the disabled person holds a higher status (boss, professor), this can counter stereotypes and facilitate more positive attitudes. On the other hand, contact of unequal status (the typical disabled patient-doctor relationship) does not improve attitude and in some cases, seems to make it more negative (Olkin, 1999).

Of course, the interaction between social participation and cultural representations is a reciprocal one. Just as material disadvantage and barriers to participation reinforce cultural stereotypes, distorted and absent representations exacerbate social and material disadvantage. I will use my own experience as an example. I can walk short distances with a walker on even terrain and can get around at home by "hanging on" to walls. Given that I fall frequently and have taken some nasty falls, switching from a scooter to a wheelchair seemed logical. However, I'm unable to independently rise from a chair (or wheelchair) so my evaluating physiotherapist recommended one with an elevator (it's amazing what technology can do)!

My physiotherapist planned to highlight the risks associated with the falls in order to make a strong case for insurance coverage. Knowing that I am a part time university lecturer, she considered describing how a power chair with an elevator would enhance my functioning in the classroom (standing is not difficult and I often like to lean on the desk). However, both she and I quickly thought better of it. One can probably make a case that such an elevator will facilitate independent self care (I can't transfer) and will reduce the risk of falling. However, arguing that such a device will enhance my mobility in the classroom is a much harder sell. Teaching is probably not your typical Activity of Daily Living (ADL) that most insurance brokers are accustomed to.

Theoretically, not having this devise will be unnecessarily limiting and may even make teaching altogether not feasible. Not only would I lose out on an important source of fulfillment, I would also be financially compromised by cutting off this source of income. Furthermore, it would deprive students of the opportunity to have a disabled instructor, an experience that may call into question possible assumptions and stereotypes. I hasten to point out that this is a speculative argument that, in this particular case, has not been tested. However, my own experience in another context in conjunction with situations relayed to me by other people with disabilities, attest to its relevance.

Wendell (1996) makes a similar point when she enumerates the loss of contribution that results from exclusionary practices. People with disabilities gain important knowledge from their lived experience, including the knowledge of how to live well despite physical and mental limitations. Even in situations where pain and suffering are part of the experience, this does not preclude a fulfilling life. This is an important source of knowledge for everyone. Many disabilities are acquired later in life, either as a result of an accident or a chronic illness. Many people will thus be affected by disability – either their own or that of a partner, parent, child, or friend. However,

> Because disabled people's experience is not integrated into the culture, most newly disabled people know little or nothing about how to live with long-term or life-threatening illness, how to communicate with doctors and nurses and medical bureaucrats about their problems, how to live with limitation, uncertainty, pain, and other symptoms when doctors cannot make them go away. Nor do they have any idea that they might gain something from their experiences of disability.   (Wendell, 1996, p. 65)

Most important of all, marginalization and exclusion of people with disabilities present a significant risk to their psychological well-being. This risk and the steps taken to attenuate it will be discussed throughout this book.

Concluding comments

In this chapter I described the development of a socially based understanding of disability that arose as a reaction to a functional limitation approach. Integrating examples from my own lived experience with professional and research literature, I demonstrated the numerous ways in which social structures and cultural forces impact on the experience of disability at the individual level.

Within the past two decades, Disability Studies has emerged as a new academic discipline dedicated to a critical sociopolitical analysis of disability. The term Disability Studies was traditionally used to describe applied work in such specialized fields as rehabilitation and special education. Recently, it has been reclaimed by academics dedicated to the exploration and understanding of disability as a social, political and cultural phenomenon (Linton, 1998). According to Olkin and Pledger (2003), the field of Disability Studies focuses on issues of power, oppression and civil rights; is committed to the empowerment and self-determination of people with disabilities; and regards disability as a basic human condition that must be studied as part of the diverse fabric of human experience. Disability studies scholars highlight how disability as a field of study continues to be neglected and/or inadequately addressed within mainstream academia and emphasize the importance of infusing a critical understanding of disability throughout the entire academic curriculum (Barnes, Mercer & Shakespeare, 1999; Linton, 1998; Olkin & Pledger, 2003).

The critical perspectives outlined in this chapter and currently represented in the still emerging field of disability studies, have informed my research on women with disabilities and motherhood. Whereas I had some critical understanding coming into this research, I admit that it was rather narrow in scope. In the five years since this research was conducted, my perspective has been further informed by the steady growth of scholarship in the field, my work as a clinician and a university instructor, and my own lived experience as a wife, mother, and woman with a progressive disability.

This chapter has focused on the commonalities that unite the various critical perspectives of disability. These common elements notwithstanding, there are some differences in how disability is defined and conceptualized, most notably between the British and North American explication of the social model of disability. These differences were briefly noted earlier in the chapter and a more thorough review is beyond the scope of this book. Nonetheless, I attempt here to address my own engagement with these differences as I endeavor to arrive at a position that most resonates with my worldview and lived experience.

For a number of years now, I have been both intrigued and empowered by the rich and thought-provoking writings of British Disability Studies scholars. The work of such scholars as Mike Oliver, Jenny Morris and Tom Shakespeare, just to mention a few, have greatly contributed to the field as a whole and to my own growing conscientization. The social model, as a concept, has been widely embraced by theorists and activists within Britain and without;

anyone who espouses a critical perspective of disability would likely be in "heated agreement" regarding the mediating role of socio-structural factors. This was a major focus of a recent special issue of the *American Psychologist* titled Fundamental Changes in Disability and Rehabilitation (*American Psychologist*, April 2003, Volume 58 Number 4). In the work of British scholars, nonetheless, this model invariably goes hand in hand with a conceptual separation of impairment, the underlying condition from disability, the "externally imposed disadvantage and social restriction" (Oliver & Barnes, 1998, p. 18).

The social model has been critiqued as an "oversocialized" conceptualization by medical sociologists (Bury, 1997; Pinder, 1997). The reader is referred to Thomas (1999) thorough review of the distinction between a social model and a medical sociology view of disability. More importantly, those who affiliate themselves with the British social model have also not shyed from critiquing it. For example, Crow (1996), Morris (1996, 2001), and others, have warned against a thrust within the disability rights movement, to focus on socially constructed barriers while neglecting to acknowledge impairment effects that are not amenable to social solutions. Thomas (1999) has pointed to conceptual inconsistencies between different definitions of disability associated with the social model. She has proposed a definition that would both rectify this discrepancy as well as reflect the psycho-emotional impact of exclusion and marginalization.

Thomas agrees that impairment effects cannot be seen as a strictly biological phenomenon; are an important aspect of lived experience; and should be addressed in critical disability theory. She further asserts, "From the point of view of disabled individuals, 'lived experience' is such that disability and impairment effects interact, and meld together in a holistic fashion" (p. 43). However, despite making a number of references to the interactive effect of disability and impairment, Thomas concludes her book as follows:

> The lived experience of many people with impairment in society is shaped in fundamental ways by the interaction between, and the accumulative impact of, disability (or disablism) and impairment effects. However, a careful *analytical* distinction needs to be made between the consequences of disability and impairment effects. The most fruitful way forward is to develop an approach which understands disability as a form of social oppression, but which finds room for the examination of impairment effects. (p. 156)

More recently, Morris (2001) has stated the importance of this distinction in more passionate terms:

> Separating out "impairment" (that is, the functional limitations of our bodies and minds) from "disability" (that is the disabling barriers of unequal access and negative attitudes) is the cornerstone of what is known as the social model of disability. This has enabled us, as disabled people, to challenge the assumption that impairment is an inevitable tragedy... (p. 2)

In reference to the use of the terms "disability" and "impairment" by the British disabled people's movement, Morris (2001) states that despite the movement's adoption of the social model of disability some 15 years ago, "it has take us a long time to consistently use the term 'disability' to mean oppression and to reclaim the word 'impairment' as a value-free word to describe characteristics of our bodies" (p. 4). She demonstrates this progression in her own writing, where she previously used "disability" to mean both oppression and impairment (1991), and later used it solely to mean oppression (1996). While Morris clearly articulates the need to address impairment effects, she sees this as contingent upon a separation of the terms. With this, I struggle.

If what is meant by a social model of disability is a commitment to locating individual experience within a socio-political structure, and highlighting oppressive (and preventable) barriers in disabled people's lives, then I can both support it and use it as a framework for my own lived experience. At the same time, I am uncomfortable with the unfaltering insistence that espousing a social model perspective is inevitably contingent upon an adherence to the above separation. Notwithstanding my respect for the work of Jenny Morris that has significantly contributed to my own thinking, I admit to being more comfortable with her former use of disability (impairment and oppression), than the latter (oppression only).

To claim the word disability for externally imposed restrictions, or even for the combined impact of structural and psychological barriers, would rob me of the very word that encapsulates my experience. I find the claim that impairment effects do not constitute disability, to be highly problematic. Can we also say that they are not disabling? I will use my own experience to demonstrate this point. My continual loss of muscle mass due to MD, and the increased bodily struggles that ensue, are undeniable. At the same time, some recent environmental modifications (switching from a scooter to a power wheelchair with an elevator), have contributed to an increased sense of independence and an improved quality of life.

Being in a progressive university community also means that I am relatively protected from prejudice, or at least its explicit manifestation. The combined effect of improved technology and enlightened social milieu, has paradoxically resulted in my experiencing my impairment as less limiting, in some ways, despite its obvious progression. At the same time, for someone to suggest that I'm now less disabled, would be an outrage. Perhaps this would hold if, hypothetically speaking, my condition were to stay static from here thereon. This, however, is not the case, and I am fully cognizant of the challenges that lie ahead. A true representation of my lived experience is not possible without recognizing the dynamic interplay between organic and social ailments. They exist in tandem, and denying their synergistic impact on my life would silence my experience. Would surrounding myself with increasingly more sophisticated devices and progressively minded people eliminate my disability altogether? Would I then claim to no longer be disabled, despite being increasingly more impaired?

This simply does not work. Whilst I resonate with the rationale behind a conceptual separation of disability and impairment, I second the question posed by Sally French (1993): "does it make sense to separate symptoms which so clearly interact?" (p. 19). I venture to say that the plausibility of such a separation is related to the context of the impairment and its ubiquitous entanglement with the environs. Ultimately, it is every person's lived experience that may justify one conception of disability or another. Common misperceptions of "disability as tragedy" are problematic, and a misrepresentation of most people's lived experience. This is a political concern that, as grave as it may be, cannot be rectified by fragmenting lived experience into impairment effects and disability effects.

As noted earlier, the *American Psychologist*, a prestigious and widely read journal of the American Psychological Association, has recently dedicated a special issue to disability studies. The issue is dedicated to the so-called paradigm shift in the conceptualization of disability and rehabilitation and its implications for psychological research and practice. Admitting that psychology has lagged behind other disciplines in adopting a critical perspective (Olkin & Pledger, 2003), the various articles provide useful information on how psychologists can use their skills and expertise to advance the well-being of people with disabilities. In the opening article, Pledger (2003) discusses the shift from the "old" to the "new" paradigm in definitions of disability: "Disability is not inherent; although a disability condition may be evident, risk factors, rather than the condition, are the true determinants of disability. This philosophical perspective espouses the belief that biological, environmental, social, cultural, and behavioral factors interact and often serve as the precursor to disability" (Pledger, 2003, p. 282). Gill, Kewman and Brannon (2003) further elucidate the difference between the old and the new paradigm:

> New paradigm proponents acknowledge physical or mental impairment as a common aspect of human experience and view people with disabilities as hindered primarily not by their intrinsic difference but by society's response to those differences. In a sense, then, new paradigm is compatible with viewing disability as a policy-linked phenomenon in that disability is determined significantly by social practices and underlying values.   (p. 306)

These are conceptualizations of disability that I can relate to unreservedly. I welcome the shifting focus from biological to sociopolitical explanations of the disadvantage experienced by people with disabilities. To me, this can be achieved without attempting to partial out biological factors altogether.

2
Sexuality, Disability and Women's Lived Experience

The disability rights movement has been highly instrumental in promulgating a socio-political understanding of disability and high-lighting barriers to social and economic participation by affected individuals. Its commitment to the elucidation and eradication of barriers to education, employment and civic participation has contributed immeasurably to the well being of women and men with disabilities.

These contributions notwithstanding, the movement has been criticized by disabled feminists for its traditional silence on issues that are most relevant to the lives of women. The psychological impact of social devaluation and the distress that is sometimes associated with the impairment itself are being increasingly articulated by disabled feminists and incorporated in disability theory (Crow, 1996; Morris, 1991, 1996, 2001; Thomas, 1999; Thomson, 1997a, 1997b). Utilizing the feminist slogan "the personal is political", disabled feminists have argued that the incorporation of lived experience can enhance rather than derail efforts to bring about social change (Thomas, 1999).

The disability rights movement which was dominated by men in its early years, neglected to explore the manifestation of disablism in the arenas of relationships, sexuality and reproduction – domains that are particularly relevant to the lives of women. This resulted in disabled women feeling marginalized by the very movement that purported to represent them as individuals with disabilities. Furthermore, the movement's struggle for a greater share of societal resources overlooked needs pertaining to the private world of family and relationships (Morris, 1996).

While the disability rights movement neglected disabled women's particular concerns as women, the feminist movement neglected their specific circumstances as disabled (Asch & Fine, 1988; Lloyd, 1992,

2001; Morris, 1996, 2001; Thomas, 1999). This exclusion has been most apparent in feminist theorizing on the sexual objectification of women, the institution of motherhood, and women as caregivers. I explore these topics in this chapter that focuses on sexuality and sense of self, and the next chapter that deals with reproduction and motherhood for women with disabilities.

Despite their critique of the disability rights and the women's movement respectively, disabled feminists acknowledge the contribution of both to the understanding of disability in general and to the lives of women with disabilities in particular. They further point to the important parallels between the oppression of women in a patriarchal society and the oppression of people with disabilities in a disablist society. Both the disability rights and the women's movement have emphasized the deleterious impact of oppressive contexts and practices. As Rousso and Wehmeyer (2001) contend, "any 'disadvantaged status' associated with being female and/or disabled is rooted not in biology, but rather in society through pervasive biases, stereotypes, and discrimination" (p. 2). Both female and disabled bodies are imbued with cultural meanings that have far-reaching implications for those that inhabit them (Fawcett, 2000; Thomson, 1997a, 1997b). Another important similarity is the belief that distress experienced at the individual level must be considered in light of power imbalance, inequality and unjust distribution of societal resources.

Exploring the ways in which gender intersects with disablism is critical to any attempt to advance the understanding of disabled women's lived experience. As Thomas (1999) contends, "the forms and impacts of disablism are always refracted in some way through the prism of gendered location and gender relations" (p. 28). These constructs further interact with other markers of identity such as race, class, and sexual orientation. The disabled people's movement has also recognized the importance of changing the perception that "the young, male, white wheelchair user is the classic disabled person" (Shakespeare, 1996, p. 195). An increasing number of political essays, research accounts, and theoretical papers highlight the synergistic potential of feminism and disability to theory and practice. While people with disabilities and particularly women with disabilities are the most obvious benefactors of this synergy, it also has the potential to contribute to such diverse fields as the study of oppression and empowerment, human resilience, and the social construction of gender.

Disabled women's lives, once silenced and invisible, have been gaining more attention in the past two decades. Autobiographies and edited compilations of personal narratives, along with political and academic writings are enhancing our understanding of disabled women's lives. Much (but not all) of this literature is written by women with a first hand experience of disability, in the spirit of the feminist tradition of "writing the self". The value of such work, while potentially empowering for the writers, extends far beyond them: "the experience of individuals tell us not simply about the particular, the micro-environments in which individuals live out their lives, but also about the general, the macro-environments which make up the broader social context of these lives" (Thomas, 1999, p. 84).

In this chapter I focus on issues of particular relevance to the lives of women: sexuality, body image, family dynamics and intimate relationships. I do not wish to imply that these issues are unimportant to the lives of men, or that disabled women are not interested in advancing their education, career options and economic status. At the same time, the centrality of relationships to the lives of women is undeniable and women with disabilities are no exception. Furthermore, this chapter provides the context for the subject of this book, reproduction and motherhood in the context of disability.

Women with disabilities and their bodies: culture, flesh, and lived experience

I live in a body that is becoming increasingly more impaired. Along with decreased mobility, more frequent falls and a greater need for assistance, my body also looks different from the "norm", and this difference is increasing. To claim that I perceive my impairment in neutral terms, as just another quality like height or eye color, would be dishonest. I have a loving son and husband, good friends and a fulfilling job, and consider myself reasonably happy and well adjusted. At the same time, I cannot deny that my progressive impairment, and all that it entails, is at times a source of distress.

But admitting only to the impairment effects will also not do. Despite the blessings I just mentioned, I couldn't claim total indifference to deviations from societal standards of female appearance. The best example of this is my preference for skirts (I only wear pants at home) that do a better job of camouflaging my swaying gait. At the same time, I have no issue with the visibility of my leg brace and am comfortable with using a walker and a scooter.

By beginning this section with a personal narrative (in an otherwise theoretical review), I hope to convey the possible complexity that is entailed in how physically disabled women relate to their bodies. I must qualify this by stating that I in no way purport to speak for all or even other women with physical disabilities. "Stealing" an idea from Susan Wendell (1996), I would like to claim that I do not represent all women with disabilities, or all women with physical disabilities, or all women with Muscular Dystrophy, or all married, Jewish, feminist, academic mothers with Muscular Dystrophy who have lived in Israel, Canada and Australia prior to moving to the USA (well, maybe). At the same time, the value of personal experience to theoretical analysis has been repeatedly demonstrated in feminist work.

In this section I explore the cultural representation of female disabled bodies as well as bodily experiences that are sometimes associated with a physical impairment. By separating the two I wish to avoid a conflation of cultural representation with bodily experiences, an issue raised by a number of disabled feminists (Thomas, 1999; Thomson, 1997b; Wendell, 1996). At the same time, such a separation is unavoidably artificial; our relationship with our bodies is based on a dynamic interaction of bodily experiences, cultural messages, and social interactions.

Women with disabilities and social constructions of the body

The Rejected Body, the title of Susan Wendell's book on disability, is reflective of western society's collective fear, repulsion, and repudiation of bodies that deviate from the norm.

> In the commercial-media-soaked societies of North America, the body is idealized and objectified to a high degree; these cultural practices foster demands to control our bodies and attempt to prefect them, which in turn create rejection, shame, and fear in relation to both failures to control the body and deviations from body ideals.   (Wendell, 1996, p. 85)

The idealization and objectification of women's bodies has been front and center of much feminist work. Sex sells, and media images of tantalizing female bodies are virtually everywhere: in movies and television; newspapers and fashion magazines; billboards and shopping malls (Daniluk, 1998). These images reflect and perpetuate societal standards of physical beauty and appearance that are unattainable by the vast majority of women. In fact, the waif-like models portrayed in most media images have shapes and body sizes representative of only 5% of women in the normal weight distribution (Daniluk, 1998).

Surrounded by such images, it is little wonder that most girls and women judge their own bodies as inadequate. Alarming rates of eating disorders, poor body image and low self-esteem are some devastating consequences.

The most recent edition of "Our bodies ourselves" sadly concludes, that "despite changes in fashion and in attitudes towards women, today's ideal woman is in fact not so different from the original blond Barbie doll" (Boston Women's Collective, 1998, p. 34). One only needs to study the images reflected from the nearest billboard or the most recent television commercial to recognize the validity of this assertion. In a recent class discussion with undergraduate female students, I was struck by how these bright, successful young women are continuing to internalize these messages, despite their ability to offer a sophisticated critique. Perhaps I shouldn't be so surprised; my own struggles with normal appearance shared earlier, are also a product of years of subtle cultural indoctrination.

From a consumerist point of view, the distance between such images and the bodies of real women ensures large profits to those in the business of beautifying them. From fashion to dieting to cosmetics to plastic surgery, the success of these industries depends on convincing women that they don't look good enough and are therefore socially devalued (Boston Women's Collective, 1998; Thomson, 1997a; Wendell, 1996). The invaluable work of feminist mothers and teachers, writers and journalists, activists and academics, is little match for the multi-million dollar industries that profit from the objectification of women's bodies. Rather than forced upon women, such "disciplinary practices" (Wendell, 1996, p. 87) of dieting, hair removal, and corrective surgery are internalized and self-imposed.

> Whereas feminists claim that women are the objects of the evaluative male gaze...the disabled body is the object of the stare. If the male gaze makes the normative female a sexual spectacle, then the stare sculpts the disabled subject into a grotesque spectacle. The stare is the gaze intensified, framing her body as an icon of deviance. (Thomson, 1997b, p. 26)

This quote conveys both the similarity and the difference between the objectification of the female and the disabled body. However, if many women feel stymied by narrow standards of acceptable appearance, "most people with disabilities cannot even attempt to make their bodies fit the physical ideals of their culture" (Wendell, 1996, p. 91).

Some may feel shame and frustration for bodies they cannot have; others may critique and reject socially produced ideals. Others yet, may find themselves fluctuating between acceptance and non-acceptance (Wendell, 1996).

The socially disabling consequences associated with deviations from norms of appearance are particularly apparent in situations where such deviations are not accompanied by functional limitations. In other words, the degree of visibility affects social relations. Impairments that are more visible are associated with higher level of social devaluation, even in the absence of any physical limitation (Thomson, 1997b; Wendell, 1996). Thus, individuals (and especially women) with facial scaring may be disadvantaged in job interviews, social interactions, and especially romantic encounters, and may thus experience their condition as disabling.

Living in bodies that deviate from the norm, people with disabilities are often considered asexual. They are frequently subject to infantilisation and may thus be perceived as having no need for sexual expression (Shakespeare, 1996). They may further be perceived as physically incapable of sexual encounters or seen as inevitably incapable of attracting a mate (Milligan & Neufeldt, 2001; Shakespeare, 1996). Relationships and intimacy is a topic on its own and will be explored in greater detail later in this chapter. I merely touch here on the "myth of asexuality" (Milligan & Neufeldt, 2001, p. 91) to convey its inseparability from any discussion on cultural constructions of the female disabled body and the well being of women with disabilities.

Beyond social construction: bodily experiences and impairment effects

Discourse on the disabled body as a cultural representation and site of oppression must be balanced by the acknowledgement that it may also be the site of bodily suffering. The social stigma associated with a disability accounts for some of the similarities in the experiences of individuals with very different impairments. At the same time, these similarities should not obscure critical differences in bodily experiences.

Wendell (1996) asserts that while feminists have theorized on cultural prescriptions of appearance and on the resultant alienation of women from their bodies, they tended to ignore "bodily frustration and suffering that social justice cannot prevent or relieve" (pp. 92–93). The central role that culture plays in the experience of disability is central to Wendell's theory. At the same time, she is critical of some constructivist approaches that "deny or ignore bodily experience in favor of fascination with bodily representation" (p. 93).

In an effort to help women become more at home in their bodies, feminist discourse has encouraged them to focus on pleasurable bodily experiences and competencies rather than appearances. Notwithstanding the potential benefits of this approach for all women, it runs the risk of undermining experiences of bodily weakness and suffering. "One consequence is that women with disabilities may feel that feminists have an ideal of the female body or of female bodily experiences in which they cannot participate any more than they can in the idealized images of sexist society, and that their experiences cannot be included in feminist understandings of the body" (Wendell, 1996, p. 167).

The danger of ignoring bodily struggles has also been raised by some disabled feminists in relation to the British social model of disability (Crow, 1996; French, 1993; Morris, 1991, 1996, 2001; Thomas, 1999). As noted in the previous chapter, this model is premised on a conceptual separation of impairment, the biological disorder, from disability, the social barriers to participation. Liz Crow (1996) is effusive about the transformative impact that the social model, with its emphasis on social oppression, has had on her life:

> My life has two phases: before the social model of disability, and after it. Discovering this way of thinking about my experiences was the proverbial raft in stormy seas...For years now this social model has enabled me to confront, survive, and even surmount countless situations of exclusion and discrimination...It has played a central role in promoting disabled people's individual self-worth, collective identity, and political organization. I don't think it is an exaggeration to say that the social model has saved lives.   (Crow, 1996, pp. 206–207)

At the same time, Crow (1996) and others contend that the social model's exclusive focus on the impact of oppressive attitudes and practices has tended to silence and thus invalidate some people's struggles with their bodies. Notwithstanding her staunch support of the social model of disability, Crow (1996) boldly contends:

> The experience of impairment is not always irrelevant, neutral, or positive...many of us remain frustrated and disheartened by pain, fatigue, depression and chronic illness...many of us fear for our

futures with progressive or additional impairments; we mourn past activities that are no longer possible for us; we are afraid we may die early or that suicide may seem our only option; we desperately seek some effective medical intervention; we feel ambivalent about the possibilities of our children having impairments; and we are motivated to work on the prevention of impairments. Yet our silence about impairment has made many of these things taboo and created a whole new series of constraints on our self-expression.   (pp. 209–210)

The acknowledgement that impairment may be associated with suffering that is not caused or easily alleviated by the removal of social barriers, is risky and fraught with challenges. Proponents of the social model have fought long and hard to dispel the myth that impairment is a personal tragedy that inevitably leads to a restricted life. Although they do not deny some individuals' experience of impairment-related hardship, they may question the value of publicizing struggles that are not amenable to change (Finkelstein, 1998; Oliver, 1990; Oliver & Barnes, 1998; Barnes, 1998). Not only can the explication of such struggles perpetuate the personal tragedy model, it can also divert energy from the struggle to eradicate socially constructed barriers.

Indeed, we cannot discount the risk that highlighting impairment effects may be (mis)used as ammunition to undermine social barriers and invoke pity. Jenny Morris has articulated the importance of giving voice to impairment effects in a number of publications (Morris, 1991, 1996, 2001), while highlighting the complexities of doing so:

We need to put back the experience of impairment into our politics. We need to write about, research and analyze the personal experience of our bodies and our minds for if we don't impose our own definitions and perspectives then the non-disabled world will continue to do it for us in ways which alienate and disempower us...however, we do not feel that the public world, dominated by non-disabled people, is yet a safe place to fully share our experiences...there is a limit to which we can publicly explore this.   (Morris, 1996, p. 14)

These issues are of particular relevance to disabled women who have pointed to the gender division within the disabled people's movement regarding the place of lived experience. These risks notwithstanding, disabled feminists have insisted on the incorporation of the personal into disability theory, including struggles that directly relate to impairments and are not easily rectified by social manipulation (French, 1993).

Girls with disabilities: messages, perceptions and experiences

This section focuses on the intersection of girlhood and physical disability through an exploration of three core themes: parental perceptions and messages; contacts with professionals; and peer relations. In concert with the rest of the chapter, the focus is on sexual identity, sense of self, and relationships.

Many women, myself included, become disabled in adulthood, having grown up as able-bodied girls. Conversely, women with early onset disabilities have been exposed to disability-related stigma from a young age. Exploring the experiences of girls with disabilities is important for a number of reasons. For one thing, it provides a context for an exploration of sexuality and self-esteem amongst their adult counterparts who grew up with disabilities. Secondly, it can elucidate challenges and possibilities for present and future generations of girls with physical disabilities. Finally, it can add to the diverse tapestry of girls and thus enrich the discourse on girlhood. Notwithstanding possible differences in the experiences of girls with and without disabilities, gender is an overarching category of identity formation and girls with disabilities are, first and foremost, girls.

Parental perceptions and messages

From 1992 to 1996, the Center for Research on Women with Disabilities (CROWD) has conducted qualitative and quantitative studies investigating sexuality and sense of self amongst physically disabled women (Howland & Rinalta, 2001; Nosek, 1996a, 1996b; Nosek et al., 2001; Nosek & Hughes, 2001). The qualitative study was based on in-depth interviews with thirty-one women and served to inform a questionnaire that was ultimately completed by 504 and 442 women, with and without physical disabilities, respectively. These studies have made a significant contribution to our understanding of this much-neglected topic and will be referred to throughout this review.

Relevant to the present discussion is the childhood experiences of those disabled at birth or as young children who have thus grown up as girls with disabilities. Although exact numbers are not reported, many women were told by their families that they are incapable of looking after a home and children; that no one would want to marry them; and that they should focus on their studies instead (Howland & Rinalta, 2001; Nosek & Hughes, 2001; Nosek et al., 2001). This corroborates the results of an earlier retrospective study that compared 31 women with pre-adolescent disabilities with 12 who had acquired their disabilities after adolescence. Although the two groups did not differ as far as general parental attitudes and expectations, parents of girls with pre-adolescent disabilities had lower expectations in the social and sexual arena and higher expectations in the educational and vocational arena. The mothers of these daughters were also less likely to have discussions with them about dating, sexuality and motherhood (Rousso, 1996). Indeed, many of the women in the CROWD studies reported having no information growing up on how their disabilities may affect their ability to have sex and bear children (Nosek et al., 2001). Parental expectations of vulnerability and life-long dependency may further contribute to the over-protection and infantilization of girls with disabilities.

A host of factors can account for parental ignoring, undermining or actively resisting a disabled daughter's budding sexuality. For one thing, parents are not immune to societal stereotypes about disabilities, and the birth of a disabled child is often their first encounter with the actual lived experience (Olkin, 1999). One need not go back far to discover that much professional literature tended to describe children with disabilities as a burden on families and their placement in an institution was often encouraged. Furthermore, parents were conditioned to discount their own grounded knowledge and expertise regarding their children in favor of adherence to professional advice (Ferguson, Gartner & Lipsky, 2000; Olkin, 1999). According to Ferguson, Gartner and Lipsky (2000), it is only within the last two decades that a more favorable research trend has begun to emerge.

This should be considered in tandem with a conclusion based on a comprehensive literature review that "before the 1970s, the clinical and empirical literatures were virtually silent on the issue of sexuality and disability" (Milligan & Neufeldt, 2001, p. 95). A similar zeitgeist existed in the school system where many disabled girls were routinely "excused" from Sex Education (Nosek et al., 2001). In a society that values women based on their ability to attract men, and objectifies people with disabilities as asexual, some parents likely surmised that broaching the topic of intimacy would engender false hopes and lead to experiences of rejection.

Alicia Contreras writes about a meeting she attended in Mexico where parents of youngsters with Muscular Dystrophy were encouraged to talk with their kids about sexuality. "There was one woman who immediately said, 'why should I talk about sexuality with my daughter? What for? Nobody would want to marry her'" (Contreras, 1999, pp. 25–26). This is indicative of the ambivalence experienced by some parents who may implicitly or explicitly convey to a disabled daughter that sexual intimacy should be neither expected nor sought (Begum, 1992; Kocher, 1994; Rousso, 1996).

It is important to note that not all women were exposed to negative messages and some tell of parents who went out of their way to foster a healthy sexual identity. They did so by acknowledging their daughter's sexuality; expressing confidence in her ability to form relationships; and assisting her in overcoming physical and attitudinal barriers (Howland & Rinalta, 2001; Nosek et al., 2001; Rousso, 1996). This created a strong foundation for future relationships and was an important factor in general well being.

Encounters with service providers

As the literature on disability attests, encounters with attendants, health professionals, and the health care system also has a bearing on how girls with disabilities perceive their bodies and their sexuality. Whereas some girls do not have any more contact with service-providers than their non-disabled peers, others require medical interventions and/or monitoring that result in frequent contact with providers. Others yet, may need assistance with self-care. The manner in which such services and procedures are conducted can have a long-lasting effect on body image, self-esteem and overall well-being (Cole & Cole, 1993; Olkin, 1999).

Disturbingly, studies and personal narratives of adult women with disabilities point to insensitive and even damaging treatment that some incurred as children in hospitals and clinics. Some women recount the detrimental impact of being poked, prodded and put on display in front of interns and medical students (Begum, 1992; Lonsdale, 1990; Mason, 1999). This is particularly invalidating when it involves exposure of the body during puberty, a time when youngsters typically have a greater need for privacy. Such practices are clearly counter-indicated with the development of a positive body image and a healthy sexuality. They can also interfere with the development of clear boundaries and thus increase a youngster's susceptibility to sexual abuse: "The medical experiences I had made me very vulnerable to being abused, it just seemed the same as everything else that had been done to me so I wasn't able to discriminate" (Wescott, 1993, p. 17, in

Shakespeare, 1996, p. 206). Indeed, children with disabilities, in comparisons with their non-disabled counterparts, experience higher rates of all forms of abuse (Nosek, 1996c; Olkin, 1999; Shakespeare, 1996).

According children an appropriate level of control over medical procedures and ensuring that their dignity is maintained in the process is being increasingly emphasized in professional literature (Cole & Cole, 1993; Olkin, 1999). As the above quote attests, having a sense of ownership over one's body, and control over who is allowed to observe and manipulate it, can reduce (but not eliminate) the risk of abuse. It further reduces the likelihood of putting oneself in potentially dangerous situations in the future and/or remaining in relationships that become abusive.

Of course, the importance of being treated with dignity and perceived as a whole person has ramifications for well-being in general. A practitioner's exclusive focus on the child's functional limitation and possible reference to "good" (nondisabled) and "bad" (disabled) limbs and body parts can be further undermining. Women with disabilities have reported childhood experiences of such medical encounters and their potentially damaging consequences (Finger, 1990, 1993; Mason, 1999).

Less than two years ago I attended a conference on Muscular Dystrophy where a medical researcher made a similar reference from the podium to "good genes" and "bad genes". He seemed completely oblivious to the problematic nature of making such comments to an audience largely comprised of affected individuals (who have "bad genes"). I include this story here as a reminder that objectifying, invalidating practices are not merely a thing of the past. This gains further credence from the following quote from a recent book on disability: "Impairments are often treated as if they are isolated body systems unrelated to the whole of the child. A club foot may be held up, examined, bound and exercised, all as if the fact that it is attached to a child at the other end is at best irrelevant and at worse a nuisance" (Olkin, 1999, p. 99).

It is unlikely that such practices have been completely eliminated. At the same time, they probably occur with less frequency and hopefully are being increasingly replaced by more progressive ones. If professional literature is any indication of perceptions and practices, then there is room for cautious optimism. In a chapter titled *Teaching Providers to Become our Allies*, Marsha Saxton (1996) describes a workshop she and other disabled women taught on the subject at Harvard Medical School. This paralleled a workshop for women on how to assert themselves in their contacts with the health-care system. Hopefully, an increase is such practices will ensure that not only women with disabilities are targeted for change, but also the practitioners that treat women as well as men, and boys as well as girls with disabilities. As I demonstrate next, issues of sexuality, peer relations and self-esteem are being increasingly addressed in professional literature on children with disabilities.

Social and romantic encounters

"The family is the child's gateway to the school and peer worlds" (Miller, 1999, p. 71). If this statement is true for families in general, it is particularly relevant for families of children with disabilities. Parents set the tone for how a child's disability is perceived by siblings and extended family members (Olkin, 1999). Furthermore, the way they deal with and adapt to challenges associated with the disability has implications for how the child will negotiate his or her condition (Miller, 1999).

Retrospective studies with adult women with disabilities emphasize the facilitative role that parents can play in helping youngsters negotiate their social environments. First and foremost, sense of self and body image are highly influenced by parental attitudes and girls who are valued by parents learn to value themselves. If they are consistently given the message that disability need not preclude the possibility of friendship and intimacy, they are more likely to behave in a manner consistent with such a message (Howland & Rinalta, 2001; Nosek et al., 2001; Rousso, 1988, 1996). In the words of one woman, "I was a social success in part because my mother expected me to succeed. In fact, she gave me no choice" (Rousso, 1996, p. 112).

Notwithstanding the relevance of this quote, parents are not omnipotent in their ability to determine their youngster's social success. In fact, helping their child form satisfactory friendships is probably one of the most challenging aspects of parenting a youngster with a disability. Disability is highly stigmatized in society and may be the basis of ostracism from peers (Olkin, 1999). Social isolation, especially during adolescence, has been consistently reported in the literature (Asch, Rousso & Jefferies, 2001). To deny this and imply that social success is solely contingent on effort and skill, would be a disservice to parents and children alike. Furthermore, adolescence is a time of separation and individuation and a teenager may decline and even resist parental efforts to facilitate social interactions (Cole & Cole, 1993; Kewman, Warschausky, Engel & Warzak, 1997; Miller, 1999).

Disability discrimination manifests itself most in the romantic realm (Olkin, 1999) and this is probably felt in adolescence more than at any other stage of development. Intimacy and relationships for women with disabilities will be discussed in the following section. Nonetheless, it is important to emphasize the role that this plays in the lives of adolescent girls. More so than older women, teenage girls are large consumers of fashion magazines and highly impressionable by the images they convey.

The growing popularity of beauty spas for teens has been the subject of full-length articles in recent editions of *Time* magazine and *Newsweek*. Photos of girls, some as young as nine, depict them in various phases of makeovers and manicures. This is a sad testament to the pressure on ever-younger girls to beautify themselves, as well as the many parents who collude in these efforts. Girls with disabilities are also exposed to these images and may feel further marginalized by their inability to "compete". In a similar vein, adolescent boys more so than grown men, are highly impressed by appearances.

In other words, there is no point denying that girls with disabilities are likely to encounter challenges and barriers, not for lack of interest but due to limited opportunities (Howland & Rinalta, 2001). In comparison to non-disabled peers, they are less likely to go out on dates and are typically older when they have their first date. Both attitudinal and practical barriers can present challenges to dating. Nonetheless, parents who are sensitive to their daughter's needs can help her overcome some of those barriers. For example, some women reported that parents assisted them in and out of cars but were sensitive enough to give them privacy at the end of a date (Howland & Rinalta, 2001).

Furnishing youngsters with information about sexuality and giving them privacy to explore their own bodies (Cole & Cole, 1993), can also have an affirming impact. A youngster with a disability may require parental assistance despite a growing desire for independence. However, parents and teens can explore creative ways of providing the former while enabling the latter and help youngsters move towards greater autonomy. Finally, opportunities to interact with other youngsters with disabilities as well as meet adults who lead satisfactory and productive lives can be hugely beneficial to both children and their parents. Doing so can engender optimism regarding future possibilities, facilitate social networks, and plant the seeds for a proud membership in the disability community.

Relationships, intimacy and well-being for women with disabilities

"When the term sexuality is viewed holistically, it refers to the totality of a being" (Whipple, Richards, Tepper & Komisaruk, 1996, p. 69). Indeed, sexuality and its expression are important components of self-esteem, emotional well-being and quality of life in general (Milligan & Neufeldt, 2001). People with disabilities have the same need for love and intimacy as their non-disabled counterparts. Yet, the road they must travel in their attempt to fulfill this need is often fraught with challenges and barriers. This is particularly complex for women who, more so than men, tend to define themselves through their attachments and relationships with others. As Carol Gilligan's (1982) research has demonstrated, males and females differ in the way they experience relationships and interdependence and in the value they attribute to them. (Gilligan, 1982; Keith, 1996; Nosek et al., 2001; Nosek & Hughes, 2001).

Many women with disabilities are ultimately successful in forging loving relationships and, more importantly, developing a strong sense of self. However, "there is a long journey of discovery that many women with physical disabilities go through to acknowledge their value and their womanhood" (Nosek et al., 2001, p. 10). I explicate this journey through an exploration of the external and internal barriers that women encounter in their quest for love and intimacy. Most importantly, I summarize research that points to disabled women's resilience in the face of barriers and to the success that many experience in meeting goals, forming meaningful relationships and enhancing well-being.

External barriers and challenges

Research on the lives of adult women with disabilities has consistently demonstrated that their social and sexual rejection is not limited to the adolescent years. They are less likely to be partnered than either non-disabled women or disabled men and, if they acquire their disability in adulthood, are more likely to be left by their partners (Asch & Fine, 1988; Crewe, 1993; Fine & Asch, 1985; Howland & Rinalta, 2001; Olkin, 1999). One recent study reported that while young women with learning, emotional and speech disabilities were found to have the same marriage rates and even higher parenting rates than nondisabled women 3–5 years after leaving school, an opposite trend was found for those with physical disabilities (Wagner, 1992, cited in Rousso, 1996).

The CROWD studies found that compared with the nondisabled control group (N = 406), participants with physical disabilities (N = 475) perceived more constraints in the realm of dating; were less satisfied with its frequency; and reported a lower level of satisfaction with their sex lives. Nonetheless, most women with disabilities had experienced at least one serious relationship (87%), with 52% being involved in such a relationship at the time of the study, versus 64% of those without disabilities. Of those who were not in a serious relationship, 42% said that it was because no one had asked them, a reason given by only 27% of non-disabled participants (Nosek et al., 2001). The authors concluded that "women with physical disabilities have as much sexual desire as women in general; however, they do not have as much opportunity for sexual activity" (Nosek et al., 2001, p. 8).

Gill (1996b) suggests that the disadvantage that women with disabilities face in this sphere can be explained in terms of aesthetics and function. The aesthetics explanation refers to stereotypical standards of feminine beauty according to which women with visible disabilities may be perceived as flawed or defective. The functional explanation refers to patriarchal notions of the role of women as caretakers and nurturers in conjunction with erroneous assumptions about the inability of women with disabilities to care for and nurture others.

Indeed, the CROWD studies found that even if women were outgoing and had many friends, these friendships were less likely to evolve into romantic relationships for women with physical disabilities versus those without. This is consistent with other research that indicates that people with disabilities are more likely to be accepted as co-workers and platonic friends than as intimate partners (Milligan & Neufeldt, 2001). The lack of reference to people with disabilities in most courses and textbooks on human sexuality (Linton, 1998; Olkin & Pledger, 2003) makes it even less likely for them to be considered as potential partners by those without disabilities.

Men who do not shun women with disabilities as potential partners may nonetheless fear that they will be stigmatised and criticized for their choices (Gill, 1996b). They may be perceived as "settling" for a disabled partner as a last resort (Milligan & Neufeldt, 2001) and/or pitied for sharing their lives with such an individual. Those who married before the onset of impairment may be regarded as staying in the marriage merely out of a sense of duty and may thus be admired for their willingness to do so (Gill, 1996b; Olkin, 1999). I always feel ambivalent when friends remark on how wonderful my husband is, not because I disagree but due to the unarticulated role that I believe my disability plays in such comments.

Beyond the attitudinal barriers noted above, potential partners may also be deterred by the extra costs associated with some disabilities. As a group, people with disabilities, and particularly women with disabilities, have significantly lower incomes and are less likely to be employed than those without disabilities. Those who receive government funding for health costs (personal assistance, adaptive equipment, etc.) are at risk of having their benefits cut off or "adjusted" if they marry. "This practice effectively crushes a new relationship under the weight of instant financial hardship...by withdrawing supports, government marriage penalties ensure the burdened life many people incorrectly assume is inevitable when loving a person with a disability" (Gill, 1996b, p. 122). It may also set up a dynamic whereby the non-disabled partner provides personal care as a cost-saving measure, a practice that may be counter-indicated with intimacy (Crewe, 1993; Gill, 1996a, 1996b; Olkin, 1999; Parker, 1993). Similar barriers to those described above, can be found in lesbian relationships between women with and without disabilities.

In a Muscular Dystrophy conference I attended in Melbourne, one of the speakers was a civil servant who was invited to address the issue of benefits. Following her talk, a young woman with a disability asked what would happen to her government pension when she marries next month. The speaker confirmed that it would indeed be cut; given that the woman's spouse is employed. This same civil servant was completely dumbfounded when, in lieu of the technical question she was expecting, I used the floor to voice the injustice inherent in such policies. Although she looked at me as though she had no idea where I was coming from, the nods of agreement from around the room assured me that other people did.

Internal barriers and challenges

Thus far I have reported on barriers that affect, but are outside of, the woman herself. However, the interactive effect of negative messages, disempowering practices and practical concerns, run the risk of further erecting barriers on the inside as well. Carol Thomas (1999) refers to this as "barriers on the outside, inside" (p. 47): "These impact upon disabled people in diverse ways and can lodge themselves in their subjectivities, sometimes with profound exclusionary consequences by working on their sense of personhood and self-esteem" (pp. 47–48). Thomas (1999) further demonstrates how such barriers that she refers to as the psycho-emotional dimensions of disability, can indirectly restrict activity. She provides an example of a woman who decides not to apply for a certain job not for lack of skill or confidence in her abilities, but due to her wish to avoid the negative reactions of others to her body.

Carol Gill (1996a) provides another example of this phenomenon in her account of a seminar focusing on self-esteem at a health centre for women with disabilities. Several women with disabilities in the audience related the difficulties associated with developing positive relationships and having a good self-esteem when they experience so much social rejection. The psychologist leading the seminar explained that Different does not mean Inferior; in a restaurant, some customers will choose the lemon meringue pie while others will prefer the banana cream pie. Just because one pie is chosen over the other, that does not make the unchosen one inferior. Like pies, women too, are different. "A hand shot up in the back of the room. A middle age African American woman with a visible physical disability quickly brought the discussion back to basics. She asked, 'But what if you are considered a smashed pie?'" (Gill, 1996a, p. 5).

As this powerful story suggests, "barriers outside, inside" are nowhere more apparent than in the realm of relationships and sexuality. Women who received negative messages in the past regarding their attractiveness and desirability or whose attempts to form relationships were previously thwarted, may retreat from intimacy as a way of shielding themselves from painful experiences (Milligan & Neufeldt, 2001). In a qualitative study with thirty-one women with physical disabilities, fear of rejection was found to be a strong theme that affected both the quality and quantity of dating. Thus, even in the absence of current experiences of rejection, those who were demeaned by such experiences in the past may be unwilling to place themselves in a position of emotional vulnerability where they can be hurt again. This may result in reduced opportunities to learn and practice important social skills as well as curtail the likelihood of meeting a potentially compatible partner. Most importantly, it can further reinforce a negative belief about oneself that may then become a self-fulfilling prophecy.

Women that internalise negative messages about themselves, a phenomenon known as internalised oppression, may be sceptical of anyone who attempts to get close to them. The CROWD researchers reported that some of their participants perceived themselves as damaged goods and thus devalued any one who expressed an interest in them; one woman in a lesbian relationship kept wondering about why her non-disabled girlfriend stuck around (Howland & Rinalta, 2001). Other women had a clear preference for non-disabled partners based on the belief that "being seen with someone with a disability increased their own stigmatisation, or that they deserved better than a person with a disability" (Howland & Rinalta, 2001, p. 54). Interestingly, other researchers (Asch & Fine, 1988; Gill, 1996b) note this phenomenon in relation to men with disabilities, many of whom eliminate women with disabilities as potential partners. Gill (1996b) refers to these men as seeking "a majority culture partner to offset rather than mirror their own socially devalued status" (p. 119). Indeed, the insidious nature of internalised oppression can work its way into the psyches of men as well as women with disabilities.

I regard internalised oppression as a useful concept in explaining the reported tendency of some women to form a relationship with anyone who is willing to do so (Howland & Rinalta, 2001; Nosek et al., 2001). Of course, this risk is not unique to women with disabilities. I am reminded of a former client of mine at a University counselling service who felt literally unable to turn down any man who attempted to court her. Nonetheless, women with disabilities are certainly more likely to have been exposed to implicit and/or explicit messages that they are not desirable. This is a critical contextual factor in explaining the lack of selectivity reported in some studies (Howland & Rinalta, 2001; Nosek et al., 2001). As Lisi (1993) notes, "Not all of us take being a sex object for granted. For someone who does not expect to be viewed as attractive, a wolf whistle from a passing truck can be a great experience" (p. 202). The likelihood of becoming involved in an unhealthy and possibly abusive relationship is undoubtedly higher for women who feel that they should be grateful for sexual attention of any sort.

Some women may attempt to compensate for their perceived inferiority by being overly agreeable and pleasing their partners while undermining their own needs and wishes (Howland & Rinalta, 2001; Nosek et al., 2001). Again, this is a risk factor for women in general who have been traditionally socialized to meet the needs of others. On the other hand, or perhaps in addition, people with disabilities utilize various strategies including humour, charm and at times deference, in order to put other people at ease and lessen their discomfort (Thomson, 1997a). Cheerfulness is required; anger is disallowed (Keith, 1996; Olkin, 1999). As an example of the common expectation that people with disabilities are supposed to smile, Olkin (1999) writes about the 1997 arrival of Matel's first Barbie in a wheelchair, befittingly named "Share a Smile

Becky". It should be clear even without the Barbie doll example that women with disabilities are at an increased risk for negating their own needs and emotions for the sake of others. In the words of Lois Keith (1996), "our desire to make everything easier for ourselves by always being bright and pleasant in our dealings with the world and our need to have everyone think well of us, can be destructive" (p. 85).

Fulfilling relationships, strengths and a positive sense of self

Thus far I have discussed common barriers for girls and women with disabilities in forging fulfilling relationships and developing and maintaining a high self esteem. Given the presence of these barriers, it is particularly heartening to point to research that clearly indicates that a high self esteem and a physical disability are by no means mutually exclusive or even rare. In the CROWD studies, 78% of the 476 physically disabled women who completed the national survey reported having a high or moderately high self-esteem. Furthermore, self-esteem was not related to age of onset of the disability or to level of severity.

More importantly, these studies provide valuable information regarding possible pathways to a positive sense of self in the context of physical disability. While women with disabilities on average reported lower self-esteem than those without disabilities, this between-group difference was eliminated for women who were working or were fulfilled with their activities; who were in a serious romantic relationship; or who had not experienced physical or sexual abuse (Nosek et al., 2001). Women characterized as such, reported a high self-esteem regardless of whether they were disabled or not. On the flip side, between-group differences in self-esteem were significant for women with opposite characteristics to those noted above. Amongst those not employed or in fulfilling activities, not in a serious relationship or who had experienced abuse, women with disabilities had much lower self-esteem than their non-disabled counterparts. A low self-esteem was also more likely to be reported by women with disabilities whose families did not expect that they would marry or live independently.

The CROWD researchers emphasize that while work, relationships and absence of abuse were found to be significant correlates of high self-esteem, "noticeably absent are factors related to the disability itself" (Nosek et al., 2001, p. 12). Of course, correlation does not equal causation and it is difficult to establish whether a high self-esteem has primarily contributed to these factors (employment, romantic relationship, absence of abuse as adults) or has developed as a result. Nonetheless, human beings both shape and are shaped by their environments and a high self-esteem is predicated on positive and affirming experiences and relationships and at the same time serves as a foundation for purposeful, goal-directed behaviour.

The importance of esteem-building activities for girls and women with disabilities in multiple settings and context is thus indisputable. In a similar vein, eradicating structural and attitudinal barriers to education and employment would increase options for meaningful employment and at the same time enhance the prospects of forming health-enhancing social networks. Without a doubt, the likelihood that a woman with a disability would meet a potential partner is increased if she is in the work force or is otherwise an active member of her community. Given that people with disabilities may be more restricted in the range of leisure activities that they can partake in, work can fulfil an important need for social engagement in addition to providing a source of income.

Notwithstanding the reported challenges in forging intimate relationships, women with disabilities look for similar qualities in a mate than those without disabilities. They seek partners who share their interests, who they are friends with as well as being attracted to, and who are likewise interested in forming lasting relationships. While some have a clear preference for a non-disabled partner, others are more comfortable with a partner with a disability. "Either choice can represent self-acceptance and esteem or self-loathing" (Olkin, 1999, p. 225). It is not the choice itself but the meaning attributed to it that is important. Regardless of a partner's (dis)ability status, a fulfilling relationship can only be had with someone who is fully accepting of the woman's disability and of the various assistive devices and medical equipment that she may need (Howland & Rinalta, 2001).

I distinctly remember the first time I sat in a wheelchair. It was a beautiful Sunday morning more than 12 years ago and we had taken my mother and our then four-year-old son to a large safari-like park a few hours from our home. Although I walked without assistance at that stage, I would tire easily and long walks were becoming more burdensome than fun. Matan was eager to see the animals and to go on some of the rides while I visually scanned the park's vast terrain. "Why don't we just take one of those wheelchairs?" Isaac cautiously suggested. Matan's palpable excitement and boundless energy was the deciding factor. I didn't want my impairment to stand in the way of my four-year-old's ability to enjoy all that the park had to offer.

I remember the feeling of being suddenly "shorter" than the rest of the adult population, the realization that everyone I see is now smiling at me, and the strangeness of it all. The fact that Matan was rather excited about the novelty of riding in mommy's lap was comforting; beyond the obvious pleasure of cuddling him, it somehow felt good to hold my child, a testament of both my sexuality and my role as a caregiver. At some point my mother and I joined Matan on the Ferris wheel while Isaac waited below. As the wheel began to turn, we spotted him comfortably stretched out in the wheelchair. I have yet to ask Isaac if this was a deliberate move on his part, but that simple act of his made a world of difference to me. It symbolized his comfort and unreserved acceptance of my disability status, an acceptance that has not wavered as the impairment progressed and the devises and aides have grown in number and sophistication.

The importance of a partner's acceptance of the disability status has been noted by a number of authors and researchers. Commenting on the reticence of many people to become romantically involved with someone who has a visible disability, Olkin's (1999) message to therapists is blunt: "For a client's well-being he or she simply cannot be in a close relationship with someone who cannot accept the disability. Most people know this already, but some need reminding" (p. 225). Lack of acceptance by a significant other of this essential component of one's identity is clearly counter-indicated with a positive sense of self. At the same time, a high self esteem can serve as a protective factor in that an individual who values her own worth and is able to integrate the disability into her sense of self, is a lot more likely to choose a partner who appreciates her as a complete person and accepts the disability as one component of her identity.

A woman, who perceives herself as a sexual being that others may be attracted to, is also more likely to be forthcoming with a sexual partner about potential barriers and ways to overcome them. As the burgeoning literature on sexuality and disability attests, even such intimately personal issues like catheters and bowel accidents can be candidly discussed and successfully negotiated within the context of a healthy and caring relationship (Howland & Rinalta, 2001; Milligan & Neufeldt, 2001). Some women report that the inevitability of having to discuss such issues with sexual partners can contribute to increased comfort and greater intimacy (O'Toole, 2002).

The challenges and barriers that many people with disabilities come across in the realm of relationships and sexuality are undeniable. At the same time, these should not overshadow the fact that many are ultimately successful in forging fulfilling relationships. As the CROWD researchers have contended, "many women reported eventually forming a long-term relationship with a partner who accepted their disability while cherishing the unique characteristics they had to offer" (Nosek et al., 2001, p. 15). Furthermore, "whether the woman had slight difficulty in walking or used a power wheelchair with a ventilator, her concept of her value was much more important than the level of her disability in predicting satisfaction with relationships and her practice of healthy behaviors" (Nosek & Hughes, 2001, p. 20).

Those who write about these issues from a disability culture perspective, point to the paucity of research on successful relationships between people with and without disabilities. Such strength-based research could potentially highlight important pathways toward fulfilment and well-being, along with possible obstacles and ways to overcome them. Being in a loving relationship not only contributes to quality of life and psychological well-being but is also associated with greater resilience to physical ailments and with longevity itself (Ornish, 1997; Putnam, 2000). The evidence for focusing on relational aspects of people with disabilities is thus compelling.

The past decade has seen a burgeoning of literature on this topic, some of which has been generated from within the disability community. Publications such as New Mobility (www.newmobility.com) provide a wealth of information on a multitude of issues including relationships and sexuality. "In true advocacy spirit, these articles recount personal stories which, by example, seek to inspire readers to resist internalizing the social messages that PWD receive about their sexuality – or lack thereof" (Milligan & Neufeldt, 2001, p. 94). For many people, access to the Internet has enabled them to obtain valuable information, learn from the experience of others, and become involved in the disability community if they so wish.

Professional literature and clinical practice is also moving away from an exclusive focus on physical capacity to greater exploration of interpersonal aspects of sexuality and wellness models (Milligan & Neufeldt, 2001; Sipski & Alexander, 1997). Nonetheless, some researchers caution that "Despite the pervasive rhetoric within the literature that urges the delivery of comprehensive sexual information and counseling to PWD, there appears to be a significant discrepancy between program description and service delivery (Milligan & Neufeldt, 2001, p. 101). These authors further remind us that progress in service delivery, as important as that may be, continues to focus on people with disabilities themselves. Such efforts must be supplanted by a commitment to changing societal attitudes and practices that continue to negatively impinge on the lives of people with disabilities.

Concluding comments

This chapter has focused on the development of relationships, sexuality, and self-esteem for women with disabilities. Disabled women's relationship with their bodies was explored through cultural representation of female and disabled bodies and the lived experience of impairment effects. Rather than dichotomous constructs, it is the dynamic interaction of bodily experiences, cultural messages, and social interactions that largely shape the way in which women relate to their bodies.

The experience of girls with disabilities was explored with a particular focus on parental perceptions and messages, girls' interactions with service providers, peer relations, and romantic encounters. There is little doubt that girls with disabilities face particular challenges in peer relations in general and in dating in particular. Nonetheless, there is much that can be done at home, at school, and in the community to help girls develop a strong sense of self and form healthy interactions.

Childhood experiences, current contextual factors and internal and external resources play a role in disabled women's relationships and self esteem. Like their non-disabled counterparts, they place a high premium on intimacy and connectedness and yearn to form meaningful relationships. Their attempts are at times met with resistance and rejection. Deconstructing negative attitudes and experiences of rejection is important in preventing women from internalising such messages. Not surprisingly, those who were raised to perceive themselves as lovable and worthy are better equipped to externalise negative experiences and continue to pursue loving relationships.

The growing literature on women with disabilities is pointing to possible pathways for enhancing well-being. For example, having a job and being in an intimate relationship were found to be important buffers against low self-esteem for women with disabilities, more so than for those without disabilities. Notwithstanding the barriers they face, women with physical disabilities, as a group, have a strong sense of self and are largely successful in forming meaningful relationships. At the same time, in comparison with either non-disabled women or disabled men, they are more likely to be poor, have less education, and are less likely to be in the work force. Thus, it is imperative that continuous efforts are made to eradicate physical, attitudinal, and psychological barriers that continue to impinge on the lives of many women with disabilities.

Disabled women researchers and activists like Carol Gill and Marsha Saxton in the US, and Jenny Morris and Lois Keith in Britain, are paving the way for younger women with disabilities and are working hard to ensure that the world they will inherit will be a friendlier and more tolerant one. According to a recent article, their efforts are not in vain. Younger women with disabilities are described in the literature as more confident, assertive, and fulfilled with their lives and relationships. Unlike the older generation of women with disabilities who had to unlearn internalised messages regarding relationships, sexuality, and self-worth, younger women with disabilities are more confident in their abilities and their prospects.

3
Reproductive Choice and Motherhood in the Context of Physical Disability

> I am twelve years old
> I know I'm not expected to have children.
> I don't know how I know, I just do.
> Nobody ever said anything;
> It's probably what they didn't say
> that made the difference.   (Duffy, 1996, p. 29)

If some women with physical disabilities were raised without having their sexuality and womanhood acknowledged, many more received messages that reproduction and motherhood is off limits. According to a recent article on the subject, "the training against motherhood begins when a woman is diagnosed as disabled and continues throughout her childbearing years" (O'Toole, 2002, p. 82). Ten years ago, the journal *Sexuality and Disability* published a special issue on parenting with a disability. In the preface to this issue the editor stated that "the beliefs that people with a disability are unable to conceive and raise children are as pervasive today as they were twenty years ago" (Ducharme, 1993, p. 185). On the other hand, according to a 1996 article in a major Canadian newspaper, "...in doctors' offices and on the street, the politics surrounding disabled parenthood is changing...there's an awareness on the part of disabled women that it's possible to become a parent, and an awareness on the part of health professionals not to discourage them" (Philip, 1996, p. A12).

The growing body of popular and professional literature on parenting with a disability, virtually nonexistent a few decades ago is characterized by such contradictions. Alongside narratives of some women's struggle for the right to have and raise their children, others tell of dedicated family members, friends, and caring professionals who make their lives easier as mothers with disabilities. For others yet, lived experience incorporates both hindering and facilitative interactions. In this chapter I cover the growing literature on mothering with a disability. I begin with a brief overview of feminist discourse on motherhood, disabled women's historical exclusion from mothering, and the contested domain of prenatal testing and selective abortion. I then review trends in the literature on the relationship between parental disability and the well-being of children. Finally, I present current knowledge on the lives and experiences of mothers with disabilities and their families.

Women with disabilities and reproductive choice

Feminist discourse on motherhood

Over the past several decades, motherhood as institution and lived experience have been extensively studied and theorized by feminist scholars. Common to all such explorations is the premise that the institution of motherhood has been named and interpreted not by women but by the patriarchal culture in which they live (Achilles, 1990; O'Barr, Pope & Wyer, 1990). For centuries, womanhood and motherhood were seen as interchangeable, one biologically, inevitably, and unquestionably emanating from the other. To be a woman was to be a mother and to be a mother was to spend most of one's adulthood bearing and rearing children. Women's lives were largely determined by their capacity to reproduce and their perceived tendency towards sensitivity and nurturance, given the "split between a 'productive' public sphere and a 'reproductive' private sphere" (Hird & Abshoff, 2000, p. 350).

The feminist movement has played a major role in both reclaiming motherhood from patriarchy and in legitimizing the choice of some women to remain childless. Rather than criticizing the act of mothering or undermining its significance for many women, it exposed dominant ideologies that relegated women to the private sphere, away from powerful political and economic institutions in which important decisions about their lives were being made (O'Barr, Pope & Wyer, 1990). In her classic book *Of Woman Born: Motherhood as Experience and Institution*, Rich (1976) made an important distinction between the oppressive institution of motherhood and the potentially fulfilling experience of being a mother. It was the institution of motherhood that feminists regarded as oppressive to women by placing responsibility for child-care almost entirely on their shoulders. The actual experience of mothering was varied, diverse, and influenced by a wide array of social, economic, and political factors. Feminists have fought for more equitable division of labor within the home, as well as for mother-friendly policies in the workplace. Such policies, it was argued, would expand women's choices by ensuring that their mothering status would not hamper educational and professional advancement.

Alongside efforts to alleviate societal constraints affecting mothers, feminist discourse has pushed for the disentanglement of womanhood from motherhood and for the embracing of all women, irrespective of their reproductive choices. The cultural glorification of motherhood throughout history has been particularly oppressive for women who are not mothers. Psychoanalytical theory explained infertility in terms of a woman's unconscious fear of femininity and refusal to assume an appropriate gender role (Hammer Burns & Covington, 1999; Ireland, 1992; Lisle, 1996; Sandelowski, 1990). In the 1950s, married women in America who did not have children were considered deviant and socially aberrant (Lisle, 1996).

In the 1960s and 1970s feminism on the whole questioned the inevitability of motherhood and emphasized the multiple routes to women's happiness and fulfillment (Lisle, 1996; Snitow, 1992). However, this trend had shifted in the 1980s when many women who postponed childbirth in the previous decade were becoming pregnant as "the ticking of millions of biological clocks was being heard" (Lisle, 1996, p. 31). 1988 was the year in which more children were born to first time mothers in the USA than ever before (Lisle, 1996; Snitow, 1992).

Notwithstanding the growing trend of voluntary childlessness in contemporary society, the pronatalist trend has not abated in the 21st century (Hird & Abshoff, 2000; Letherby & Williams, 1999; Park, 2002). Women who opt out of parenthood are more likely to be negatively stigmatized than men who make similar decisions or women who are unable to conceive (Hird & Abshoff, 2000). Some feminists further claim that the implicit societal assumption that motherhood is an intrinsic part of female identity has not been sufficiently challenged in feminist analysis (Ireland, 1992; Snitow, 1992). Snitow (1992) concludes, "In the long run we were better able to attend to mothers' voices than we were able to imagine a full and deeply meaningful life without motherhood, without children" (p. 33). In the same vein, Hird and Abshoff (2000) state that recent feminist focus on female biology and motherhood "...presents problems for childless women whose experiences of their femininity without maternity tend to be silenced" (p. 357).

When motherhood is not expected: disabled women's reproductive journey

The pronatalism discussed thus far was never directed at all women, irrespective of race, class, sexual orientation and disability. Indeed, history attests to the selective pronatalism that was directed at healthy, wealthy white women, whereas women with disabilities, along with poor women, immigrant women, women of color, and lesbians, have been historically discouraged from procreation (Franzblau, 1996; Park, 2002). If the former experienced the pressure to bear children as oppressive, women with disabilities were perceived as childlike, dependent and asexual and were excluded from fulfilling traditionally female roles (Asch & Fine, 1988; Gill, 1996a & b; Nosek et al., 2001). As noted in the previous chapter, people with disabilities continue to face formidable challenges in having their sexuality acknowledged and in forging and maintaining intimate relationships.

Barbara Waxman, who passed away in 1999, was the former editor of the journal *Sexuality and Disability* and a fierce advocate for disabled women's reproductive rights. She has argued that "beneath the asexual stereotype lurks the belief that disabled women's reproductive capacity is a biological, moral, and economic danger" (Waxman, 1994, p. 155). Waxman, along with other disabled feminists, have exposed and condemned the restriction of full reproductive freedom that many women with disabilities have reported over the years. Restriction of reproductive freedom can take many forms. Stories of coerced abortions (Gill, 1996a) and pressure to undergo tubal ligations and hysterectomies (Ridington, 1989; Rogers, 1996) can be found in the literature on women with disabilities and were probably more prevalent in the past. Other more subtle pressures to refrain from reproducing are more commonly reported. A recent American study reported a childbearing rate of 38% in their sample of 475 physically disabled women, compared with 51% in the nondisabled comparison group. Women with physical disabilities also had a higher rate of hysterectomy (22% versus 12%) and were more likely to have this procedure done at a younger age (Nosek et al., 2001). Based on this data The CROWD researchers contend "it seems like the default recommendation for women with severe physical disabilities to have a hysterectomy" (Nosek et al., 2001, p. 33).

In the following section I explore these issues in relation to the growing popularity and sophistication of prenatal testing. Relevant to the present discussion are the frequent difficulties and frustrations that women with physical disabilities encounter in their quest for information on sexuality and reproductive health (Howland & Rinalta, 2001; Kallianes & Rubenfeld, 1997; Nosek et al., 2001). Historically, medical and professional literature were virtually silent on issues pertaining to the sexual functioning and reproductive health of women with disabilities, while in private offices physicians tended to discourage these women from having children. Consequently, there exists an astounding disparity in knowledge about the reproductive health of disabled versus non-disabled women; little is known about the number of disabled women of childbearing age, or their rates of fertility, pregnancy, birth and abortions (Nosek, 1996; Waxman, 1994, 1996; Saxton, 1994).

Knowledge on sexuality and reproductive health for women with physical disabilities is steadily growing. It was a major focus in a conference sponsored by the National Centre for Medical Rehabilitation Research (NCMRR) in 1996 and was also explored in a number of recent books (Graves, 1993; Krotoski, Nosek & Turk, 1996; Sipsky & Alexander, 1997). However, as Milligan & Neufeldt (2001) have claimed regarding sexual information and counselling, there is probably "a significant discrepancy between program description and service delivery" (p. 101). In other words, the growing knowledge in this field is not necessarily finding its way into the hands of women with physical disabilities or even the doctors who treat them. The CROWD researchers claim that "it is truly astounding how little information physicians are given about the effect of disability on reproductive capacity or the value women with disabilities ascribe to the ability to bear children" (Nosek et al., 2001, p. 34). This is corroborated by some very recent narrative accounts in published form and on the internet (Wates & Jade, 1999; www.disabledparents.net) and serves as a reminder that there is still a long way to go.

The historical tension between the feminist movement and women with disabilities is highly relevant to any discussion of disabled women's reproductive issues. The women's movement has used the term "reproductive rights" in reference to the right to be free of unwanted pregnancy – preferably by prevention but also by termination (Kallianes & Rubenfeldt, 1997). This narrow definition was exclusionary and thus invalidating of women with disabilities who often framed their own struggle as the right to have children. Clearly, the fight for reproductive rights has a different meaning for these women who have been denied information and "offered" abortions and tubal ligations all too readily. So long as the feminist struggle for reproductive freedom is defined only in terms of the right to terminate unwanted pregnancies, the wishes and concerns of women with disabilities are silenced (Gill, 1996a; Keith, 1992; Lloyd, 1992, 2001). Whilst this is obviously relevant for disabled women who choose motherhood, it is no less so for disabled women who do not and will not have children, either due to choice or circumstances. As Lloyd (2001) aptly argues, "the reinstatement of childlessness as a positive state is difficult to embrace if one's status as a 'non-parent' stems from one's inability to convince others of one's capacity to be a mother, in both its biological and social meaning" (p. 720).

The risk discourse

Thus far I have juxtaposed the pressure (past and present, internal and external) to bear children that women in general experience, with the pressure reported by many women with disabilities, to refrain from doing so. In a British survey of disabled mothers' experience of maternity, a third of the 199 respondents reported that they had been advised against having children, mainly by a relative other than their partner but also by physicians and geneticists (Goodman, 1994). In the Boston-based project "Women and Disability Think Tank", all 10 participants had similar stories of being actively discouraged from considering pregnancy by health practitioners or family members (Saxton, 1994).

While pressures to refrain from reproduction can be attributed to a host of factors, they often hinge on the perception of risk to the resultant child. Two commonly held beliefs are: a) disabled mothers are likely to produce disabled children and b) children will be negatively affected by having a parent with a disability. Later in this chapter I explore the latter assumption. In this section I discuss the perception of risk to the foetus, an issue that is inseparable from the larger debate on prenatal testing and selective abortion. Contrary to a commonly held belief, most impairments are not hereditary and are thus not transmitted from mother to child. This rudimentary fact is known to many and stating it may seem superfluous. Nonetheless, some women report being "warned" by co-workers, family members and even total strangers of the "risk" that they will produce a child with a disability. Furthermore, some forms of impairment are genetically transmitted and are quite likely to affect the foetus. Some people will undoubtedly question the decision of such parents to have a baby who may inherit their condition.

Francis Galton who launched a movement to improve the human race through selective breeding coined the term eugenics. By the 1920s such movements were prevalent all over the world and were ultimately associated with the compulsive sterilisation of thousands of individuals with intellectual impairments (Wikler, 1999). As Parens and Asch (2000) note, "the history of discrimination against people with disabilities, including episodes of infanticide and compulsory sterilisation, is long, ugly, and well documented" (p. 5). Today, few would support such violations of reproductive rights (Wikler, 1999). This, however, does not preclude people from making moral judgements about the reproductive decisions of others.

In 1991, a talk show host in California invited listeners to comment on the pregnancy of Bree Walker, a Los Angeles television news presenter with Ectrodactyly, a hereditary condition that results in the fusing of fingers and toes. Walker's decision to carry to term a child who is likely to inherit her condition was questioned by the host and criticised by some of the callers: "I would rather not be alive than have a disease like that when it's a 50–50 chance" (Campion, 1995, p. 136). If this incident can be attributed to prejudice born from ignorance, the following quote is from an article by a professor of bioethics: "I do not think that anyone should be prevented or prohibited from making his or her own choices about reproduction. However...it does not follow from this that reproductive choices are not open to moral condemnation...to make a reproductive choice knowing that the resulting child will be significantly disabled is morally problematic, and often morally wrong" (Harris, 2000, p. 96).

The above quote is in relation to the issue of prenatal testing and selective abortion, a practice that is growing in popularity yet marked by controversy. When I was pregnant some 17 years ago, I vaguely remember a casual comment by my obstetrician as she obtained my written permission for the multiple marker test, a commonly used screening test for birth defects. Although I signed my name and even agreed to pay for this procedure (it was not covered by Canada's publicly funded health care), I must admit to being mostly if not totally oblivious to the possible ramifications of a positive result. This was a long time ago considering the growth in this field. The human genome project has led to significant advancement in the ability to detect foetal abnormality or "mutation" associated with certain conditions. It is now possible to detect gene mutations associated with hundreds of conditions, with almost daily growth in the number and variety of conditions that new tests are able to detect (Parens & Asch, 2000).

Professor of Psychiatry Dorothy Wertz speculates that "In the future through DNA chip technology it may be possible to offer tests for thousands of conditions for mere pennies per test" (Wertz, 2000, pp. 273–274).

Prenatal diagnosis (PND) is becoming a routine part of prenatal care (Saxton, 2000) and most women (over 80%) choose to terminate a pregnancy when the foetus is found to have Down Syndrome, Spina Bifida, or Cystic Fibrosis (Gillam, 1999), amongst other conditions. For a number of years now, disability rights activists have been articulating the need to critically examine this practice and the often taken-for-granted assumption that abortion will follow a diagnosis of disability. For one thing, critics point to the disparity between how people with disabilities perceive their lives and how those same lives may be perceived (and thus described) by professionals. Carol Gill (1996a) writes about her encounter with a gynaecologist who remarked on how incredible she must be to be happy despite her severe disability. The gynaecologist disagreed with Gill's comment that happiness is more closely related to one's ability to meet goals and have fulfilling relationships than to the extent of the disability. As Gill later found out, this gynaecologist also served as medical director of genetic services: "I shudder to think about what this Ob/Gyn is telling her patients about bringing people like me into their lives"   (Gill, 1996a, p. 11).

The equation of disability with tragedy and with a life not worth living has been long decried by people with disabilities who describe their own lives in very different terms. Notwithstanding the harmful consequences of socially created barriers, many disabled people, like their non-disabled counterparts, lead lives that they perceive to be enjoyable, meaningful and fulfilling. They worry that in the absence of first hand knowledge about life with a disability, prospective parents are at risk of making critical decisions based on information that is at best incomplete and at worst marked by doom and gloom (Parens & Asch, 2000; Saxton, 2000). Furthermore, medical references to disability typically do not include the negative impact of socially constructed (and thus preventable) barriers. Rather, any disadvantage is attributed to a bio-medical reality. Conversely, people with disabilities often regard social and attitudinal barriers as more troubling than the impairment itself.

The argument is often made that PND benefits women by expanding their reproductive choices. At the same time, those who choose to forego prenatal testing are likely to be criticised for such choices and often have to contend with the clear disapproval of their doctors

(Stewart, 1996). An even greater concern raised by some critics is the potential risk to medical coverage for those who choose to bring to term rather than abort the "flawed" and "expensive" foetus (Blumberg, 1994a, 1994b; Rioux, 1996; Saxton, 1994). Decreased tolerance for individuals living with "preventable" impairments may also threaten public funding for resources that can enhance the quality of their lives (Andrews & Hibbert, 2000). Of course, until such time that science will enable us to use gene therapy in order to correct detectable impairments, prevention in relation to PND is really prevention of the individual herself.

Some critics contend that the societal pursuit of perfect babies suggests that people living with disabilities are really a tragic mistake of nature, "defective faulty machines that should have been recalled" (Blumberg, 1994b, p. 139). The risk of being stigmatised as preventable people, ones who have "slipped through the net of prenatal screening" (Andrews & Hibbert, 2000, p. 320), cannot be ignored. Saxton (2000) reminds us that "the first generation of potentially 'screenable' disabled people is just now coming of age" (p. 159). Like Saxton, these people may ask themselves: "would my parents have 'chosen' me?" (p. 159). Individuals with disabilities, those who love them, and others, who share their concerns, are increasingly articulating the potentially devaluing impact of membership in such "screenable" categories.

There is a diversity of views on PND, not only in the general population but also amongst physicians, scientists, and ethicists. For example, John Harris whom I quoted earlier refers to disability as a "harmed condition" (p. 97) and to those who knowingly give birth to disabled children as "morally wrong" (p. 96). He is further at odds with a view of disability as entirely socially constructed and only problematic due to social constraints. Steinbock (2000) also disagrees with the social construction view, while acknowledging both the impact of socially constructed barriers and the fulfilling lives that are had by most people with disabilities. Steinbock (2000) and others (Baily, 2000) further postulate that the decision to terminate a pregnancy following PND is not tantamount to devaluing the lives of individuals living with impairments.

The issue of PND and selective abortion is charged, complex, and fraught with challenges. Many people with disabilities including those who point to the problematic nature of PND, do not deny that some impairments are associated with restrictions that cannot simply be removed by social change. At the same time, they worry about the implications of "letting the part stand in for the whole" (Asch, 2000,

p. 14), when "a single trait stands in for the whole (potential) person" (p. 14). "When we present the diagnosis of a genetic disease condition to the parents, do we also remind parents that this baby would also still come with a full set of other human characteristics?" (Saxton, 2000, p. 161). Saxton's conclusion is that this is rarely done. Neither are prospective parents typically encouraged to meet families who are currently raising children with disabilities, or with disabled adults who have jobs, families and lives that are otherwise similar to people without disabilities.

While highlighting the danger of an uncritical embrace of this technology, disabled activists like Adrienne Asch and Marsha Saxton believe that the ultimate decision lies with prospective parents. They further acknowledge that the disability community does not hold a uniform position on this issue. Some individuals may decide to undergo the very procedures that, had they been available at the time, would have prevented their own existence. Irrespective of their own views on PND, disabled feminists in particular, are not advocating for restricting the options available to parents. In fact, "virtually all the major work in the disability critique of prenatal testing emerges from those who are committed to a pro-choice feminist agenda" (Parens & Asch, 2000, p. 12).

What disability rights activists do advocate for is a fundamental change in how PND is offered, options are discussed, and life with a disability is presented to prospective parents. Research suggests that families of children with disabilities are more alike than different from those without disabilities and on average, fare no better or worse than families in general (Ferguson, Gartner & Lipsky, 2000). Prospective parents would benefit from such information, especially in light of early professional literature that tended to portray children with disabilities as a burden on families. I conclude with a quote from Adreinne Asch, herself a disabled feminist and academic: "If parents can make their choices about selective abortion after information that helps them to imagine a worthwhile life for child and family, I support parents in the decision they make" (Asch, 2000, p. 254).

Parental disability and the well-being of children

In her book titled *Who's Fit to Be a Parent*, Campion (1995) asserts that "today, the focus of assessment for parental fitness has shifted away from whether people can produce the right quality of genetic offspring to whether they are up to the actual task of child-rearing" (p. 132).

People with physical disabilities are amongst those Campion refers to as "parents on the edge" whose fitness to rear children has been traditionally questioned. The discouragement of motherhood for women with disabilities can only be partially explained by societal fears that they will produce disabled children. Another commonly held belief, and one that has been supported by some of the literature is that children's physical and psychological well-being is at stake when they have a disabled parent. In this section I review some of the research studies and professional literature on the relationship between parental disability and the well being of children and families. Research and professional literature is both affected by prevailing social trends and also serves to shape them by challenging or reinforcing common beliefs. Thus, professional literature on parenting with a disability is an important contextual factor in the experiences of disabled mothers and their families.

Disabling discourses

Compared with the myriad of studies on children with disabilities and policies regarding their educational integration and accommodation, parents with disabilities continue to be primarily ignored by research and social policy (Meadow-Orlans, 2002; Olkin, 1999). Olkin (1999) contends, "It is as if families have children with disabilities and then these children disappear from the face of the earth" (p. 126). The sparse literature that can be found on the topic typically focuses on the relationship between parental disability and children's well being. In some cases a negative impact is hypothesized, studied and "verified" (Peters & Esses, 1985); in other cases the correlation between indices of dysfunction in children and parental disability is explored (LeClere & Kowalewski, 1994); and in others yet, the negative impact on children and the need to counsel them is taken as a given (Kennedy & Bush, 1979).

In the very first sentence of an article titled *Counseling the Children of Handicapped Parents*, Kennedy and Bush (1979) recommended counseling for these children in order "to facilitate their adjustment to deficiencies in parenting behaviour and family structure that may have resulted from the parent's handicap" (p. 267). They further speculated that "handicapped parents, because of their frustration, may make their children scapegoats and assign them additional responsibilities" (p. 267). The article is replete with such terms as "afflicted", "stricken", "bed-ridden" and "physically defective" in its description of disabled parents and concludes by portraying these parents as frustrated individuals who "become increasingly disagreeable" (p. 270). Published less than 25 years ago in a reputable counselling journal, this article was undoubtedly read by many professionals who came in contact with children of parents with disabilities. Its potentially iatrogenic impact is clear.

Whereas the negative biases of the authors are crystal clear in the above-mentioned article, they can be more insidious and therefore escape detection in other publications. One such Canadian study (Peters & Esses, 1985) investigated the effect of parental chronic illness (Multiple Sclerosis) on family functioning. Thirty three research participants and the same number of controls aged 12–18 years and matched for sex, age and socioeconomic status, were administered the Family Environment Scale. Based on statistically significant differences between the groups, the authors concluded that children who have a disabled parent perceive their families significantly differently than those who do not. More specifically, they regard their families as having more conflict, being less organized and less involved in cultural activities and intellectual pursuits, and as placing less emphasis on moral and religious issues.

The grim results of this study and its implication for parents with disabilities must be considered in light of a major methodological drawback that receives no more than lip service by the authors. While the research subjects were recruited through the local MS society, all of the controls were students at a local religiously affiliated school (Mennonite Brethren). The authors give no other information about the school other than its religious affiliation. Nowhere in the article is it mentioned, for example, that this is a private school rather than a publicly funded one. The reader would not have this information unless they, like me, lived in the city where the study was conducted and worked in its school system. Would we not speculate about possible differences between families whose children attend one religiously affiliated private school and those who attend various public schools? The authors only mention the religious affiliation of the school, refer to it very briefly as a methodological drawback, then minimize its impact by arguing that most of the control group scores were "reasonably similar" (p. 307) to standardized scores. These methodological drawbacks cannot be considered minimal given the possible ramifications of the results.

Another study (LeClere & Kowalewski, 1994) which explored the effects of adult disability on children's well-being, analyzed data from the 1988 U.S. National Health Interview Survey on Child Health

(NHIS-CH). Adults in the household were classified as disabled based on a self-reported limitation due to health problems in the ability to perform major activities. Information on one randomly selected child per family was gathered from the parent (typically the mother) via a 28-item Behavioral Problem Index (BPI). The results of this study indicate that the mean number of severe and common behavioral problems was significantly increased by the presence of a disabled family member. After controlling for covariates (income, education of the responsible adult, family structure, marital status of mother), children living with a disabled parent or with more than one disabled relative were found to be the most affected. The authors conclude that the magnitude of these effects should not be understated and that more attention should be paid to the families of disabled individuals.

While I do not dispute the need to pay more attention to families who live with a disability, I question the very broad self-reported definition of disability that was used and the ability to generalize from that to families of parents with physical disabilities. For one thing, it is possible that a tendency to perceive and report limitations in one's ability to perform activities is correlated with a tendency to perceive and report behavioral problems in one's children. Furthermore, in the absence of any information on types of impairments, parents who are limited in their functioning due to mental illness or alcoholism, for example, could also fall under this rubric, while the problems they face in their parenting may be qualitatively different.

Also relevant to the topic of parental disability is the literature on young carers that has gained prominence in the last decade. A 1994 article titled *Lost Childhood* undoubtedly grabbed the attention of many readers. The article addresses the issue of children under 18 who provide care to ill and disabled relatives and emphasises the negative impact of such caring, referring to it as "a curse on children" (Sidall, 1994, p. 15). This issue has received increased attention not only from the popular media but also from researchers and policy analysts, most notably in the UK. Based on research carried out by Aldridge and Becker (1993) and others, arguments have been made regarding societal neglect of young carers and their social, economic, and educational disadvantage. Emanating from this research are a host of recommendations for respite services, drop-in centres and emotional support to these youngsters (Aldridge & Becker, 1996).

The focus on young carers has been critiqued on a number of fronts. Olsen (1996) has drawn attention to the artificial divide between this body of literature and one that explores the lives of parents with disabilities. He argues that researchers who have focused on young carers have neglected to emphasize the inadequacy of funded supports to meet the needs of their parents. He further objects to the unchallenged assumption that caring on the part of children is unquestionably associated with negative outcomes.

Keith and Morris (1996), feminist researchers and mothers with disabilities, have made similar arguments. For one thing, they contend that the very terminology of young carers is suggestive of taking charge of the individual requiring assistance. In other words, the child is assumed to be taking responsibility for the parent or even to be in the reversed role of parenting their parent. Not only is this association between the provision of assistance and role reversal harmful to children and parents alike, it is also an inaccurate description of the relationship dynamic in many such families. The misguided perception where disability is inevitably associated with dependency tends to undermine the parenting role of people with disabilities. Morris (1992, 1993, 2001) and others (Keith, 1992; Keith & Morris, 1996; Lloyd 1992, 2001; Olsen, 1996) have convincingly argued that narrow societal conceptions of care, where the caring role is equated with the caring function, have contributed to the barriers faced by parents with disabilities. Thus, parents who are unable to independently fulfill all of the physical tasks of child rearing are often subjected to others' skepticism regarding their ability to function as parents. Those requiring assistance with their own personal care are even more vulnerable to this kind of criticism.

Keith and Morris (1996) further emphasize the need to explore why children provide care in the first place. They point to poverty, disabling professional attitudes and disabling services as impediments to parental access to resources. Parents with disabilities are often reluctant to disclose their needs for services due to fear that their parental competence will be questioned (Keith & Morris, 1996; O'Toole, 2002; Thomas, 1997; Thorne, 1991). They are further wary of services that will be delivered in a manner that is inconsistent with their specific needs and circumstances or may be altogether diminishing and disempowering. Their reluctance is not unfounded; parents with disabilities are typically afforded little choice regarding the kinds of services they receive, the manner in which services are delivered, and who carries them out (Wates, 1997). Furthermore, obtaining such supports in an era of spending caps on social services can be very difficult if not unattainable (Toms Barker & Maralani, 1997; Reid, Angus, McKeever & Miller, 2003).

Those who have voiced concerns with some of the research and policy development on young carers also point to the danger of institutionalizing this phenomenon as an acceptable practice. After all, it is much cheaper to provide respite services and emotional support to young carers than to ensure that the entire family is properly serviced. Keith and Morris (1996) refer to this as a form of collusion with government whereas Olsen and Parker (1997) warn that "...there is a very real danger that providing services which support the child in the role of the carer will obstruct the development of services aimed at overcoming parental dependence" (p. 129). Indeed, a recent report on young carers in Australia (2002) makes the point that young carers need to be acknowledged and supported given that there will never be sufficient resources to meet the needs of those who require care. Arguments of this nature, coupled with instances where services are withdrawn based on the availability of a young carer, are cautious reminders of the potentially disablist policies that may ensue from this discourse. The reader is referred to Aldridge and Becker (1996) and Olsen and Parker (1997) for a thorough understanding of the controversy that surrounds this issue.

Enabling discourses

Kirshbaum and Olkin (2002) contend, "Much of the research on parents with disabilities has been driven by a search for problems in these families" (p. 66). "Not surprisingly, many studies which set out to confirm pathologizing hypotheses succeed in doing so" (p. 67). Much of this literature has been critiqued on various grounds including unexamined assumptions, methodological flaws, and lack of differentiation between disability situations (Kelley, Sikka & Venkatesan, 1997; Kirshbaum and Olkin, 2002; Medow-Orlans, 2002; Prilleltensky, 2003).

Researchers who align themselves with disabled parents emphasize the importance of the overall family constellation as well as sources of risk and protective factors external to the parental disability. The family's level of isolation versus support, the impact of poverty and disincentives for gainful employment, and inaccessible environments faced by many parents with disabilities are being raised as important contributing factors that should be considered in research (Blackford, 1999; Kelley et al., 1997; Kirshbaum, 1996; Kirshbaum & Olkin, 2002). Furthermore, some studies have found positive psychological adjustment amongst parents with Cerebral Palsy (Greer, 1985); lack of adverse effects of paternal disability (spinal cord injury) on the well being of children (Buck & Hohmann, 1981, 1982); and similar interaction patterns between mothers with Multiple Sclerosis and their daughters, and non-disabled mother-daughter dyads (Crist, 1993).

What helps some families cope well despite the presence of risk factors and what can be learned from their ability to thrive in the presence of illness and disability? What supports do parents require that would enhance their parenting? These are some of the questions that warrant researchers' attention. Indeed, some studies have been instrumental in highlighting factors associated with positive family functioning. One study found that frequent use of familial introspection, defined as the ability to reflect on the family performance and make adjustments in the face of illness demands, is associated with positive outcome for the family including better adjusted marriages and better parent-child relationships (Hough, Lewis, & Woods, 1991; Lewis, Woods, Hough & Bensley, 1989). Furthermore, fewer stressors and a perception of strong social supports, distinguished well adjusted from poorly adjusted families. Another study of parents with Multiple Sclerosis has identified specific coping mechanisms utilized by well adjusted versus poorly adjusted families (Power, 1985). Positive coping mechanisms include open communication within the family and with health care professionals, flexibility in roles and a willingness to share responsibility, outward-directed activities, and continued involvement of the disabled parent in family activities and engagement as a competent decision maker. Poorly adjusted families were characterised by poor communication, insufficient knowledge about the illness and its implication, and a tendency to unnecessarily exempt the disabled parent from daily responsibilities.

An encouraging trend among some researchers and service providers is one of approaching these families with the purpose of identifying strengths. One such example is *Talking it Out in the Family*, a video portraying real life situations of parental disability where the actors are the people living the experience (Blackford, 1990). Research conducted at Through the Looking Glass (TLG), a research, prevention and intervention centre in California focusing on disabled parents and their families, also operates from a strength-based orientation. Some examples are an in-depth study of families with at least one significantly disabled parent where the parents perceive themselves as having positive parenting experiences; a longitudinal study of children of parents with physical disabilities which explores factors that promote positive child outcomes as well as those that increase risk; and research consisting of both a qualitative and quantitative components exploring the impact of assistive technology on the transition to parenthood (Kirshbaum, 1996; Kirshbaum & Olkin, 2002).

These types of studies are helpful as they advance our knowledge about specific coping strategies associated with positive outcome. They have clear implications for practice that can be used by professionals and are potentially empowering to people with disabilities who are either parents or are considering parenthood. Rather than minimizing difficulties or potentially problematic family situations, work of this nature is based on a disability culture orientation and focuses on socially created constraints to optimal functioning. Furthermore, as more research that explicitly sets out to "document the spectrum of capability in parents with disabilities" Kirshbaum & Olkin, 2002, p. 70) is amassed, professional and public perceptions will continue to shift in a more favourable direction.

Mothering with a disability: women's lived experience

Notwithstanding the historical lack of attention to parental disability, women with disabilities have always had children and this number is clearly on the rise. Improved health care, legislative changes that have allowed for increased community participation and gradual changes in societal perceptions have undoubtedly contributed to a growth in numbers and in greater visibility. The past two decades have also seen a surge in both autobiographical accounts and studies that describe the lives and experiences of mothers with physical disabilities. A Survey of Income and Program Participation (SIPP) conducted by the US Census Bureau in 1993 reported that about seven million parents with children under 18 years of age have a disability. A person was classified as having a disability if he or she: a) used a wheelchair b) used a cane or walker for six months or longer c) had difficulty with a functional activity d) had difficulty with an activity of daily living e) had difficulty with an instrumental activity or f) had a developmental, mental or emotional disability. According to these criteria, 11% of all parents report a disability and approximately 30% of disabled adults (1/3 of disabled women and 1/4 of disabled men) are parents of children less than 18 years of age (Toms Barker & Maralani, 1997).

A national survey of parents with disabilities was conducted as part of Through the Looking Glass' Research and Training Centre (RTC). Of the 1,175 parents with disabilities who completed the survey, 90% are white, 75% are women and 80% have a physical disability. The respondents' profiles are similar to the SIPP Census in terms of distribution of disability type (about 80% physical), employment status (about 50%) and marital status (2/3 married or live with a partner). However, the respondents were self-selected and differed from the national sample in a number of ways. There are fewer minorities (10% versus 30%), more women, and a generally higher level of income and education. Approximately 50% of the RTC sample had a college or graduate degree and the same number was employed at the time of the survey with an average yearly income of under $10,000. The survey is about mothers and fathers with a range of disabilities. However, the high proportion of women (75%) and those with physical disabilities (80%) make it particularly relevant to this book. This survey, along with other studies and autobiographical accounts, provide us with invaluable information about the challenges mothers with disabilities face at different phases of their reproductive journeys.

As the subheading below suggests, many of the difficulties experienced by mothers are attributed to socially constructed factors. This is not to undermine the role that the impairment itself plays in some cases. However, many mothers describe barriers that are either external or not directly related to the impairment and can be alleviated by systemic and attitudinal changes. I first review barriers due to errors of commission: direct actions and practices that are experienced as disempowering and that can constitute a threat to well being. Errors of omission on the other hand, refer to unavailable or insufficient services and resources that their absence constitutes an impediment to well being.

Disabling practices and experiences: errors of commission

Attempts to prevent a disabled woman from becoming pregnant, continuing a desired pregnancy, or raising her own child are the most blatant and potentially most harmful errors of commission. Amongst the disabled mothers who responded to the national survey, 14% reported suggestions that they be sterilized and 13% were pressured to have an abortion (Toms Barker & Maralani, 1997). Pressure to refrain from having children was also reported in disabled women's autobiographical accounts. In one particularly shocking account, a family planning worker attempted to convince a pregnant woman with a severe physical disability to undergo an abortion. She attempted to impress upon her how difficult it is to raise a child, a task that she "couldn't possibly manage" (Litwinowicz, 1999, p. 32). When this worker realized that her "client" was undeterred, she chose another strategy: "You do realise that when your child can walk and talk it will come to you and say, 'I hate you mother because you can't talk properly, you dribble, and you're in a wheelchair and I want a new mother'" (p. 32).

This account is extreme in its cruelty and is unlikely to be a common experience. I further venture to say that we would be hard-pressed to find many if any family planning workers who would defend such behaviour. Nonetheless, personal narratives titled "expecting but unexpected"; "The right to maternity" and "Against all odds" found in a current website for parents with disabilities (www.disabledparents.net), along with a recent collection of disabled mothers' narratives (Wates & Jade, 1999), suggest that mothering with a disability is still subject to scrutiny. Often times, attempts to discourage motherhood come from family members, co-workers and even complete strangers.

Barriers have also been reported by disabled women attempting to adopt a child (Toms Barker & Maralani, 1997; Kopala, 1989; White & White, 1993), obtain custody following a divorce or separation (Campion, 1995), or even take their infant home from the hospital (Campbell-Earl, 1993; Mathews, 1992; Kocher, 1994). In one case that has received wide publicity, a young mother with Cerebral Palsy in California lost both of her infants who were apprehended at birth and eventually adopted out of state (Mathews, 1992). In the national survey for parents with disabilities, 16% of parents reported attempts to have their children removed from their custody (Toms Barker & Maralani, 1997). While such horror stories are the exception rather than the rule, many women with physical disabilities describe having to demonstrate their competency and parental fitness.

Thomas (1997) conducted a qualitative study on disabled women's reproductive journeys. She found that fear of being perceived as an inadequate mother and the consequences that may ensue from this was a major theme in the interviews. Single mothers are particularly vulnerable to being perceived as incapable of looking after their children (Morris, 2001; O'Toole, 2002; Thomas, 1997). "Without a partner, particularly a nondisabled partner, they are often perceived as questionable, potentially unsafe, and possibly unfit" (O'Toole, 2002, p. 81). Indeed, the CROWD research found that women with physical disabilities are no more likely than those without disabilities to stay in a marriage or a relationship they wish to leave. However, a different pattern emerges where children are concerned. In the CROWD sample, disabled mothers were much more likely (23%) than non-disabled mothers (16%), to remain in a bad marriage for fear of losing custody of their children (Nosek et al., 2001).

This fear is not unfounded. In most western societies, state interference in private family matters is regarded with disdain and resorted to only when children are believed to be at risk. This reluctance, however, primarily applies to middle class, heterosexual, nondisabled nuclear families. "There is plenty of interference for single mothers on welfare, mothers with disabilities, lesbian mothers and others who are considered unfit or undesirable parents" (Reinelt and Fried, 1993, p. 195). Keith and Morris (1996) contend that the debate on "young carers" who are "burdened" by caring for a parent, has typically focused on children raised by disabled mothers who are single, separated or divorced. That single, disabled mothers are also likely to be poor, and devoid of resources, rarely enters this debate. Such mothers, whom Keith and Morris refer to as "easy targets", are the most likely group to wonder: "are we considered to be good enough parents and if not is someone going to 'rescue' our child/ren from the 'burden' of having a disabled or ill parent?" (Keith & Morris, 1996, p. 12).

Disabling practices and experiences: errors of omission

Whereas disabled parents are amongst those most vulnerable to state interference in their family life, "Very little, if any, of this interference comes in the form of financial or social support" (Reinelt and Fried, 1993, p. 195). In this section I explore how the dearth in tangible resources and practical information for mothers with disabilities works to hinder optimal functioning and thus constitutes an error of omission.

In the national survey of parents with disabilities (RTC), 79% of respondents required personal assistance, most commonly with mobility-related activities. Whereas over half of the respondents used personal assistance to help with parenting, only a fraction (10%) used government-supported assistance for this. Most (68%) received unpaid help from family and friends and/or paid for the extra help out of their own money (43%). This is despite the fact that parents with disabilities have a significantly lower family income than parents without disabilities. The most commonly reported annual income level in the RTC survey was under $10,000, with the vast majority of respondents (74%) earning less than $30,000. Parenting equipment adapted for the needs of parents with disabilities was used by 30% of respondents. The vast majority (67%) used their own money to pay for it; many more indicated that such equipment would facilitate their parenting but they either have no way to pay for it or do not know where to obtain the necessary information.

Affordable housing that is both accessible and appropriate to the needs of children is a major hurdle for many parents with disabilities. In the national survey many parents (40%) reported difficulties finding such dwelling, as most accessible housing is ill suited to the needs of children. Most parents needed to make some housing modification, paid for it out of their own money, and lacked the financial resources to make further modifications. In a recent Canadian study, eleven mothers who are wheelchair users were interviewed about their home-making and parenting roles. In many instances, study participants were reportedly restricted in their ability to fulfil typical parenting and homemaking roles (diapering, laundry, cleaning children's bedrooms) largely due to constraints within their living quarters. Accessing funding for renovations or for alternative housing was a constant source of frustration for most of the women, even though they possessed knowledge about funding avenues and the skills to advocate on their own behalf (Reid et al., 2003). The authors note that the availability of non-profit housing in Ontario that has declined between 1994 and 1998, has been nonexistent for the past several years (Reid et al., 2003). This would explain the frustrations experienced by these mothers, despite their proactive stance and good advocacy skills. And if this state of affairs exists in Canada, with its publicly funded health care and social safety net, one can only imagine how mothers with disabilities fare across the border, in the wealthiest, most advanced of all nations.

Indeed, disabled parents in the national (US) survey also reported barriers to employment (76%), recreation (73%), and transportation/ community access (60%). This is despite the fact that survey participants, as a group, were found to be less racially diverse, have a higher level of education, and a higher income than the general population of parents with disabilities (Toms Barker & Maralani, 1997). Given these demographics, the authors of the survey contend that the challenges, barriers and service needs identified in the survey are likely underreported, "with even greater proportions of disabled parents likely to report these as issues if more parents with low income, low educational levels, and members of minority groups had participated" (Toms Barker & Maralani, 1997, iii).

The above statistics represent crude errors of omission as far as providing parents with disabilities with adequate resources and supports. The lack of information on parenting and disability is another error of omission that can be a source of strain. Previously, I noted the frustrations women encounter as they attempt to gather information on sexuality and reproduction in the context of disability. According to current publications, this frustration typically continues over the course of pregnancy, childbirth, early parenting, and beyond. In the RTC survey, 36% of respondents reported that their health providers lacked disability expertise and that this caused problems during pregnancy and childbirth (Toms Barker & Maralani, 1997). Similarly, 34% of the 94 respondents to a British survey on disabled mothers' experiences of maternity noted the difficulties entailed in gaining relevant information. Whereas 2/3 of the respondents had general information on pregnancy, only 2/5 had information on the effect of their condition on their pregnancy; slightly more had information on how pregnancy may affect their condition (Goodman, 1994).

Autobiographical accounts and a handful of qualitative studies lend further credence to the reported dearth of information for both women and their service providers (Lipson & Rogers, 2000; Nosek et al., 2001). A number of Canadian studies conducted in the mid 1980s and early 1990s pointed to the inadequacy of the health care system to meet the pregnancy and childbirth needs of women with disabilities. These studies identified an inadequate coordination of services, inappropriate referrals of patients, and staff that felt ill informed to meet the needs of pregnant women with disabilities (Conine, Carty & Wood-Johnson, 1986, 1987; McEwan Carty, Conine & Hall, 1990). A brief look at disabled mothers' accounts in published collections (Wates & Jade, 1999), journals and consumer magazines (i.e. Disability Pregnancy and Parenting International; Sexuality & Disability) and on the web, further attest to the gap between supply and demand of information on pregnancy and disability. Of course, "knowledge and attitudes are difficult to untangle" (Lipson & Rogers, 2000, p. 17) and an insufficient knowledge base on pregnancy and disability can negatively impact providers' attitudes and tinge their interactions with disabled women.

Inadequate understanding of disabled parents' issues extends beyond the pregnancy and infancy stage. In a qualitative study of 16 chronically ill mothers, participants experienced the health care system as ill equipped to meet their needs as both chronically ill women and mothers. They were either given medical recommendations that were highly incongruous with their roles as mothers, or, when parenting was addressed, the implications of the chronic illness were ignored (Thorne, 1991). A current study on Head Start, a comprehensive program in the US that serves over 15 million children living in impoverished environments, explored the extent and nature of contact between HS staff and parents with disabilities. In a six state region,

85% of programs reportedly served parents with disabilities. While staff attempted to meet the needs of parents by making referrals, adapting information and providing social support, the majority of programs did not have written policies to guide their work (Bhagwanji, Thomas, Bennett, Stillwel & Allison, 1998). Toms Barker and Maralani (1997) claim that "not only do services to the general population seem unaware of disabled parents and their needs, but even services that specifically target people with disabilities seem unaware that many of their constituents have children" (pp. 11–9). It is hardly surprising that parents with disabilities feel that theirs is an isolated experience and that they are, to borrow the title of a report on the topic, "the only disabled parent in the neighbourhood" (Ridington, 1989).

For the purpose of this review, I wrote separately about errors of commission and errors of omission. My decision to do so was guided not only by my wish to simplify the discussion, but also by my belief that as a society, we are more likely to ignore the latter than the former. Most professionals and progressively minded citizens would admonish crude and unjustified interference with disabled women's reproductive freedom and parenting rights. At least, I would like to believe that that is the case. I am less optimistic about the public's willingness to commit resources that would enhance optimal functioning. Moreover, I suspect that even amongst those who would agree to commit resources, many are unaware of the tangible barriers and practical constraints that mark the lives of many mothers with disabilities.

Nonetheless, I acknowledge that any separation between errors of commission and omission is an artificial one as their impact on mothers and families is interactive and exponential. In 1993, a highly publicized court case in East Lansing Michigan dealt with the potential removal of a non-disabled infant from her physically disabled parents. Both parents were severely disabled and received regular attendant care. However, state laws prevented their attendants from providing any care to their infant daughter. Instead, they were warned that they were being closely watched by social services (Bergman, 1993). Disabled activists have long protested against oppressive societal conception of independence as contingent upon the ability to perform physical tasks unassisted. For mothers with disabilities, this is combined with the likewise oppressive conception of motherhood as contingent upon the omnipotent ability to independently provide physical care to children. Women who are entitled to publicly funded attendant services for personal care, are rarely allowed to utilise this service to help them care for their children (Toms Barker & Maralani,

1997; Reid et al., 2003; Reinelt & Fried, 1993). As Waxman (1993) asserted in her court testimony on behalf of the Earls, "parenting continues to be understood as a primarily physical relationship rather than an emotional and social one" (p. 7).

The interaction between errors of omission and commission is also enacted in disabled mothers' reported reluctance to advocate for resources that can assist them in parenting. Some of the mothers with chronic illnesses who participated in Thorne's (1991) study felt that only if they became totally incapable of functioning would they get the services they require. At the same time, they worried that unless they demonstrate their independence and capabilities, they are at risk of being seen as incompetent parents and might even be at risk of losing their children. In Britain, Thomas (1997) reached very similar conclusions: "Living with the fear of losing the right to care for their children forces some mothers to go to great lengths to 'present' themselves and their children as managing 'normally' – often at significant personal costs in terms of comfort, and emotional and physical well-being" (p. 635). Under this veil of fear, even genuine attempts to lend a helping hand are at risk of being misconstrued.

A few weeks before she had a baby, Dally (1999) listened to a radio show about children who were removed from their disabled mothers. As a woman who lost an arm in an accident, she was understandably alarmed when nurses on the maternity ward asked her if she had been in touch with a social worker. "I stonily replied that the only social workers I knew were friends and that I would have plenty of help from my family. This latter remark was a blatant lie...I realise now that these nurses really did want to get some help for me. And I threw their offer back in their faces" (Dally, 1999, p. 61). Given the prevalence of attitudinal barriers that mothers with disabilities are subjected to, it is hardly surprising that genuine offers of assistance may be treated with suspicion.

Information from the RTC survey amongst other sources is suggestive of the particular challenges faced by mothers with disabilities, and particularly single mothers with disabilities. In comparison with male respondents, female respondents were less likely to be married, employed, and well educated and more likely to be single heads of households (Toms Barker & Maralani, 1997). Single disabled mothers with limited financial resources, are most likely to be affected by the interactive effects of errors of omission and commission. When my own son was an infant, I thoroughly enjoyed playing, changing diapers and especially breastfeeding – something that only I could provide him with. However, I was unable to get him in and out of the car by myself, independently care for him for an extended period of time, or even safely pick him up once he began to gain weight. Had I not had a loving partner, generously helpful mother and father and financial resources for a full time babysitter (I worked part time), would I have been prevented from raising my son?

Enabling practices and experiences: allies, strengths and possibilities

There is little doubt that socially created barriers that I described as errors of omission and commission are risk factors to the well being of mothers with disabilities and their families. While explicating such barriers is important, it is likewise important to highlight caring and empowering interactions with family members, friends and professionals. In recent years, mothers with disabilities, as a group, have increasingly articulated their experiences of insensitive attitudes and unjust policies. At the same time, they have acknowledged and paid tribute to the many allies who have helped them along the way.

Parents and family members who in some cases have been the source of disempowering messages about motherhood, have also been noted for the supportive role they play in facilitating a disabled daughter's parenting. In one study of 12 mobility-impaired women's birth and postpartum experiences, the majority of participants reported negative reactions from family members when they announced their pregnancy. In most cases, however, these reactions were replaced with support as the pregnancy progressed and concerns regarding the effect of the pregnancy on the woman's health and functioning were allayed (Lipson & Rogers, 2000). Family members and close friends were listed as the main source of help by close to 70% of participants in the RTC survey (Toms Barker & Maralani, 1997). In a need assessment I conducted in conjunction with a disabled women's organization, parents, siblings, in-laws and close friends were also identified as important sources of help and support (Prilleltensky, 1995).

On the professional front, nurses and midwives are especially noteworthy for their attempts to assist mothers with disabilities. There are various stories of nurses asking how they can be of help (Dally, 1999; Kopala, 1989); physicians who facilitate and support disabled women's reproductive rights (Goodman, 1994; Kent, 2000; Litwinowicz, 1999); and social workers who go out of their way to obtain resources and supports that could facilitate motherhood (Morris, 1993). Organizations such as the Maternity Alliance in Britain, the Childbearing and Parenting Program for Women with Disabilities or Chronic Illnesses in British Colombia, Canada, and Through the Looking Glass in Berkeley, California, are all noteworthy for their empowering attitudes and the tangible resources they provide. In my past involvement with the Centre for Independent Living of Toronto (CILT)'s parenting network, I've been moved by the commitment demonstrated by a few local occupational therapists to facilitate motherhood for women with disabilities. Themselves mothers of young children, these professionals along with women from the disability community, attended evening meetings and devoted time, energy, and expertise toward that end. Such allies, especially when they are encountered in settings that have traditionally discouraged disabled women from procreating, can be tremendously empowering.

The following poignant quote attests to the impact that a supportive professional can have: "After talking to the physiotherapist and the social worker, I stopped feeling guilty about my children suffering deprivation because of my disability. I realized that children do not have any more right to a perfect parent, that is, one who is not handicapped, than a parent does to a perfectly formed child" (Belohorec & Kikuchi, 1985, p. 33). More recently, Kent (2000) has recounted her interaction with an Ophthalmologist who explained that while her blindness is the result of Leber's, a hereditary condition, a (potential) child is unlikely to be affected unless her husband is also a carrier of the same recessive (and relatively rare) gene. "The discussion could have ended with that simple exchange of information. But the doctor had more to say. 'You have a good life, don't you?' he asked. 'If you have a child with Leber's, it can have a good life too. Go home and have a dozen kids if you want to!'" (p. 60).

The perceptive reader will rightfully argue that the mere act of imparting such unsolicited advice, in relation to such a significant and highly personal issue, should be deconstructed and critiqued. The discussion should have ended with the practitioner imparting relevant information that would enhance his patient's ability to make a truly informed reproductive decision. It is difficult to argue that unsolicited advice regarding reproductive decisions is permissible so long as it is stated in the affirmative. At the same time, Kent's conclusion that "even from a total stranger those were wonderful words" (p. 45) is completely understandable. So long as the lives of people with disabilities are devalued and deemed tragic, and those who may bring these lives to fruition are discouraged from doing so, any message to the contrary is bound to be embraced.

Beyond loving family members, devoted friends and committed professionals, the resolve and resourcefulness of many mothers with disabilities is central to successful parenting experiences. A recent Canadian study examined the homemaking and parenting experiences of 11 mothers who were wheelchair users (Reid et al., 2003). While securing accessible housing that met the needs of their families was a constant source of frustration for most women, this was not for lack of effort, knowledge, or ability to self-advocate. In fact, participants were knowledgeable as well as proactive in seeking out possible sources of funding and negotiating for possible modifications. Most participants perceived their wheelchairs as liberating devices that increased their sense of control, and they actively lobbied for greater accessibility within their neighbourhoods. In fact, these mothers played a role in many such changes including the placing of ramps in their children's schools.

Along with explicating the barriers they face, mothers with disabilities are telling heart-warming tales of fulfilment of a dream (Goodman, 1994; Killoran, 1994; Willig Levy, 1999), loving relationships and positive communication (Blackford, 1990; Dick Gomez, 1999; Reinelt & Fried, 1992; Rogers & Matsumara, 1990), and pride in children who are well-adjusted, caring, and appreciative of human diversity (Armstrong, 1999; Goodman, 1994; Ridington, 1989). Dick Gomez (1999) contrasts her young daughter's comment "I'm so lucky, my mommy's accessible" (p. 138) as they joyfully "zoom down the street singing" (p. 139), with a comment by one grim observer that "it must be hard for her to see you like this" (p. 139). Philippa Armstrong (1999) humorously writes about a chuckle she shared with her 13-year-old daughter as the daughter dramatically mimicked a comment someone made to her about her mother: "she's a remarkable woman!" I suppose we all like to feel remarkable once in a while. In this case, however, both mother and daughter were keenly aware of the paternalistic undertones of this comment. In my own family we have adopted a somewhat peculiar sense of black humour that includes reference to various societal prejudices and misconceptions regarding disability. Recently, I jokingly asked my 16-year-old if his reluctance to be seen in public with his dad and me has anything to do with my disability. "You're joking, right?" was his immediate response. He was quick to "assure" me that his non-disabled and highly physically fit father is "way more embarrassing than you are". With teenagers, you learn to appreciate such "compliments".

Concluding comments

This chapter has focused on different aspects of mothering with a physical disability. I reviewed disabled women's historical exclusion from motherhood; professional and research literature on parental disability and child well-being; and the lived experience of mothers with disabilities and their families. Mothers with disabilities have only recently emerged as a group with some shared, socially constructed, struggles and challenges. These commonalities notwithstanding, disabled women, like their non-disabled counterparts, experience motherhood in diverse and multiple ways. More than the type of impairment, its course, or level of severity, it is the braiding of disability status with other markers of identity (class, ethnicity, sexual orientation), as well as with individual mothers' particular contexts, support systems, and personality attributes, that shapes their unique and diverse experiences.

Furthermore, disabled mothers' lives and the stories they tell about those lives, do not lend themselves to simplistic dichotomising of hardships versus joys. Rather, stories of joy and fulfilment are at times laced and intertwined with frank explication of barriers, frustrations, and even worries. This is beautifully captured in "Intervals", a short piece by Sylvia Dick Gomez (1999). In a mere four-and-a-half pages we read about this single mother's joys and tribulations with a teenager step-daughter who has chosen to live with her younger sister and disabled step-mother rather than her own biological (and non-disabled) father; the younger daughter's comment that with a disabled mother "you can get lots of attention...and you can cut the lines at Disneyland" (p. 174); along with the mother's admission that the girls "have seen me hang my head and weep in frustration, in anger, in fear, in pain. I try to shield them from the worse of it, but sometimes my grief just boils over" (p. 174). Dick Gomez writes about her seven-year-old's "assurance" that "I will help you, mommy, we (a long list of family and friends) will all help you. We love you", and a few moments later: "I'm hungry. Will you make me French toast? Can I have a friend over?" (p. 174).

This humorous combination of out of sync maturity and age-appropriate expectation of care is not suggestive of a "parentified child". Rather, it stretches the boundaries of what we consider an appropriate parent-child relationship and speaks to the diversity of acceptable parenting practices, family constellations, and home environments. To me, this piece's rich tapestry of intense love, physical and emotional pain, concerns for the future, humour and joy, are not to be silenced but accepted and embraced. Life may not always be easy, but, as one disabled mother has noted, being a good parent "does not reside in the ability to chase around after a toddler, nor in the ability to teach your child how to ride a bike. Being a good mother has to do with making sure your child has a strong sense of self-worth, and an appreciation of the wonders and abundance of life" (Killoran, 1994, p. 122).

4
The Research Process

In the first three chapters I examined disability from a socio-political perspective and outlined how this perspective can advance our understanding of the lives of women with disabilities and motherhood. My approach is consistent with a paradigm shift that increasingly amplifies social, cultural, political, and economic determinants of disability (Gill, Kewman & Brannon, 2003). The shift toward an understanding of disability as a social phenomenon largely shaped by a host of contextual factors has significant implications for research. These implications span the entire research process: How research agendas are determined (Tate & Pledger, 2003); "who gets to ask the questions" (Olkin & Pledger, 2003) and control the process and product of the research (Oliver, 1992); and most importantly, what is the epistemology that undergirds the research.

Disability rights critics point to the atmosphere of distrust that historically characterised the relationship between researchers and people with disabilities (dubbed subjects). Oliver (1992) and others (Barnes, Mercer & Shakespeare, 1999; Olkin, 1999; Olkin & Pledger, 2003) claim that most research on disability has contributed to the problems faced by disabled people by reinforcing the dominant idea that disability is an individual problem. As Olkin and Pledger (2003) contend, "research about persons with disabilities is both personal and political, and conducting research as if it were only personal perpetuates stigma and discrimination" (p. 298). Increasingly, people with disabilities, demand more than token participation in research projects. They are interested in research projects that go beyond the personal experience of disability to explore the impact of ableist policies and practices. They want to see research projects that expose, examine, and attempt to transform disempowering and ableist policies and practices in schools, hospitals, and other meso-level organizations. Finally, critical disability theorists and activists are interested in exploring and challenging dysfunctional societal practices that perpetuate ableism, oppression and discrimination (Prilleltensky, 2004a).

In this chapter I discuss the underlying assumptions that guide my research and the specific techniques used to gather, analyze, and interpret the information. I present the theoretical underpinnings that frame my research as qualitative, feminist, and informed by a disability rights perspective. I then move to an elaboration of the research process and to the various phases of data collection, analysis, and interpretation. With the theoretical underpinnings as backdrop, I conclude the chapter by outlining the major methodological issues that I came across in the process of the research and my attempts to deal with them along the way.

Research paradigm

Guba and Lincoln (1994) define paradigm as the "basic belief system or worldview that guides the investigator, not only in choice of method but also in ontologically and epistemologically fundamental ways" (p. 105). Questions of method are secondary to those of paradigm. My own worldview guiding this research is couched within a qualitative, feminist, and disability rights perspective. Like a paradigm, qualitative research is an approach to knowledge rather than merely a set of techniques. Broadly speaking, qualitative approaches to research are based on the belief that methods used to investigate the physical world are inappropriate for the investigation of human lives. Unlike the physical world that is predictable and largely unaffected by the act of investigation, the social world is forever shifting and evolving, constructed and reconstructed by people's values, goals, and particular contexts. Whereas the overall purpose of quantitative research is to explain and predict, qualitative research seeks to understand people's lives and the multiple meaning they give to their lives as they negotiate their existence. The process of investigation cannot be separated from what is being investigated and from who is doing the investigating. Researchers are part of the world they research and their own experiences, beliefs and value systems impact every aspect of the research process (Denzin & Lincoln, 1994; Howe, 1992; Hunt, 1992; Morgan & Smircich, 1980; Smith, 1983).

Feminist research is also classified as an approach rather than a particular method of data collection (Campbell & Wasco, 2000; Maynard,

1994; Maynard & Purvis, 1994; Reinharz, 1992). At the core of this approach is a commitment to the production of knowledge that is useful and empowering to women and which can contribute to their growth and well-being (Edwards, 1993; Fine, 1992; Maynard, 1994). Of prime importance is the openly ideological, value-laden nature of feminist research which focuses on the oppressive factors in women's lives and on the inter-relation between gender and other social constructs such as race, poverty, and disability (Fine, 1992; Lather, 1986, 1991; Maynard, 1994). The centrality of the political and ideological nature of feminist research is evident in every phase of the research process with more and more emphasis being placed on research that is transformative, empowering and action-oriented (Acker, Barry & Esseveld, 1991; Fine, 1992; Kelly, Burton & Regan, 1994).

There are many similarities and parallels between what the feminist movement has attempted to do for women and what the disability rights movement has attempted to do for people with disabilities. Both have emphasized the role of oppressive contexts and have advocated for macro level changes in the social structure and for a more equitable distribution of resources. Researchers such as Oliver (1990, 1992), Fine and Asch (1988) and Zarb (1992), to mention a few, have documented and exposed the anti-disability bias that undergirds a lot of the mainstream research on disability. More often than not, people with disabilities have been depicted as unfortunate individuals who are forever trying to come to terms with their tragic reality. In this kind of research, problems encountered by people with disabilities are seen as inherent in the physical condition itself, rather than mediated by environmental, social and political factors.

I now present some of the fundamental principles associated with qualitative, feminist, and disability rights research paradigms. I focus on refuting positivism, importance of context, research relationship, participant and researcher voice, and research from an openly ideological perspective.

Refuting positivism

The main tenet of positivism is the existence of a single reality or truth that can be studied and apprehended in an objective, value-free manner. Unearthing truth and reality through research is contingent upon the scientist's ability to remain neutral and value free in relation to the object under investigation. Internal validity, external validity, reliability and objectivity are the four criteria used by positivists to evaluate their research. Applying these criteria, especially that of objectivity, ensures that investigator and investigated "object" remain independent and uninfluenced by one another and that the ensuing data is uncontaminated (Alvesson & Sköldberg, 2000; Willig, 2001). "Inquiry takes place as though through a one-way mirror. Values and biases are prevented from influencing outcome, so long as the pre-scribed procedures are rigorously followed. Replicable findings are, in fact, 'true'" (Guba & Lincoln, 1994, p. 110).

Over the course of the century, positivism has been transformed by post-positivism, which contends that reality can only be approximated and not fully apprehended. Using multiple methods to capture as much of reality as possible, post-positivists remain highly traditional in their emphasis on the discovery and verification of theories and in the evaluation criteria they utilize. For both positivism and post-positivism, the aim of inquiry is to explain, predict and control phe-nomena, be it physical or human (Denzin & Lincoln, 1994; Guba & Lincoln, 1994; Oliver, 1992). Positivism and post-positivism have been criticized by those who believe that all research is conducted within a particular social context, that it cannot be value free, and that it should cast a wider net in terms of the goals of inquiry (Danziger & Dzinas, 1997; Murray & Chamberlin, 1999).

Like most other social research, "the history of research on disability is undoubtedly one that has been dominated by the positivist research paradigm both in terms of the research undertaken and the assump-tions underpinning it" (Oliver, 1992, p. 107). Oliver (1992) identifies two main pernicious outcomes stemming from the dominance of pos-itivism over disability research. The first relates to the portrayal of dis-ability as residing solely within the individual and emanating directly from a medical condition. This supposedly value-free portrayal of "reality" served to obscure any relationship between socio-political conditions and the individual experience of disability. The second detrimental impact of positivism has to do with its naive assumption that a non-problematic relationship exists between research findings and policy change.

Feminist researchers have refuted positivism on similar grounds. Feminist researchers share the belief that their values and life experi-ences impact every stage of the research process – from deciding what to investigate, to the formulation of research questions, to conducting and analyzing the research. They object to notions of neutral, value-free research that culminates in objective knowledge that is not con-taminated by the researcher's subjectivity. Rather than asking whether values, beliefs and experiences influence the research, the question becomes one of clarifying those values and beliefs and explicating the particular lenses through which the research is conducted. Given that the researcher is part of the social world that she is investigating, her own presence in the research is acknowledged rather than neutralized (Edwards, 1993; Fine, 1992; Lather, 1986, 1991; Maynard, 1994).

The importance of context

Many qualitative researchers emphasize the importance of context. As Denzin and Lincoln (1994) claim, "there is no clear window to the inner life of an individual. Any gaze is always filtered through the lenses of language, gender, social class, race, and ethnicity. There are no objective observations, only observations socially situated in the worlds of the observer and the observed" (p. 12). The wide range of qualitative methodologies, vary, among other things, in the degree to which they focus on context as an important organizing principle.

Phenomenological research which focuses on participants' experience of meaning attempts to actually strip away context in order to come to the essence of meaning. Although context is not negated or ignored, a distinction is made between what exists inside, which is the focus of phenomenological research, and what exists outside, which is of little interest (Moustakas, 1994; Polkinghorne, 1989; VanManen, 1990). Context is also afforded a limited role in Heuristic research as described by Moustakas:

> Only the co-researchers' experience with a phenomenon are considered, not how history, art, politics, or other human enterprises account for and explain the meaning of the experience....the depiction is complete in itself. Interpretation not only adds nothing to heuristic knowledge but removes the aliveness and vitality from the nature, roots, meanings, and essences of experience. (Moustakas, 1994, p. 19)

As a researcher, I situate myself within the contextualized, constructivist approaches to qualitative inquiry. From the narrative approach, I resonate with the notion of people leading storied lives and telling stories about the lives they lead (Crossley, 2000; Clandinin & Connely, 1994). The telling of life stories is an interpretive process that has a formative impact on one's identity (Ochberg, 1994). As stories are told, new meanings and interpretations come to the forefront, shaping not only the story but also the life on which it is based (Widdershoven, 1993). With life story as its starting point, life history research is "a way of understanding life as lived in the present and influenced by personal, institutional, and social histories" (Cole & Knowles, 1995, p. 18). Its purpose is to understand people's lives and meaning-making through a reconstruction of past events and within particular personal, social and political contexts (Cole, 1991, 1994). While context is also considered in the narrative approach, it is more prominent in life history research which often considers other sources of data in addition to life stories. At times, the externally-gathered information is conflicted with or contradictory to the personal story that unfolds and may require challenging on the part of the researcher. As a result, researcher and participant engage in a jointly negotiated co-construction of knowledge (Cole & Knowles, 1995; Cole, 1991, 1994; Goodson, 1992; Measor, 1985).

Goodson (1992) discusses the danger of studying subjective experience apart from its restrictive or facilitative context. He underscores the importance of researching lives within the constraints imposed on them by broader social forces such as race, gender, and ethnicity. Having the privilege of the bigger picture, this knowledge can be shared with participants, thereby facilitating their understanding and meaning-making. Similar assertions are made by Bertaux (1981), who feels it is the responsibility of the researcher "to put together bits of knowledge that might be found everywhere...and to draw a picture of the whole and its movements" (p. 40).

I consider the social, political, and historical context central to life history research, as imperative in the study of women with disabilities and mothering. Neither motherhood nor disability is located solely in biology; both emanate from a complex interaction of biological, psychological, social, environmental and political factors. I share Goodson's "concern for telling the story with an equal concern to provide a broader context for the location, understanding, and grounding of those stories" (Goodson, 1992, p. 243).

The importance of attending to context is also emphasized in feminist approaches to research (Acker, Barry & Esseveld, 1991; Fine, 1992; Holland & Ramazanoglu, 1994). "Although we view people as active agents in their own lives and as such constructors of their social worlds, we do not see that activity as isolated...rather, we locate individual experience in society and history, embedded within a set of social relations which produce both the possibilities and limitations of that experience" (Acker, Barry & Esseveld, 1991, p. 135). Gender is seen as a major organizing principle in women's lives and the social construction of gender is at the heart of feminist inquiry (Lather, 1991).

In more recent feminist work, it has become increasingly apparent that to study the oppressive factors emanating from the social construction of gender, without its relation to other social attributes such as race, class, and disability, is to add insult to injury to marginalized women. Consequently, a lot of the more recent feminist inquiry has focused its efforts on studying the particular ways in which gender braids with other social constructs (Edwards, 1993; Fine, 1992; Lather, 1991; Maynard, 1994; Phoenix, 1994). Much feminist research has begun to focus on women who have been most invisible and understudied in order to bring their experiences and realities into the mainstream, as the following quote indicates:

> Much feminist research claims to name new topics, to examine the invisible, to study the unstudied, and to ask why it has been ignored...we have demonstrated how certain people are ignored, their words discounted, and their place in history overlooked. We have shown how certain things are not studied and other things are not even named.   (Reinharz, 1992, p. 248)

This trend has wide implications for women with disabilities who have been critical in the past of both the disability rights movement and the feminist movement for neglecting their needs. While the former did not value their particular concerns as women, the latter neglected their specific circumstances as disabled (Lloyd, 1992; Oliver, 1990). For example, early research on disability focused exclusively on the experiences and needs of disabled men; disabled women were rendered invisible. As to the second charge, disability and feminist theorists like Jenny Morris (1992) and Lois Keith (1992) demonstrated how women with disabilities have been left out of the feminist agenda, as if their issues and concerns are of no importance to feminists. In a compelling article titled *Who cares wins?*, Keith (1992) is highly critical of the apparent insensitivity to women with disabilities demonstrated in feminist research and in debates on community care. In their advocacy of women-centred issues of care, most feminists have totally aligned themselves with women as care providers (for it is usually women who do the care giving), and have failed to identify with the recipients of care, many of whom are disabled women. In fact, those on the receiving end of care have often been categorized simply as dependent people of no specific age or gender. Taking context into consideration entails, among other things, the inclusion of both disability and gender as important organizing principles. The growing body of literature on women with disabilities in recent years suggests that these criticisms have not gone unheeded.

The centrality of the research relationship

Whereas traditional research seeks to separate researchers from those being researched (Kincheloe & McLaren, 1994), this separation is counter-indicated in qualitative studies. Qualitative researchers and theorists place a major emphasis on the relationship with study participants. When we enter into a research relationship with participants and ask them to share their stories with us, there is the potential to shape their lived, told, relived and retold stories as well as our own. These intensive relationships require serious consideration of who we are as researchers in the stories of participants, for when we become characters in their stories we change their stories (Clandinin & Connelly, 1994, p. 422). Recognizing that research can have either a negative or a positive transformative impact, researchers acknowledge the care that has to be taken when personal experience methods are used. The importance of upholding the dignity, respect and well-being of participants is consistently emphasized in this literature, as is the need to consider issues of reciprocity and to search for ways in which the research can have a positive impact for participants.

In traditional methodologies there is little question as to the separate, and very distinct roles of the researcher and the researched. Other than the right to withdraw at any time, participants don't have much control over the research process. Their role is one of being a source of data for the research and ends once the data have been collected. Participants play a much more substantive role in personal experience methods where they are often interviewed several times, may be asked to review transcripts for any mistakes or misunderstandings, and may even provide input at the level of analysis and interpretation.

Many feminist researchers emphasize their attempts to minimize the distance and power differential between themselves and their participants. Feminist studies often entail a greater sense of connection between researcher and participant and possibly some sharing of her own experiences by the researcher. In her much quoted article about her research on motherhood, Ann Oakley (1990) discusses her departure from conventional, male-oriented interviewing ethics by establishing a non-hierarchical relationship and investing herself in the research process.

Researchers with a disability rights perspective have also discussed the nature of the research relationship. The negative experiences that many people with disabilities have had as research subjects and the ensuing feelings of distrust and suspicion towards researchers is demonstrated by the following quote: "A few of us have escaped the researchers' scrutiny of their seemingly pathological fixation on the limitations and negative aspects of disability. We have been portrayed as sick, helpless, and incompetent; incapable of living independently" (Woodill, 1992, preface). Those who critique research from a disability rights perspective advance similar arguments raised by feminists regarding the traditionally powerless and passive role of research participants. An emancipatory approach to disability research "seeks to change the established social relations of research production which presume an asymmetrical relationship between researcher and researched. The power of the researcher-as-expert is enshrined in their control over the design, implementation, analysis and dissemination of research findings. The end result is that the 'subjects' of research are treated as 'objects', who are simply conduits for supplying information required by the researcher" (Barnes, Mercer & Shakespeare, 1999, p. 217). Critical disability theorists are increasingly demanding efforts be focused on ameliorating disabling environments rather than helping disabled individuals adapt to these environments. They are further demanding an emphasis on strengths rather than deficits, and a shift in the balance of power from professional control to consumer control. This paradigm shift has led to many research partnerships between researchers and people with disabilities (Nelson & Lord, 1996).

Voice of participant, voice of researcher

Participant voice is a central concept in qualitative research. Unlike positivistic research whose large scale designs all but drown out individual voices, these same voices are often front and centre in qualitative studies. Giving room for participants to tell their stories, their version of life events and their priorities for action, can be validating and empowering experiences and ones that may facilitate change. As Yow suggests, "This validation is especially important to people our society devalues" (Yow, 1994, p. 117). Both women and people with disabilities have traditionally suffered from devalued social status. Good social research is one way of bringing their issues and priorities to the forefront.

Participant voice is a major concept in both feminist and disability studies. Feminist researchers emphasize the importance of amplifying women's voices in research. After decades of having men speak for them and interpret their experiences, women tell their own stories and reflect on the multiple meanings of those stories. Reinharz (1992) asserts that feminist researchers favour interviewing as a research tool as it "offers researchers access to people's ideas, thoughts and memories in their own words rather than in the words of the researcher. This asset is particularly important for the study of women because in this way learning from women is an antidote to centuries of ignoring women's ideas altogether or having men speak for women" (p. 19).

Similar arguments have been advanced by disability rights theorists and researchers. Early research on disability focused more on non-disabled people's reaction to disability than on the subjective experience of living with a disability. While this type of research can enhance our understanding of prejudice and stereotypes, it tells us nothing about the personal experience of living with a disability in a disablist society (Asch, 1984; in Fine & Asch, 1988). The subjective experience of disability, rendered in the first person, can give insight into its socio-political embeddedness. As Olkin (1999) asserts, "it is phenomenal how undeterred we are from pursuing 'outsider' research by the able-bodied about disability. For no other out-group is the pervasive exclusion of voices from within so silent and stilled" (pp. 319–320). As an example in point, a national symposium about different approaches to disability research held in the UK in 1989, did not include any disabled presenters (Barnes, Mercer & Shakespeare, 1999).

While the importance of representing the voices of participants is an uncontested terrain in research conducted from the aforementioned paradigms, this cannot and should not replace the voice of the researcher. Like participants, researchers too are situated within a host of attributes such as class, race, age, gender, and health. Situating participants advances our understanding of their experiences and the meaning they attribute to those experiences. By the same token, not situating ourselves as researchers presumes an objective, non-contaminated account of these lives. "Researchers must first accept their own personhood, their co-participation in the human venture they seek to understand. The failure to acknowledge this is probably the largest single reason for the failure of social science research to influence practice" (Hunt, 1992). While these warnings may sound redundant, the fact that they continue to resound in the most current literature suggests that researchers continue to omit their own signatures from their work.

Edwards (1993) describes the research process as an interaction of two subjectivities, that of the researcher and that of the researched.

Researchers are not merely recording instruments (Edwards, 1993) and the experience of research participants cannot speak for itself (Holland & Ramazanoglu, 1994). Fine (1992) is critical of feminist work that uses the voices of participants to provide a critical social interpretation. Doing so without acknowledging the researcher's own stance is, according to Fine, an exploitation of voices.

As researchers struggle with "how to be there in the text" and how to inscribe a signature that is neither too thin or too thick (Connelly & Clandinin, 1990), they become increasingly more aware of the indelible mark that they leave on their work. The need to not only acknowledge the researcher's voice and unique contribution but also to monitor and keep track of biases and subjectivities, is emphasized by a number of qualitative researchers (Glesne & Peshkin, 1992; Holland & Ramazanoglu, 1994; Lather, 1986; Riddell, 1989). Alan Peshkin (1993) writes about his own process of accepting and making the most of his subjectivity that is central to conducting research from a qualitative paradigm. He warns, however, against the possible perils of neglecting to reflect critically on subjectivity. "One's subjectivity, however, has the capacity to not only enable but also to disable. It is necessary, therefore, to try to see what you are not seeing, to detect what you are making less of than could be made, so that you can temper as necessary that which your subjectivity is pressing you to focus on" (p. 104). By journaling the process of coming to conclusions and continuously attending not only to the emerging understanding but also to gaps, surprises and counter-patterns, subjectivity can become a research asset, rather than a liability.

Researching from an openly ideological perspective

Most qualitative researchers acknowledge the value-laden nature of research and the need to navigate carefully the relationship between researcher and researched. They vary, however, with respect to the degree to which they use research to advance socio-political ideals. Critical theorists attempt to use their work as a form of social criticism (Flyvbjerg, 2001; Kincheloe & McLaren, 1994; Reason & Bradbury, 2001; Smith, 1999). Their aim is

> the critique and transformation of the social, political, cultural, economic, ethnic, and gender structures that constrain and exploit humankind, by engaging in confrontation, even conflict. The critique for progress is that over time, restitution and emancipation should occur and persist. Advocacy and activism are key concepts. (Guba & Lincoln, 1994, p. 113)

Most qualitative researchers who frame their work within a feminist and/or disability rights perspective would probably align themselves with the criticalist camp.

The centrality of the political and ideological nature of feminist research is evident in every phase of the research process with more and more emphasis being placed on research that is transformative, empowering and action-oriented (Acker et al., 1991; Brydon-Miller, 2001; Fine, 1992; Kelly et al., 1994). While acknowledging the importance of starting from women's personal accounts and meaning-making, many feminist researchers indicate the inadequacy of remaining at the level of personal accounts and subjective experiences. They further warn that describing experience as an end in itself can serve to hinder rather than enhance women's well-being (Maynard & Purvis, 1994; Kelly et al., 1994).

> To repeat and describe what women have to say, while important, can lead to individuation and fragmentation, instead of analysis. Feminism has an obligation to go beyond citing experience in order to make connections which may not be visible from the purely experiential level alone.   (Maynard, 1994, p. 24)

By going beyond the personal experience to analyze factors that are oppressive in women's lives and produce a critical socio-political analysis, feminist research can help women understand their experiences in relation to the larger social structure. This may facilitate a re-evaluation of the experience that may, in turn, stimulate action.

Similar calls have been made for situating the experience of disability within a larger socio-political context (Fine & Asch, 1988; Goodley, 1996; Morris, 1992; Oliver, 1992; Olkin, 1999). The aforementioned paradigm shift in disability research can "help strengthen the thesis that disability is a social phenomenon largely shaped by the environment and can downplay the characterisation of disability as individual deficit" (Tate & Pledger, 2003, p. 294). This paradigm is being increasingly incorporated by disciplines that have adopted a historically conservative, individualistic approach to disability. For example, I was pleasantly surprised to read that the National Institute on Disability and Rehabilitation Research (NIDRR) have framed "a comprehensive research agenda, focusing on developing new methods, technologies, and approaches for eliminating the environmental, cultural, and social barriers that prevent people with disabilities from full inclusion in all aspects of society" (US Department of Education, 1999, in Melia,

Pledger & Wilson, 2003, p. 288). Nonetheless, rehabilitation psychology places greater emphasis on factors related to the individual with a disability, while critical disability theorists emphasize societal transformation (Olkin & Pledger, 2003). Given the debates in the literature, it is clear that those who conduct research from a disability rights perspective do not speak in a uniform voice. For example, while Oliver (1992) and Barnes (1998) have been critical of any research that is not under the full control of disabled consumers and does not lead to direct policy change, Shakespeare (1996) argues that policy change is not the only criteria for evaluating research. Nonetheless, disability theorists share a general commitment to research that can advance social justice and contribute to self-empowerment for people with disabilities (Barnes, Mercer & Shakespeare, 1999).

Conducting the research

Having framed my worldview and approach to research as influenced by feminist and disability rights principles, I now turn to the actual research process and to the various phases of data collection, analysis, and interpretation.

The research story

My story begins with a session I attended at the American Psychological Association Convention (APA) during my first year of doctoral studies. The topic of the session was women with disabilities. It proved to be a formative event in my life as it marked my first contact with the disability movement or, for that matter, with other women with disabilities. Sitting in a session where the entire panel and most of the audience were comprised of women with disabilities was a moving and empowering experience. I decided that my doctoral research would be on the topic of women with disabilities and began to do a lot of reading in this area. As I immersed myself in the literature, I became increasingly more interested in focusing on motherhood in the context of disability and began to seriously consider it as a possible research topic for my dissertation – luck would have it that a symposium on mothering with a disability was planned in my region by a women's health organization. Attending this symposium and connecting with disabled feminists marked the beginning of my working relationship with a local disabled women's organization.

The research project that was ultimately conducted was "conceived" at an evening meeting which focused on ways of meeting some of the mothering needs of women with disabilities in a large Canadian city. At that point, the organization was gearing up for a three-day symposium on mothering issues as members had identified motherhood as an important area for women with disabilities. We decided that the symposium would be a good opportunity to gather data that would help identify the experiences, issues and priorities that women with disabilities had with regards to mothering. I volunteered to take prime responsibility for developing a needs assessment survey and for running focus groups at the symposium. We thought that the data that would emerge would help inform the organization's work and may also be beneficial for funding purposes. I regarded it as an opportunity to do community work which could also be beneficial for a future research project.

The background to this project is important in that it demonstrates the bottom up, grass roots approach that was taken. It was a case of a community project turned dissertation, rather than an academically initiated project that enlisted people with disabilities as partners and participants. Although it was very small in scope and was conducted without any financial assistance, this study was commensurate with the paradigm shift in disability research mentioned earlier. It had a community rather than an institutional locus of intervention, focused on the needs and experiences of the target group and, most importantly, was largely controlled by the consumer organization. I took responsibility for developing the needs assessment and focus group guides as well as facilitating the discussions. However, I was accountable to the organization's board and executive every step of the way and incorporated the feedback I got from them on an ongoing basis. An example in point is the needs assessment survey which was a lengthy and involved process where input was provided at various stages of its development. After coming up with a version that was satisfactory to the organization, it was sent out to seven women with disabilities in the community who agreed to provide feedback and make suggestions. Their input was incorporated and represented in the final version of the survey.

In terms of outcome, the survey and focus groups were instrumental in identifying the top barriers and concerns that women with disabilities face either as mothers or as those who were considering motherhood. It also identified the services and resources they considered to be most important and their ideas on how the well-being of women with disabilities with and without children could be enhanced in the community. The results of this study were published as part of the symposium report and were widely disseminated (Prilleltensky, 1995). Although I had secured permission to utilize the data for dissertation purposes, I was ultimately a lot more interested in the qualitative component of the study. Hence, the needs assessment informed this research and was used for triangulation purposes but did not stand on its own as a quantitative component of the study.

The abbreviated version of this story does not allow me to expand on the issues that came up as we worked on this project and on some of the lessons that we learned along the way. Participation in another APA session, this time as a presenter on a panel, provided the avenue for describing the research process (Prilleltensky & Odette, 1996). For the purpose of the present discussion I prefer to focus more globally on my experience of doing this work. Having spent my adult life either working for large school boards or studying in academic institutions, working in partnership with a grass roots consumer organization provided me with a new perspective on things. It also served to challenge some of my inflexible notions of how things should be done. I learned, for example, that relying on the parallel transit system (for people with disabilities) requires a more flexible attitude to meeting times, as do fluctuating health needs. Interestingly, this enabled me to be more attentive and respectful of my own health needs and consider it as a factor in my professional life. This split between the public and private worlds has been discussed by several feminist and disability researchers. As Susan Wendell reminds us, "The public world is the world of strength, the positive (valued) body, performance and production...(whereas) weakness, illness, rest and recovery are generally hidden and often neglected. Coming into the public world with illness, pain or a devalued body, we encounter resistance to mixing the two worlds" (Wendell, 1996, p. 111). I realized, through this community project, that in my professional capacity in the public world, I myself re-enacted this split. I did so by keeping hidden and private any reference to my own health issues, fully expecting myself to transcend any weakness or fatigue that may interfere with "normal" performance.

The experience of the symposium was most illuminating and rewarding for me, both as a physically-disabled mother and as a student researcher. Surrounded by other women with disabilities, I was delighted and rejuvenated by the atmosphere of warmth, support, and connectedness that marked the symposium. Any early reservations that I had (should I do this research? who would benefit from it? who would be interested?) were put to rest by the support and encouragement I got from the symposium participants. I felt that I was given a mandate to conduct this kind of work. Furthermore, the women I met at the symposium and through my dealings with the organization readily agreed to participate in in-depth interviews which comprise the main source of data for this dissertation. Consequently, 2/3 of the women I interviewed also participated in the pilot project. Although I bring the "official" section of the research story to an end here, its thread continues throughout the book.

Research participants

Data for the research were gathered via 26 in-depth interviews with 13 participants and four focus groups with women who were at different stages in relation to motherhood. Over half of those interviewed were mothers with children at different stages of development. The rest were women who were either in the process of weighing their reproductive options or had already decided to remain childless. All were women with physical disabilities who had varying levels of mobility/limb impairment. Most were wheelchair users. Participants were well educated as a group; approximately 2/3 of those interviewed held a university degree. None of them belonged to a visible minority group.

The focus groups predated the interviews and were held at the symposium mentioned above. Thirty five women altogether attended the focus groups. The goal of this conference was to meet the mothering-related needs and interests of women with a range of disabilities, physical and otherwise. Consequently, most, but not all of those who partook in the focus groups were women who have a mobility/limb impairment. All those quoted in the study belonged to the latter category of mobility-impaired women. The interviews took place 18 to 24 months after the focus groups. At the time of the conference, women who were willing to participate in in-depth interviews were asked to provide their names and phone numbers. Consequently, most of those who were interviewed for the study also participated in one of the focus groups. At least 10 types of physical disabilities are represented in the study.

Data collection

Focus groups. Typically used in market research, focus groups are a way of collecting information from a group of people on their perceptions and feelings towards a certain issue. It is based on the assumption that people both influence and are influenced by others around them and that this will be reflected in the focus group discussion (Krueger,

1988). As indicated above, data for this research included four focus groups that were held during a weekend symposium on women with disabilities and motherhood. Each group was geared towards a specific group of women with disabilities: women considering motherhood, mothers of young children, mothers of older children, and women who were not mothers. This last group, titled "Not every woman is a mother", was facilitated by a woman with a disability who did not have children and who was trained as a social worker. I facilitated the other three groups.

The groups were held concurrently with other sessions and workshops to ensure that symposium participants had a choice about participation. Sessions were chosen by participants several weeks before the symposium took place. Those who signed up for the focus groups were informed that it was part of a research project and may be used for publication purposes. In addition, a statement was read at the beginning of each session indicating that participation is voluntary and may be withdrawn at any time. Participants then signed a consent form indicating their willingness to participate in the research. They also consented to my taping of the session and using direct (albeit anonymous) quotes in a research report and/or publication. Unfortunately, one session (for mothers with young children) could not be taped due to a last minute technical problem. Instead, detailed notes were taken by a co-facilitator.

In preparation for the focus groups I developed guides which would tap on participants' experiences, issues and priorities in relation to motherhood. Although the guides served to provide some parameters, the focus group discussions also centred on the particular issues and interests presented by participants. Each group had a life of its own. All were characterized by intense, thought-provoking and highly interactive discussions. Stories were shared, advice was sought and offered, and new meanings were in the making. The data that emerged from the focus groups have been integrated with data gathered via in-depth interviews. Together, they are the basis for the four Findings chapters of this book.

In-depth interviews. Marshall and Rossman (1989) emphasize the importance of choosing a method within qualitative research that is best suited for the question under investigation. The need for consistency between research question and research method notwithstanding, it is also the preference of the particular researcher for certain methods over others that guide the research. Alan Peshkin demonstrates this, as he describes his passion for ethnographic fieldwork: "Rather than pursuing research with questions in search for the 'right' methods of data collection, I had a preferred method of data collection in search for the 'right' question" (Glesne & Peshkin, 1992, p. 102). In the same vein, interviewing is often appealing to feminist researchers due to its emphasis on avoiding control, connecting with others, and researching women's lives on their own terms (Edwards, 1993; Oakley, 1990; Reinharz, 1992). I regard the choice of in-depth interviewing as my main source of data collection as both appropriate for the question under investigation and consistent with my preference for a relationship-based, interactive approach.

I interviewed 13 participants (eight with children, five without) and conducted a total of 26 interviews. Most women were interviewed twice, one was interviewed only once due to time constraints, while another was interviewed three times due to a combination of mutual interest and faulty taping during the first interview. Nine women also participated in the focus groups a year and a half earlier. The rest were recruited either through some other disability-related work I did in the community or through the snowballing technique in which key informants suggest the names of other potential participants.

Most of the interviews took place in the home of participants, one was conducted at a work setting while two others were carried out at the university. Average length was 90 minutes. Informed by the literature and by the pilot study, I came to the first set of interviews with an interview guide. As I expected, it was used loosely and flexibly, given the dynamic and interactive nature of in-depth interviewing. Some interviews were completely participant-led. Others required more structure and therefore a greater reliance on the interview guide. The questions were open-ended and phrased and ordered in such a way as to "make words fly" (Glesne & Peshkin, 1992, p. 63). Beginning with questions that are less personal and revealing is likely to increase the participant's comfort level and enhance the quality of the interviewing process (Glesne & Peshkin, 1992; Measer, 1985; Seidman, 1991; Yow, 1994).

Participants signed a consent form indicating their willingness to participate in the interview and to have it audiotaped. They received a copy of the transcripts and were given the opportunity to change and/or clarify information. Together with the transcript of the first interview, participants were mailed a 3–5 page summary. The second interview focused on reflections from the first interview and a co-construction of knowledge using information from the first interview, from the focus groups, and, in some cases, from the survey filled out by the particular participant. Whereas the first interview was more information-driven, the second interview dealt with the more sensitive issue of exploring possible contradictions and engaging in clarification and co-construction of the emergent knowledge.

Data analysis and interpretation

Glesne and Peshkin (1992) refer to data analysis as "the prelude to sensitive, comprehensive outcomes that make connections, identify patterns, and contribute to greater understanding" (p. 146). Along with other qualitative researchers, they emphasize the time-consuming and labour intensive nature of the analysis phase, a phase which requires immersion in the data collected. My approach to data analysis has been informed by the work of Glesne and Peshkin (1992), Merriam (1988), and Seidman (1991) and consisted primarily of thematic organization of the data.

My official engagement in data analysis did not begin until most of the interviews had been completed. However, I produced summaries of the first set of interviews as soon as they were transcribed and sent them to participants along with the transcriptions. Without exception, the response to the summary was favourable. A number of participants noted that although they did not get around to reading the full transcript, they enjoyed reading the summary. A few said that it was instrumental in reflecting on past events and even served to trigger new understandings. One woman asked her partner to read it and used it as a stimulus for discussion. For the purpose of the research, the summaries served as a bridge to the next interview and allowed for corrections and clarifications.

When most of the interviews were completed, I entered the next phase of in-depth data analysis. Having constructed the summaries several months prior, I decided to put them aside so as not to pre-empt my analysis. My first step in this analytical process was to go through each transcript and label excerpts according to categories. For example, a participant's account about a recent issue with her child might be labelled in the margins as relationship with child, along with 2–3 words specific to the story. While some categories span several pages, others are no more than several sentences. The next step was to transfer the information from the margin of the transcript into a computer file, noting the page for each category. This process was repeated for each transcript with little concern for repetition of themes and categories. The end result was a list of categories for each participant and for each interview. The next step was to study what now amounted to a booklet of categories. I spent several days reading and re-reading the categories, looking for connections not only within interviews as I had done before, but also between interviews of different participants. Gradually, this process led to categories being clamped into broader themes and to the emergence of a framework for the data.

Methodological reflections

In my introductory comments to this chapter I indicated my intention to write about methodological reflections apart from the step-by-step description of the research. Although this division facilitates the writing process, it is clearly an artificial division given that the entire research process is guided, facilitated, and often impeded by methodological issues and dilemmas. For example, the above description of the analysis and interpretation of the research is incomplete without acknowledging my own voice and signature as the researcher. My own gaze, to use Denzin and Lincoln's term, is filtered through my stance as a disabled academic and a mother, and one who is white, heterosexual and married to a non-disabled academic. These latter characteristics are just as important as the former as my experience of disability and motherhood are mediated and filtered through my relatively privileged social standing.

Being a feminist and a disability rights advocate, I am interested in the production of knowledge that aims to contribute to the well-being of women and people with disabilities. My lens is further filtered by my belief that unequal power structures and oppressive ideologies play a major role in framing the personal experience of womanhood and disability. Hence, I approached this research with the explicit intent to study the braiding of gender, disability, and other social constructs. Doing so, however, is not counter-indicated with having an open mind, coming as a learner, and conducting rigorous research. It is simply acknowledging my own role in the research process. In the same vein, I do not apologize for my openly ideological perspective that aims to present the oppressive underpinnings of personal experience on the one hand, and to highlight the strengths of study participants on the other. At the same time, I agree with Lather's (1986) claim that an ideological stance must be accompanied by a commitment to conduct rigorous research that can produce credible, trustworthy data.

My own attempts to enhance the rigor of my research prompted me to adopt a very careful and conservative approach to data analysis. I initially marked and categorized almost every transcript excerpt in the fear of leaving out meaningful information. As time consuming and labour-intensive as this process was, I chose to err on the side of over-incorporation and not under-incorporation. Only after everything in each transcript was marked, coded and categorized, did I feel comfortable, the second time around, to be more reductionist and economical in my approach. My other attempts to enhance research rigor include a triangulation of data sources (interviews, focus groups, information from the survey), explication of the process of coming to conclusions, and keeping a running record of hunches, surprises, insights, and dilemmas. My commitment to rigor notwithstanding, I recognize and acknowledge my role as the elicitor, editor, and interpreter of data and as the weaver of events, life stories, and meaning-making. There are various plausible stories that can be told in any research project (Glesne & Peshkin, 1992) and the particular one I tell is inextricably bound to my own subjectivity and way of being in the world.

Various methodological issues and dilemmas came up for me over the course of the research. Some of these issues had rather simple solutions while others continue to present a source of discomfort. The centrality of the research relationship and the inherent challenges in conducting ethical research are at the heart of these issues and this discussion. Earlier I discussed the centrality of the research relationship and the importance of upholding the dignity, respect and well-being of participants. I also noted the more flexible and permeable research boundaries that are characteristic of feminist methodology. As Reinharz (1992) states, "blurring of the distinction between formal and personal relations...is characteristic of much, although not all, feminist research" (p. 263).

My own approach was to be very informal and forthcoming with participants. I knew some of them on a more personal level before the start of the research and our relationship was enhanced in the process. All participants knew that I was a mother with a disability and most learned more about me over the course of the research. Although I took care to maintain the focus of the interviews on participants' experiences and meaning making, I shared some of my own experiences usually in response to direct questions. Mobility impaired mothers are too scarce and difficult to come by for me to withhold information that can be of use. On other occasions, I made spontaneous and brief references to my own family over the course of a discussion. It seemed as though the attributes we shared as women with mobility impairments provided an immediate connection. Despite my informal approach and the reduced distance that marked the research relationship, I was careful not to exploit this sense of intimacy for research purposes. Participants were invited to share according to their level of comfort and were given the opportunity to delete any information that they wished from the transcript. Furthermore, they had a chance to review and edit the direct quotes that I use in the manuscript. I inserted this additional check-in point in order to provide participants with greater control of the data and provide myself with ethical peace of mind.

The reduced distance that marked my research style contributed to some non-research like interactions with participants. For example, one young mother consulted with me about various child rearing situations, from letting her baby cry, to future decisions about discipline and limit setting. In a sense, I was the perfect candidate for such consultations given my presence in her home, therapeutic background with children and adults, and personal experience as a mobility-impaired mother. My approach was to respond as openly and helpfully as I could while constantly monitoring my role in this relationship. Over the course of three interviews, this participant and I had various opportunities to discuss child-rearing and family issues. I felt that these discussions enhanced the interview process and were also useful for her. Without losing sight of the distinction between research and counselling, I was nonetheless available for questions and discussions. The informal nature of our meetings also included enjoyable time spent holding, feeding, and playing with her baby. The proud mother that she is, she seemed to take great pleasure in my obvious delight with her baby. Despite differences in age, family situation and general circumstances, there was a strong sense of mutual liking. Had this participant not moved away, it is quite likely that my relationship with her would have continued beyond the research.

I have to admit that the reduced distance and more permeable boundaries are not without their challenges. In the focus groups that pre-dated the interviews, the knowledge that emanated from the sharing of lived experience created a very intense emotional climate. My multiple roles of researcher, group facilitator and mother with a disability were challenging to negotiate at times, given my own intense feelings of kinship and validation. I was acutely aware that at times I simply wanted to be of the group, without the added responsibilities of a moderator and a researcher. In one group I shared something from my own experience to answer a question that one woman posed to the group and that only I had direct experience with. At the time, I chose to do this as I felt it would be helpful for the woman posing the question. Upon listening to the taped session, I was somewhat concerned about the space that I took to tell my story and wondered if it was not my own need that I was meeting. I had to entertain the possibility that I got carried away by the powerful experience of being surrounded by women who had similar experiences to my own.

Relaxed boundaries can also pose challenges to maintaining the researcher role separate and distinct from roles performed in other contexts. This challenge became apparent to me as I went over one of the interview transcripts. In this case, a mother was telling me about the strained relationship she has with her adolescent daughter. In her efforts to avoid conflict and prevent angry outbursts on the part of the daughter, she typically refrained from posing questions about her daughter's activities and whereabouts. Without even noticing, I provided input as to how communication could be encouraged in a non-confrontational manner: "I think sometimes parents can find a way of inviting kids to talk about things without pressuring them. So instead of saying 'why aren't you with your friends any more', another way might be 'you know, it's really nice to have you around here more. I noticed that you're not going out so much. I don't want to pressure you to talk about it if you don't want to but...I'm here and I'd like to hear you if you want to talk.'" I realized, as I read the transcript, that it was not my place to impart this unsolicited advice. I was there in a research capacity and I clearly outstepped these boundaries in this case. I recognize this as a boundary violation on my part and use this recognition to do a better job of self-monitoring. However, I do not regard this minor transgression as detracting from the overall ethical integrity of the research. Writing about boundary issues in feminist therapy, Brown (1994) states that "feminist ethical principles construe boundary maintenance in therapy as a continuous, rather than dichotomous variable....no therapist is immune from the potential to engage in violations of client boundaries" (p. 215). By recognizing the potential for such violations in their own work, conscientious therapists "can theorize the problem as learning to identify the risk factors for boundary violations, and making a commitment to seek out such risk factors in themselves" (p. 215). Brown's suggestions can also be applied to feminist research which is also marked by more flexible and permeable boundaries. Being reflective and introspective about our research relationship can go a long way in enhancing its ethical integrity.

Protecting the anonymity of research participants is another methodological issue that presents itself in my work. Maintaining participant anonymity is one of the most basic ethical research requirements. However, this is no simple matter when the population under study is as specific as women with physical disabilities. In studies that draw on more general populations, assigning fictitious names and omitting unique features is often enough to maintain anonymity. The same cannot be assumed for the narrow and specific group under study. The braiding of motherhood and physical disability further heightens the specificity of this group.

I struggled with these issues as I summarized the data from the focus groups for a research report I prepared for the disabled women's organization. All group participants signed a consent form agreeing to maintain the confidentiality of other participants, to the taping of the session for research purposes, and to the use of direct quotes in a research report or publication. However, after analyzing the data (and despite attempts to disguise personal information), I became concerned that reading their own words may make some of the women feel exposed and vulnerable. After all, it is virtually impossible to truly disguise participants from others who partook in the same group. I ended up sending each of the 35 women who participated in the groups a copy of the report prior to its publication. Along with the report I sent a letter, requesting feedback within a certain time period should anyone find any part of the report uncomfortable or problematic. Unlike individual interviews where changes and omissions can be made relatively easily, this is not the case with focus group discussions where it may be difficult to discern "who said what", To my relief, no requests were made for deletions or omissions.

I faced similar dilemmas with respect to the data I obtained via in-depth interviews. Beyond sharing transcripts with participants and granting them editorial powers, I felt a responsibility to present them with the direct quotes that I ultimately chose for the final manuscript. Interview transcripts are generally lengthy and may not be read in great detail. Furthermore, it is difficult for participants to know what they should edit when it is not clear what will ultimately be used for public consumption. Most importantly, the relatively small and interconnected nature of the disabled community presented particular challenges as far as anonymity was concerned. As researcher, I struggled with the uncomfortable knowledge that "anonymity of individuals and collectives can create tension with the desire to write thick, rich descriptions" (Magolda & Robinson, 1993, p. 12). My commitment to confidentiality and anonymity was a major factor in my decision not to present complete profiles of participants. Instead, I chose to present quotes in the context of a thematic analysis in the hope of obscuring and protecting the identity of participants. I realized during the writing phase, however, that some of my chosen quotes may indeed make it possible for some women to be identified by others in the community. I also realized that doing away with all such quotes would seriously compromise the quality of the research. I chose to deal with this dilemma by deleting some quotes, changing others, and allowing participants to be the final judges as to what stayed in and what was taken out. A number of my participants had shared their experiences in presentations, publications, and documentaries. For some, being identified as research participants was not uncomfortable or problematic. I have therefore decided to concentrate my efforts on ensuring that participants are the final judges over the inclusion of quotes and other potentially identifying information.

5

Growing Up as a Girl with a Disability

In this chapter I focus on the early experiences of study participants as girls and young women with disabilities. Of the 13 women who participated in the in-depth interviews, 10 were either disabled from birth or had incurred their disability at a young age. This chapter is based on the stories they shared with me about growing up as girls with disabilities. Childhood experiences were not explored in the focus groups, nor were they directly queried in the in-depth interviews. Nonetheless, most participants chose to provide some background information and discuss salient childhood experiences. In some cases this was further explored in the second interview.

The stories that were relayed to me provide an important backdrop to participants' present day experiences and dilemmas. Their value, however, extends far beyond the provision of a context for this research on motherhood. As I listened to participants' stories about growing up as girls with disabilities, it became increasingly evident that they need to be presented for their own merit. They provide a glimpse into life on the margins of mainstream girlhood, the socially constructed oppressive factors that often pervade such lives, and the resilience and determination that sometimes shield adverse outcomes.

I begin by focusing on expectations both at home and at school for girls with physical disabilities. I then discuss issues pertaining to psycho-sexual development followed by social development and peer relations. I conclude by highlighting the risks to self-determination that these stories convey as well as the courage and persistence with which it was sought.

It's a girl...and she has a disability: what does the future hold?

Parental expectations and family dynamics

It is probably safe to say that most expectant parents wish for a healthy, non-disabled baby. The love they feel for their baby even prior to its birth usually entails dreams and hopes for the future, for what he or she will become. The diagnosis of a disability in a newborn baby unquestionably requires some adjustment on the part of parents, with shock, sadness and guilt, commonly reported. This cannot be divorced from cultural representations of disability, nor from a past legacy of professional portrayal of disabled children as burdens on families. The nature of information and the manner in which it is presented to parents can further impact their perceptions of their baby. In the present study, two participants reported that their parents were told to anticipate the early death of their daughters:

> My folks didn't have a lot of support in terms of what to do with me. They were told in the hospital to take me home and that I was going to die...they just said "take her home, there is not much hope"...like what a thing for them to have to live with...I think that has always stuck with them, especially my mom...she's always been very protective of me.

In at least three cases parents were advised to place their disabled daughter in an institution whereas another set of parents was told that their daughter would always require a special school. This is quite consistent with the prevailing attitude towards people with disabilities some 30–40 years ago when most of the participants were born and raised.

Study participants told varied and diverse stories of how their parents regarded their disability and the coping mechanisms that they enlisted. Two described a home environment where their disability was perceived as tragic and severely limiting. This is unrelated to the extent of the impairment as both cases involved girls who were highly mobile and physically independent. One participant noted her mother's young age and the financial strain that her family was under as important contributing factors. The other woman situated her own devalued status within a cultural context that perceived women as inferior to men and having limited opportunities:

> Some of it had to do with the culture...a family of immigrants, not having a really good understanding of the cause of the disability,

with religion tied in to that...was this disability the result of a cross, something that somebody had done in the past? And also the protectiveness of the culture where women didn't get out...and then the disability on top of it. It was just a monster to try and cope.

The other participant experienced rejection by her mother. She recounted the numerous and futile attempts she made as a child in order to gain her mother's love and acceptance:

I remember making efforts to try to make her love me in some way...I remember specifically trying to do things that would sort of make her accept me...I just could never do anything right...I remember feeling "I really hate this person" and then I remember other times feeling "I wish I could just make her love me."

Rejected by her mother, this participant had a very loving father who provided physical care-giving at a young age and emotional nurturance throughout life. Of the 13 women interviewed for this study, this was the only indication of rejection on the part of a parent. Two other women noted that while their parents were clearly committed to them as individuals, they fell short of fully accepting their disability. In one family the daughter's disability was never discussed. The parents provided physical accommodations and consistently followed through with various therapy regimes. However, they never talked with their daughter about her disability and its impact on her life. Lacking any information about her impairment and sensing that this is not a topic to be discussed, she went through a phase where she worried that her condition would worsen; a concern that had no realistic basis:

It (disability) was never discussed and I didn't want to bring it up...I hated going to camp for children with disabilities because I saw kids with more serious disabilities and worried that my disability would get worse, just like them...at the other end, I thought that if I were really tried, perhaps the disability would get better, go away.

Interestingly, the other participant who felt that her parents did not fully accept the disability was also reluctant to associate with disabled peers. The message that she would walk again and resume pre-injury functioning interfered with her ability to fully integrate the disability into her sense of self.

Contrary to some of the negative and ambivalent messages noted above, several participants emphasized the affirming messages they got from their parents, either explicitly or implicitly. One noted that her parent's attitude that one must make the best of every situation has helped her cope in difficult times. Throughout her childhood this woman perceived her family as affirming and supportive without stifling her independence. Another participant recounted similarly positive experiences:

> I always knew that yes, I had a disability but for the most part I could pretty much do and be almost anything I wanted to be...I don't know if my parents really worked at it or they were just lucky or they had a gift for instilling a very powerful and positive self image.

Families varied quite a bit in the extent to which they encouraged independence and self-efficacy. One woman, considered highly fragile as an infant, was sheltered and protected throughout her childhood and adolescence. Even when her survival was no longer in question her parents were somewhat reluctant to let her go out with friends; neither did they expect her to partake in any family chores and responsibilities. Antithetically, another participant, also considered fragile, was encouraged to become as independent and self sufficient as possible:

> She (mother) felt that I would have to be tough in order to survive...she would say "you have to figure a way to fight back"...she was teaching me to be independent in a way or to fight my own battles and use my smarts...to talk my way out of a fight because I couldn't do anything about it physically.

Despite the severity of her daughter's impairment, this mother had high expectations in behavioural, social, and academic domains. Having a limited education herself and experiencing financial difficulties, she instilled in her daughter that a good education and a good job was her ticket to independence. Several other participants also noted that their parents were instrumental in enhancing their independence, while one became self-sufficient and independent by default as her mother did not participate in her care. For another participant, independence was promoted as far as getting chores done at home; if she could not do something one way her parents taught her an alternate way. Nonetheless, given these parents' belief that their disabled daughter would always live with them, they did little to encourage self-efficacy and independence beyond domestic chores. They were strongly opposed to her decision to attend university, also due to a cultural background that did not envision women as professionals:

> My family were mainly farmers and everybody had a function in a family...and on a farm you would have to pull your weight and yet you know what could I really do?...I don't think there were any professional women in my world, in my sphere...so I didn't have that role model and with being disabled and not being able to pull my weight the question was what actually could I really do?

As children, none of the women I interviewed were encouraged to see themselves in long-term relationships or as mothers to children. Some were explicitly told it was not to be, others got implicit messages to that effect, while others just never remember it being discussed or alluded to. Whereas most girls grow up knowing that they may well become partners and mothers, these girls were either given messages to the contrary, or experienced a total silence on this subject. This will be further explored later in this chapter.

Expectations in educational and institutional settings

Four participants had received some of their education in a segregated setting, either at a school for children with disabilities or in a residential institution. Consistently, they commented on the lack of emphasis placed on academic achievement and on the poor quality of the education that they received:

> There was such an emphasis on students doing things like physiotherapy and so kids would be pulled out of class to go to therapy...the level of the school was not the same as it was in the integrated programs...it was also like this huge playground...there weren't the expectations that you do your homework or that you have any movement towards adult responsibilities or any kind of responsibilities.

According to participants' accounts these settings were largely based on a medical model and targeted physical and medical needs more than academic and educational ones. This was particularly prevalent in an institutional setting that focused almost exclusively on physical care while academic achievement was blatantly underplayed. One participant who clearly excelled academically recounted "fighting tooth and nail to get a study space that was away from the general chaos and mayhem". Another woman entered a residential setting in middle childhood. Notwithstanding the institution's policy of admitting youngsters with physical but not intellectual disabilities, she was significantly more advanced in relation to same-aged peers whose entire schooling was at the institution:

> Everybody my age was in a much lower grade...they were shocked that I was in a grade 5 reader, these kids my age, and they were like in 2 or 3...it was just the way it was there.

The disparity in education became most apparent during the transition to "regular" school at the end of elementary; several participants were placed at a lower grade level in the integrated system. One spoke of the social disadvantage that this created for her:

> I remember going to the guidance counsellor once a week and saying "I can't deal with it"...I mean the workload was tough but that's not what was bothering me...it was the maturity level of these kids...they were 12, 13, and I was 15...I just felt like I was babysitting a lot of the time.

Set apart by her disability, this student was also set apart due to the significant age discrepancy between herself and her non-disabled peers. Another recounted the catch-up work she had to do in order to keep up with peers who did not experience educational disadvantage.

As they reflected on their school experiences several participants noted that many youngsters in segregated settings were not expected to live. Most of them had known at least one child who had died. The perception that a significant percentage of the student population is not expected to live to adulthood would explain the present-oriented focus of these settings, as well as the emphasis on physical and medical care. The primary function of schools is to enhance children's development, thereby planting the seeds for adult roles and responsibilities. Teaching students who may not make it to adulthood can generate a great deal of anxiety and ambivalence on the part of educators. Confusion may ensue as to what purpose the school actually serves. Unless these issues are explored and resolved, a school may indeed be turned into a huge playground, compromising the education of many of its students and possibly limiting their options.

Psychosexual development: messages, perceptions, and experiences

Parental messages and perceptions

Consistent with some of the research I reviewed earlier, some participants grew up in families where their sexuality was ignored, undermined, or actively discouraged. One noted that in her family "there was not an expectation that I was going to date...certainly no expectation that I was going to get married and be in a relationship". During adolescence her mother steered clear of any conversation about relationships and sexuality. When the daughter shared her frustration at not getting asked to dance at parties, she was told that she had plenty of time and should not concern herself with these matters. Now a mature woman, this participant offered the following reflection: "I don't think she (mother) knew what to do with that...I think she really struggled with what to do with my pain".

One participant was explicitly discouraged from thinking about relationships and intimacy. Growing up in a culture where women assumed traditional gender roles, her only role model for adult female identity was that of a wife and mother. Although she grew up wanting to assume these roles, she was explicitly told that this will not happen:

> My family always said "you can't think about boys, you can't think about relationships, focus on your studies...you're not going to have any children...this is not for you".

Exploring these issues some 25 years later, she now attributes these messages to her family's wish to protect her from the pain of rejection. They could not envision that anyone would find her sexually desirable and wished to spare her the heartache of unrealistic dreams and hopes. Her adult perspective notwithstanding, she experienced these messages as devastating and invalidating during adolescence.

Another participant remembers talking with her mother at age 11 about marriage and children. The mother said not to worry; "everyone finds someone and it would take time". The message was quite different several years later when this woman was no longer a child:

> A week after my sister got married we were looking at the wedding pictures...there were some other close friends there at the time and someone said "well, that's one wedding down, one to go" I was a

month short of being 19 at the time and my mother said right in front of me and them and everybody else, "well, no, there won't be any more weddings in our family". I remember feeling incredibly devastated.

This insensitive and hurtful remark was made by a mother who was otherwise described by the daughter as very caring and supportive. This participant was not treated differently from her non-disabled sister in other domains and was encouraged to become independent and self sufficient. She contextualized her parents' perceptions about sexuality and disability within the larger societal framework: "a lot of people have biases when it comes to people with disabilities and certainly your own family is not exempt from that".

Attempts to protect a disabled daughter from sexual rejection and exclusion are common to all accounts of parental reticence to acknowledge sexuality. In at least two cases parents were also concerned about safety issues: "my mother's words to me when I was dating were 'just remember that you can't run away'". This participant was not exposed to any negative messages about sexuality. Other than the above warning, her family was generally silent about these matters, a factor she attributes more to their general discomfort with discussing sexuality than to any disability-specific factor.

Beyond the home: interactions with health professionals and service providers

Invalidating messages about sexuality, or ignoring the subject altogether, were not limited to the home front. Several participants noted the absence of any such discussions in the segregated schools or residential facilities they attended as children. The basic information students received on reproduction and the menstrual cycle was not connected to the broader topic of human sexuality:

The head nurse would give you a brochure from the makers of Tampax or something that says this is how an egg gets fertilized… but you didn't have the concept that there were human beings involved. It could have all been in a laboratory the way it was described in the brochures…as far as teenagers going out together, that was highly discouraged…staff were strongly discouraged from having talks with us about sex, and in fact, some staff were fired because they thought it was stupid and if you had a question they would try to answer it.

Another participant noted the open door policy of the residential setting where she was raised; doors had to be left open at all times as staff wanted to monitor adolescents' behaviour. Some of this changed towards the end of her stay there, with one of the staff members initiating a series of expert-led discussions about sexuality. Despite these reforms, most of the staff remained suspicious and resistant to any attempts to broach the subject. In the words of one former resident, "you weren't to be a sexual being and if someone was attracted to you sexually then they must be deviant". Another participant, whose only experience with segregated settings was in a professional capacity, also noted the glaring absence of any discussions about sexuality. She had contact with a number of physically disabled teenagers who lacked the most basic information about sexuality and reproduction:

> They would ask me questions and I would bring in books with illustrations because they knew nothing about their bodies, their sexuality, and they wanted to know...most of them were at the age where they just wanted to know about their bodies and the sexual part of it but some also wanted to know about children.

The importance of obtaining relevant information about sexuality was emphasized by another woman, one who acquired her disability as a pre-adolescent. She attributes the dearth of information she had on the subject to her attempts as an adolescent to come across as knowledgeable and self-sufficient in this domain. Consequently, it was not until she was in university that she found out that her disability should not preclude her from expressing her sexuality. She described the excitement she felt after attending an information session about sexuality and disability:

> I wasn't really certain that I could have sex...once I discovered that I could, it was such an eye-opening experience...I was so excited, I felt like I was electric that night.

Several participants recounted situations where privacy around the body was not respected during medical procedures and which left them feeling objectified. One recalled her experiences as a young child of having to demonstrate her walk to physicians and medical students:

> All these medical students were there. I was almost completely naked, walking in front of everyone...I hated that. I never felt comfortable walking, I would become tense and walk ten times

worse...and I got the message "you don't walk right, you've got to do better". When I was home, I could do most things. I got tired, but I could walk...but when I went for a check-up I got the message "there is something defective about you".

Another participant described similar experiences both at the segregated school she attended and during visits to medical clinics. She was highly critical about the manner in which physiotherapy sessions were organized at the school:

There would be no privacy screens or anything...they'd have us literally running around in our underwear...at ages 9, 10, 11, 12. You know, when you become painfully aware of your body and you're becoming aware of the opposite sex as well...so you've got a number of things impacting on you and they weren't sensitive at all to how it would make you feel and how it would impact on you later on...I really see this as a form of systemic abuse in a way.

As a grown woman, this participant can reflect critically on these painful childhood experiences and refer to them as a form of abuse. As a young girl, she felt totally powerless to change things, even though she clearly attributed the frustration and resentment she felt to the manner in which she was treated:

Even if I had verbalized to them what I was feeling it wouldn't have mattered. They weren't going to change the way that they were going to do anything anyway.

She would become resistant and uncooperative during treatment sessions and medical exams even though she knew that this distressed and embarrassed her mother.

My mother couldn't understand why I would resist so much and why I was so stubborn and headstrong...I didn't even at that point know why I was doing it...I do realize it now and you know, it's only been very recently that I've begun to realize why I was so resistant...that was my only way of being able to protest.

Two other participants, who also experienced privacy violations as children, described a sense of discomfort without being able to pinpoint its source. Unlike the participant quoted above who could define it for herself but not protest out loud, these participants could not even name it for themselves; "there was no point of reference to say that this isn't what it should be". Despite the inability to name the source of the oppression, these experiences have left one child with the impression that she doesn't really own her body.

Differing levels of privacy violations were noted by half of the participants who had a disability in childhood. These issues did not even come up in some interviews; others described medical exams that were conducted in a respectful and affirming manner. Regardless of the prevalence of this phenomenon, the fact remains that feeling a lack of ownership and control over one's body can pose a significant risk to a healthy sexual identity.

Messages from peers

In an article about girls with disabilities and sexuality, Rousso (1996) notes that "their more limited social and sexual involvement results not from lack of interest, but rather, lack of opportunity"   (p. 109). The social development and peer relations of study participants will be discussed in the following section. Pertinent to the present discussion is the experience of sexual rejection during adolescence, a theme common to most of the accounts. Whereas some participants experienced explicit and direct sexual rejection, others were "passed over" or sexually ignored. One participant relayed a particularly painful experience of being mocked for saying that she likes someone:

> I remember having this crush on a boy and telling a non-disabled friend about this and it got back to him. Well, that was it, it was the biggest joke...it was very painful because I felt a lot of shame about it...they thought it was totally weird.

Another participant was excluded from a "girl talk" by a non-disabled peer who considered it irrelevant for her:

> I remember in elementary school the girls were talking about boyfriends and about getting married...we were guessing who was going to get married first...I was very quiet, I wasn't making any guesses...and one girl, she just turned to me and said "oh well, you won't ever get married".

These types of encounters are hurtful, demeaning and potentially damaging, even when they are experienced as isolated incidents rather than as the defining feature of one's psycho-sexual adolescent experiences. Furthermore, sexual rejection need not be as explicit and mean-spirited as that described above for it to have an undermining impact and pose a risk to self-esteem. One participant recounted her pain as she watched all her friends being asked to dance while she was left to sit by herself:

> There were times when I'd be at a wedding and all the kids would get up and dance, my friends would be asked to dance and I would usually be left sitting by myself. It was because the fear of the disability in that culture...the fear that maybe I would have children like that...so here I was a teenager with all those hormones and wanting to fit in like the rest of them but not looking the same...and coming home crying.

It is important to note that the nature of this participant's impairment would not have precluded her from dancing or even made this activity particularly difficult. Her exclusion from the dancing arena can be accounted for by her deviation from norms of acceptable female appearance more than by any functional limitation. This gains further support from another participant's adolescent experience. Due to the specific nature of her impairment, she appeared a lot less disabled than she actually was. She remembers taking pride in the fact that boys found her attractive and paid attention to her. She was both angry and perplexed, however, at the different treatment afforded to another disabled girl, a friend of hers.

> What bothered me was not the way girls treated her but the way guys treated her...they weren't very nice to her...the sort of looks they were giving her and stuff like that...and they treated me differently than they treated her...even though she could carry my books, and she could run, and she could sit on the floor, she could do all of the things that I couldn't do, but it was the way she walked, you know, the CP walk.

The lasting impact that such experiences can have are underscored by another participant's comment that to this day she finds it difficult to walk in front of a group of kids as it reminds her of her own devaluation by adolescent boys some 25 years ago. Adolescent women in general tend to be alienated from their bodies and judge them through the prism of the male gaze. To the extent that the beauty myth is devaluing to all women, it can be especially detrimental to young disabled women who may construct their self concepts from these male appraisals (Riger, 1993). The impact that sexual devaluation can have on self-esteem is reflected in several of the accounts. Reflecting on a relationship she had as an adolescent, one woman noted that the best thing about it was that someone found her attractive; she had always considered herself fat and ugly. Another participant indicated the excessive emphasis that she and some of her young disabled friends had placed on being in a relationship. Beyond a longing for intimacy, being in a relationship for these young women was equated with a sense of wholeness and self-worth.

Social development: relationships with disabled and non-disabled peers

As a child grows and develops, her initial social circle expands beyond her family to include other children and adults. Adequate peer relations are important for a child's social and emotional well-being and are also associated with success at school. As young girls, most study participants had some contact with neighbourhood children. When they reached school age some joined their non-disabled peers in the regular school system while others attended segregated schools with other children with disabilities. Without exception, all were integrated in junior and senior high school.

Two participants who attended a special school spoke very favourably about the opportunity it afforded them to meet other children with disabilities:

> There weren't any kids with disabilities when I was really really young, I was pretty much on my own...but when I went to (special school), that's when my world opened up...there was one young girl that we're still friends, very close...that was the first time when I connected with her, and her mom and my mom got to know each other so I would go over there on weekends and whatever. That was the first time having someone in my life not in school.

The other participant also emphasized the importance of the social ties that she formed at the segregated school she attended. Amidst criticism of lack of privacy at school and low academic expectations, the social opportunities it afforded were seen as highly favourable. Both participants noted that they formed many lasting friendships that carried them over the years and are still important to them today:

> I got a lot out of that. I didn't get anything academic, that's for sure, but I got some incredible friendships...I still have a lot of these friendships and I think that that was really important for me in terms of having a solid base of friends with disabilities who I could relate to in ways that I maybe couldn't relate with non-disabled peers.

Although segregated settings by their very nature provided opportunities to meet other children with disabilities, many of their practices were actually counter-productive to healthy socialization. Commenting on her experience at a residential facility, one participant noted that daily routines (such as temperature taking) were carried out at times that suited staffing schedules rather than children's social activities. Describing many of these practices as unwarranted, this participant noted that they could have at least been scheduled with the children's needs in mind.

As I indicated earlier, all of the participants had experienced regular school settings either for their entire schooling or following elementary school. One participant had predominantly positive social interactions:

> I was in a regular school...if there was a fire drill, the two biggest boys made a fireman's lift and carried me out...there was no fear of insurance claims at that time...Kids knew I had a disability, I knew I had a disability, but it was put in perspective. It was part of who I was.

This participant, as well as another one who only attended a regular school, experienced some disability-related adjustments when they made the transition from elementary to junior high school. One found herself having to explain her disability to peers, something she had never encountered in elementary school where everyone knew her as disabled. She described going through a phase when she wished she didn't have to answer such questions as why was she limping and why she had a key to the school elevator. The participant quoted above had similar concerns, although the transition she ultimately experienced was a smooth one. She described the doubts she had when, due to accessibility issues, she began attending a different high school than her neighbourhood friends:

> I only knew one person who was going to that school, another girl, and we didn't particularly like each other...so it was a case of being in a new school situation, making a whole new group of friends...so for that brief time I had a little bit of self doubt...I realized that all the neighbourhood kids and the ones I had gone to school with, they always knew me for who I was and yes, they knew I had a disability but that was just part of the package...and here's a whole new group of people who I don't know who don't know me...they don't know that I'm okay.

Both participants were integrated throughout their schooling; their peers in primary and junior high school were familiar with their disabilities. The transition to a new situation and to peers who were not familiar with them precipitated some degree of concern and discomfort. A positive adjustment had ultimately been made in both cases.

A number of participants described more difficult transitions, usually from a segregated primary school to an integrated junior high school. Most reportedly went through a stage where they did not want to be associated or "lumped together" with other students with disabilities:

> We had our own home room. We were called OH students or something like that, I don't know. But we were labelled...in the lunch room they had a special table for us, and I didn't want that. I didn't want to be segregated.

Some resisted any kind of special treatment that clearly set them apart from their non-disabled peers. One noted how one of her teachers in junior high school would exempt her from a detention that the rest of the class got. Another recounted her discomfort when she was called to a meeting over the school's PA system along with other students with disabilities:

> Various students in the school had disabilities and I guess in their mind (the administration) they were thinking: "what can we do to make it easier for them, we'll call a meeting for all students with disabilities". Well, that's fine when I think about it as an adult, but when you're in high school you don't like to be singled out...and that's exactly what they did when they called us over the PA

system...it was so clear, so and so is in a wheelchair, and so and so uses crutches, and so and so well, she limps...they're calling all the crippled kids...it just bothered me that I had to be a part of that group.

Along with resisting an association with other students with disabilities, several participants recounted their attempts to make friends with non-disabled peers and some of the barriers that they came across. Some had to overcome personal barriers such as extreme shyness or a lack of exposure to a non-segregated environment:

It was a bit harder for me to make friends at high school because there was such a huge gulf in my cultural experience compared to theirs. I was removed from the community...for 6 years I hadn't really had interactions with non-disabled kids...in the institution a volunteer would come up to you and say "do you want to do this and do you want to do that", so in high school I sort of thought well, if a kid wants to hang out with me they'll approach me...but they didn't because they were just as shy as I was.

Another participant remembers making a conscious decision to overcome her shyness and make the first move to establish contact. She ended up connecting with two non-disabled girls who told her that they had been wanting to approach her and several other students with disabilities but did not know how it would be received. These accounts suggest that if left unaddressed, reservations on the part of youngsters with and without disabilities can inhibit the development of friendships.

Although some participants recounted experiences of active rejection by non-disabled peers, the more common experience was one of subtle exclusion and lack of acknowledgement. One participant noted how she would be used as a "late ticket" by non-disabled peers who would take her books just as she was about to enter class and claim to be late because they were helping her. Another attempted to connect with non-disabled peers by choosing one of them to be excused from class a few minutes early in order to push her chair to the next class:

There was an agreement among the teachers that students with disabilities could leave five minutes before the class ended...I grabbed that moment and took advantage of it because it was my way of connecting with one student in the class. I would pick somebody out and say "I need so and so's help"...a lot of the guys wanted to do that because they got a blast out of taking risks with my chair and we'd go racing down the hall...but it was my way of being connected with these people.

Despite the enthusiasm to help her from class to class, this participant clearly understood the limits of this friendship even as a young teenager: "I knew that after class I wasn't going to be asked to join them at the mall". A few had found their social niche by linking with other students who were either less popular or otherwise non-mainstream. The participant quoted above recounted the important transition she went through in high school when she decided to re-establish contact with her disabled peers from elementary school. Abandoning previous attempts to be fully accepted and integrated with non-disabled peers, she re-connected with peers with disabilities and found a strong sense of support and community:

A lot of us were struggling with the same stuff of you know, not having relationships, not feeling connected with our non-disabled peers...I had a friend who was not allowed to go on a school trip because he had a disability...I think that the systematic ways that some of us were being excluded really brought us together.

This participant's reference to systematic exclusion was mentioned by another study participant and is fundamental to the discourse on integration and participation. Some of the same physical and attitudinal barriers that hinder adults with disabilities from full community participation were also at play in participants' early experiences of social integration. Being integrated into the regular school system still meant that at the end of the school day they were bused right back to their home or residential setting. There was little opportunity to participate in extra-curricular activities or otherwise connect with non-disabled peers outside of the school milieu, a connection which becomes increasingly important during adolescence. A shared day at school does not guarantee social integration, especially in the absence of opportunities for social connection after school hours:

I had no choice about getting involved in anything because the school bus came and took me right after school...so I wasn't involved in any after school activities. I never went to dances and nobody ever asked me out.

Physical barriers are further confounded by attitudinal ones; a number of participants resented the assumption that they would only associate with other disabled individuals. Such assumptions are demeaning in their portrayal of the disability status as the defining feature of one's identity. Reflecting on her relationships with disabled and non-disabled peers, one participant noted:

> It's not that I didn't like them (disabled peers) as people, it's that I didn't want to be labelled...I didn't want to restrict myself to this group of people and be seen by them (non-disabled peers) as being part of this unit...I wanted to be seen for me.

The reluctance to associate with disabled peers can also be explained as a form of internalized oppression. In a social context where disability is perceived as a medical condition inherent to the individual and where those who are labelled as such are devalued, a child may indeed attempt to disavow that part of her self by associating only with non-disabled, non-stigmatized individuals.

Fighting for self-determination: narratives of risk and survival

Narratives of risk

Thus far I have described the salient childhood experiences of study participants as they pertain to family dynamics, psychosexual development, peer relations, and contacts with educational and institutional settings. Permeating most of these stories are the multiple barriers that many have faced in their quest for self determination and control over their lives. Self determination can be defined as "the individual's ability to pursue chosen goals without excessive frustration" (Olson, 1978, p. 45). Pursuing chosen goals cannot take place in a vacuum; it is contingent upon the ability to first imagine oneself in various roles and then perceive oneself as having capabilities and opportunities to attain them.

A number of study participants noted the absence of role models of adults with disabilities as they were growing up. Children are constantly emulating the adults around them as they try out different roles and identities. Having no exposure to adults with disabilities can significantly hinder a disabled child in her attempts to imagine herself in the future and consider different options. Having spent most of her childhood in an institution, one woman emphasized the difficulty for a child trying to imagine life beyond the institution:

> You didn't see kids there leaving or getting married or having kids... they left and you just never heard from them again....and then a lot of the kids who lived there died.

The antithesis to this was experienced by another participant who became involved in disabled sports as an adolescent:

> Being involved in sports, I was exposed to all kinds of people with disabilities older than me who were living very normal lives...they were working and driving and they had kids...it opened up a whole new other world.

Having trepidations about the future due to an absence of role models was not limited to those who were raised in an institution. Two other participants struggled as youngsters with who they may become, as all the women in their sphere were so visibly different from them. Lisi (1993) conveys the sense of powerlessness and frustration that can emanate from this void: "Growing up...I often felt alien in the homes of my parents and our neighbours, as though I faced people from different cultures across the dinner table and living room floor" (p. 202).

Whereas an absence of role models poses a subtle and indirect risk to self-determination, crude and tangible obstacles were also reported. Participants provided numerous examples of feeling powerless as children over various aspects of their daily lives, above and beyond the relatively little power afforded to children in general. One participant recounted the lack of control she felt as a pre-pubescent youngster following her injury:

> I found it really hard, this sense of having no control over my body...when you're in the hospital, medical staff determine when and how often your bowels will move and whether you're going to have a catheter or diapers or...you know, all those things that are so intrinsically personal...I always had a sense that you can't say no in a hospital...you just abdicate control.

Further discussing this issue, this participant made it very clear that the most troubling aspect for her was the lack of self-determination that she felt, much more so than the loss of physical control over some of her bodily functions. The most blatant and compelling description of having one's self-determination completely disregarded came from a participant who reflected about her early years in an institution for children with disabilities:

> You had no say in anything...you didn't have a say about what you ate or when you ate it. You didn't have a say about when you got up or when you went to bed. You didn't have a say about what times you could play or have free time. Even what you were wearing... they were going to open the closet door and pick item a or item b...it was a power issue...they were in charge.

The same controlling, undermining attitude that characterised decisions of daily living, was later applied to such critical decisions as where residents would be "placed" as adults:

> You had to leave when you were 18...and they would just dump people wherever there was a spot. I mean they didn't really care. They would place you out to a nursing home or some convent...it didn't matter, wherever there was an opening.

The logical conclusion that children may come to under such circumstances is that it really doesn't matter where they go, because they don't really matter. Maintaining a sense of self worth is an uphill battle when the pervasive message is one of helplessness and lack of agency and control.

Narratives of survival

Alongside and often intertwined with accounts of adverse interactions, lack of control, and multiple risks to self-determination, are participants' narratives of fighting for control over their lives and destinies, resisting oppression, and surviving multiple adversities. Two participants commented on the role that anger played in their fight for self-determination. For one woman, the anger she felt over her exclusion in the community and her parents' bleak outlook about her future options, mobilized her to leave home despite her family's objections. She described her decision to move out as a matter of survival:

> If I had stayed there I may not have gone on to university, I may have been in the home and taken care of...I just wouldn't have had the strength and the determination, it was almost a challenge to my

spirit...here I was accepted to university and the weekend I was to go my dad wasn't going to take me...he said: "what are you going to do? where is this going to end up?"...I called up my friend and said: "are you going? come and get me". And I left. I had never ever been that determined.

The other participant channelled her anger towards resisting oppressive attitudes and practices at the institution where she was raised:

I was mad all the time, I was just always mad...and I was always in trouble. I was constantly grounded. I was always in trouble because I couldn't contain it...if a staff member was doing something that I thought was idiotic I would tell them, in whatever language I chose, what I thought of their behaviour...I knew there'd be a backlash but I didn't care...it was more important to name the score...I also knew that it would let the other kids down if I didn't fight back because they would expect me to fight back about it...in a way I think they were vicariously fighting some of their fights through me.

She later used her anger to organize her peers and, as a group, demand to be involved in planning their discharge from the institution. Rather than passively accepting the nursing home placements arranged by the institution, these youngsters successfully lobbied for consumer-directed attendant services that would enable them to live independently in the community.

Another participant, who was rejected by her mother as a disabled girl, noted that she also had blessings in her life to balance out the adversities. Her father was always loving and supportive, she had a close relationship with her siblings, and as a youngster had managed to attract older friends who served as positive role models: "I've always been able to kind of find what I needed along the way".

These are examples where participants were able to transcend some of the adversity in their lives and to keep their heads above water when the odds were stacked against them. In other cases, highly supportive and affirming families provided a solid basis for the development of self-efficacy and a good self-esteem. One participant related how she asserted herself with her orthopaedic surgeon as a 17 year-old by requesting that he make his hospital visits at a more suitable time:

I said, "I don't want you coming to see me at 1 or 2 in the morning because I'm tired and I can't listen to the things you're saying to me and I can't ask questions. I want you to come and see me during the day when I'm awake"...and he did!

From a young age, this participant had the sense that she had some measure of control over her life and her destination:

There are some things as a child that you don't have a choice about, but I always knew that I had with most things some element of choice.

Whereas parents have the greatest impact on their child's development, other people that are influential in a child's life can also play hindering or facilitative roles. As children, most participants had some encounters with callous attendants and health care professionals. Such encounters can have an adverse effect on children's sense of control and self-determination. Alongside examples of negative experiences and interactions, some participants described ones that were positive and affirming. Two women described their childhood contacts with physicians and health care professionals as predominantly positive. One woman spent extensive time in hospital as a young girl. She had fond memories of caring nurses and physicians who would make a point of coming to visit with her. When her birthday rolled around they brought a cake to her bedside and held a party. Another participant noted a particularly memorable encounter with a physician:

I always liked the doctors because they were always really nice to me...some people have really horrible memories of going to doctors, but I really don't. And I remember specifically one doctor, I must have been getting older. I must have been like 11 or 12 because he said to me, I remember exactly, he said to me: "you can grow up, and you can have kids, and you can do everything everyone else does", he said to me. And that just stuck in my head...I don't think he even realized what an impact that statement had, you know.

As this woman got older and had various questions about her progressive condition, she knew that she could count on this physician to be respectful and upfront. He candidly answered her questions and admitted to not having all the answers. Such affirming and esteem-enhancing attitudes by those in positions of power can have a profoundly positive and lasting effect.

Concluding comments

This chapter represents participants' salient childhood experiences within the family, the school system, and institutional and medical settings. Within each of these domains, participants described disempowering experiences that can undermine well-being as well as those that can shield from adversity.

The impact of parental messages and family dynamics on the well-being of children is undeniable. With the exception of one case of blatant rejection by a parent, most participants perceived their families as caring and committed, if not always supportive. None of the participants, including those who described nurturing and supportive home environments, were encouraged to see themselves in long-term relationships or as mothers to children. In some cases this was blatantly stated, whereas others were either pointed in different directions or experienced parental silence on the issue.

Parental reticence to acknowledge and foster a healthy sexual identity must be considered in light of prevailing attitudes towards sexuality and disability at the time that study participants were growing up. Furthermore, these parents were undoubtedly affected by the paternalistic professional ethos prevalent at the time. Their intimate knowledge of their children's limitations, abilities, and needs notwithstanding, parents of children with disabilities were historically undervalued as an important source of knowledge and encouraged to defer to medical authority.

Explicating accounts of disempowering experiences at home, in educational and medical settings, and in the community, runs the risk of conjuring images of disadvantage and passivity. I struggle with this presentation as I am aware that focusing on such images can be oppressive in and of itself. In the words of Jenny Morris (1992), "images of disadvantage are such an important part of the experience of oppression that emancipatory research... must consistently challenge them" (pp. 162–163).

My decision was ultimately guided by my belief that such childhood experiences must be told and exposed. My intention was to tell the stories and thereby illuminate the oppressive factors that frame these experiences. As I wrote about sexual objectification and violations of privacy, I questioned myself about the risks and benefits of such an exposure. Far from wanting to sensationalize these issues in a voyeuristic manner, my aim was to impact readers the way I was impacted, to amplify the voices of oppression and raise a collective outcry against such abusive practices.

Throughout the chapter and especially in the final section, I attempted to balance images of passivity and oppression with impressive accounts of resistance and survival. The latter, are just as important as the former, in shaping participants' experiences, meaning-making, and identities. In fact, it is the very sort of women who participated in this study who are the strongest and most passionate advocates for future generations of children with disabilities. They do so by talking and writing about their experiences, being involved in consumer organizations, and advocating on behalf of their younger counterparts, as well as other vulnerable citizens.

6
To Have or Not to Have: Motherhood, Disability, and Choice

Given the historically held belief that all women are destined to be mothers, motherhood, as choice, is a relatively modern concept. Today, most women consider motherhood as one option, with some opting for other paths of life. In fact, current statistics point to a substantial increase in childlessness in the USA, Canada, Europe, and New Zealand, with approximately 20% of women estimated to be childless around the turn of the century (Jones & Brayfield, 1997; Hird & Abshoff, 2000; Park, 2002). While medical advances in the field of reproductive technology have resulted in more treatment options for infertile couples and in extending women's childbearing years (Keye, 1999; Stammer, Wischmann & Verres, 2002), childlessness by choice is gaining more prominence.

This trend notwithstanding, the majority of women consider motherhood as a viable option, with most becoming mothers at some point in their lives. In this chapter I focus on the choice to become or not become a mother in the context of a physical disability. While motherhood is no longer prescribed for women in general, or proscribed for women who have disabilities, this group of women continues to face particular issues and challenges as they consider their reproductive options.

Over a third of the women who participated in the in-depth interviews and approximately half of those who partook in the focus groups are women without children. This chapter gives a voice to the desire for children that some participants have expressed, to the challenges and barriers that they envision, and to the ambivalence that was communicated in the interviews and focus groups. The final section of the chapter explores the lives and meaning-making of women who do not have children. Although participants without children are the main source of data for this chapter, mothers are also included to the extent that the issues they raised predate the birth of their children and are of relevance to this discussion. In order to provide a context for participants' reproductive options, I begin by exploring the various messages that they have received about sexuality and motherhood.

Messages and perceptions about sexuality and motherhood

Messages about sexuality

A common theme identified in the previous chapter on girls with disabilities, is the lack of recognition of their sexuality by family members, peers, and the community at large. Having their sexuality denied or undermined was certainly not limited to the growing up years; a number of participants recounted adult experiences of sexual invalidation. Those whose families ignored their sexuality in childhood and adolescence were also more inclined to get negative messages about dating and relationships as young adults. One participant recounted her parents' reaction to her engagement:

> When I got engaged there was this campaign to convince me that I was making the biggest mistake and there was absolutely no way that I could do this...their reaction was "how could you do this...you don't know what you're doing" and I thought: "Oh God, maybe I don't, maybe I'm just a complete idiot."

While this participant was very young at the time, two other participants, both over 30 years of age, noted that their parents were still resistant or at best ambivalent about the idea of them being in intimate relationships. In one case, this was recently manifested in the parents' reluctance to accept a dinner invitation with their daughter's boyfriend. It was this woman's first attempt to introduce her family to a boyfriend, something she had always shied away from:

> I've had other relationships but they really haven't been that serious...I always thought that I'm not going to even raise the possibility of bringing someone home until it's more definite...because for some reason I felt that if I did introduce them to my family and it didn't work out they would think that I was a failure in that area...they don't see my situation as credible.

Nonetheless, this participant was confident that her parents would eventually come around given the close relationship she had with them. She further speculated that her mother's reluctance could have been associated with a concern that she would no longer play an important role in her daughter's life. Having spent many years providing physical and emotional support, this mother's identity was strongly intertwined with her role as advocate, nurturer and caregiver.

It is important to note that negative parental messages, was not the predominant adult experience of study participant. Furthermore, most of those who received such messages perceived them as emanating from their parents' attempts to shield them from the pain of rejection. One father was somewhat uneasy when his daughter terminated a relationship with a disabled man and began going out with a non-disabled man. This participant, who later married her non-disabled boyfriend, attributes her father's disease to his concern that she was more likely to be left by a man without a disability. A number of other participants whose parents were initially resistant or, in one case, outwardly negative towards their daughter's sexuality, were clearly delighted once they realized that their daughter was in a stable and fulfilling relationship.

The majority of study participants reported some experiences of sexual rejection as women with disabilities. One focus group participant with a very mild disability, noted the discrepancy between her parents' consistent assurances that she could expect to lead a similar life to non-disabled peers, and the invalidating messages she got in the wider community:

> The message I got (at home) was "you're just like everybody else"...there was always this assumption at home that I would grow up to be like everyone else...that's all I heard when I was younger...I never thought it (a relationship) was impossible until the rest of the world started treating me differently...until my disability became an issue out there with the way men treat me.

Several participants described situations whereby men who were initially interested in them had a complete "change of heart" once they became aware of their disability.

> The guys that asked me out I met at night clubs and they didn't get to see all of me, they saw part of me... I had some very bad experiences when they did find out.

One participant recounted having several dates with a young man when she began to attend university. Their outings were date-like in that the young man picked her up and paid her way, as was considered appropriate at the time. Nonetheless, he made no attempts to hold her hand or make any move that would express a sexual interest:

> Then one time he asked me to go to this university dance. He asked me if I would mind if he brought another person along, this woman...I guess he didn't realize...he had no sense that I was considering this a boy-girl relationship even though he wasn't...it was very odd but quite demoralizing...it reinforced this whole idea of I'm just asexual and nobody will want to go out with me...they'll just continue to have these asexual relationships with me.

Interestingly, three participants reported being pursued by men who were either not available to participate in an intimate relationship or thought that being in a relationship with a disabled woman was the best they could do. Two participants were pursued by closeted gay men; in one case, a wedding proposition soon followed. The third woman was asked out by a man who told her that he has recently learned that he was infertile, and therefore considered her to be an appropriate match.

Messages about motherhood

Study participants, as a group, were exposed to numerous disempowering messages about their reproductive choices. Consequently, most related that they never envisioned themselves as having children. Several participants noted that although they never discussed the possibility of having children with their families, they knew that it was not something that their parents ever considered as an option for them. One woman indicated that the unspoken message was "if you can't help yourself with a lot of things how can you expect to look after someone else?" Another woman said that if she were to discuss this subject with her family, they would try to impress upon her just how difficult looking after a child would be for her. She tested (and verified) this assumption by raising the issue with her family between our first and second interview. While she was far from certain that she wanted to have children, she was perturbed by the fact that her parents questioned her ability to consider all of the relevant factors and make a mature and responsible choice in the matter. For a third participant, exploring this matter with her family was not an option she could even consider at that point in time:

> If I ever brought that to them I would have to be so absolutely sure about my decision because they would do everything in their power to convince me that I couldn't do it...I'd have to be so solid and I'd have to cover all the basics.

Although more participants related experiences of familial opposition to their becoming or considering motherhood, several noted that they were never exposed to such messages. In reaction to some of the stories of discouragement shared at one of the focus groups, one woman related: "My family never put pressure on me one way or the other. I always felt comfortable...I've been lucky".

Another woman noted that this subject never came up in conversations with her parents. "Reading between the silence", she reasoned that her parents did not really consider this for her and may worry if she were to become pregnant. However, she was quite confident that whatever course of action she decided to take would be respected and accepted.

A number of participants commented on the interaction they had with physicians about motherhood in the context of disability. One woman was strongly advised to refrain from pregnancy during her first gynaecological exam. In addition to a prescription for birth control pills, which she had requested, this woman also got the physician's unsolicited opinion that pregnancy would be unwise for her. Although she has since learned that the information she was given was inaccurate, the physician's warning had strongly impacted her: "it almost seemed like pregnancy was equated with death for me". Although she now believes that the doctor did not intend for her to make this association, her warnings with respect to the danger of pregnancy were indeed powerful and stifling.

Another participant also came to her physician in order to discuss reproductive choices. Although she was merely in her twenties at the time, she did not think that she wanted to have children. Growing up without any role models of women with physical disabilities, let alone mothers with disabilities, this participant, like a number of others, did not envision herself as a mother. She approached her physician about the possibility of having a tubal ligation:

> Once I asked my doctor about a tubal ligation. She was ready to pick up the phone and make the appointment. I said "wait, not now"...I

wasn't even married at the time, just dating. That doctor was not used to disabilities. Every time that I would see her she thought that everything is related to my disability...finally I switched doctors.

There is little doubt that this woman's physical disability was a determining factor in the approach taken by her physician. Most physicians would make a point of attempting to dissuade young women from choosing this procedure and suggest other, less drastic means of controlling fertility.

Notwithstanding physicians' traditional discouragement of pregnancy for women with disabilities, two other participants had antithetical experiences to those reported above. One noted the memorable experience in adolescence of being told by a physician that she could expect to lead a similar life to non-disabled peers, including having children if she so chooses. Another woman recounted her excitement following her first gynecological exam:

I had gone to a gynecologist and he said "you know, you're normal", and I started to cry...He's telling me I'm normal, and I've been told all along that I'm not normal.

It may be significant that these two women went on to become mothers. Taken together, these diverse experiences clearly attest to the prominent role that health-care professionals often play and to their potentially hindering or affirming roles.

To Have or not to have: weighing the options

If deciding whether to have a child can be difficult for many women today, it is all the more complex where a physical disability is involved. The level of complexity is likely to increase for those whose impairments are considered severe. Almost all of the women who participated in the study have reportedly considered motherhood at some point in their lives. Some eventually had children, others did not, due to choice or circumstances, and others yet, are still undecided. A small number of women who participated in a focus group discussion articulated a strong and unreserved desire for children. Other childless women were either undecided, clearly ambivalent, or had made the decision to remain childless.

Participants also discussed the challenges and barriers that they envisioned or had envisioned in the past, with respect to motherhood. The challenges they raised include, among others, their ability to physically look after a child, the possible impact of pregnancy and childbirth on their health, and the ways in which a child might affect their relationship with their partner.

Pregnancy and disability

A number of participants wondered about how a pregnancy might affect their disability, and, in some cases, how the disability would affect the pregnancy.

> Before becoming pregnant, I would need to know what sorts of risks I might be at...what to expect during a pregnancy...how it could impact on my disability, on my mobility...I'd be worried about falling and loosing the baby and that kind of a thing.

Another woman, who had always known that she wished to remain childless, noted concerns with mobility during pregnancy as one of a number of factors that she took into consideration:

> Although my body had never experienced it, I knew from observing other people that the last couple of months of pregnancy can be very uncomfortable and cumbersome...and I thought I've got enough of that without adding to it.

It is important to frame this consideration within this participant's general decision that mothering is not something that she really wants to do. Rather than concerns with mobility being the deciding factor, it was but one consideration among many. Concerns about the impact of pregnancy and the possible long-term effects on physical well-being was noted by another participant:

> I had a real fear of opening myself up to all those medical things...to sort of mess around with my body...What if I become incontinent? How am I going to cope with that? I was really terrified about putting myself at the mercy of urologists...all those things terrified me...the sense of having no control over my body.

She related these fears to childhood experiences of powerlessness in medical settings. After years of fighting for control and self-determination, the thought of being in a situation that would require increased medical interventions was perceived as a possible threat to personal liberty and agency.

Also related to this topic is the issue of giving birth to a child with a disability, something that was raised by a number of participants. Two women made reference to this issue in terms of the precautions that they would take, or have taken, during pregnancy.

> I'd be very careful not to drink, smoke, or take medication. I'm very judgmental about pregnant women who are taking these things. I would definitely not drink, I probably wouldn't even go to the dentist.

This participant went on to say that if she were to have a child, she would do so before she turned 36 so as to minimize the chances of giving birth to a child with a disability. Although she had no doubt that she would accept and love her child regardless of ability status, it was important for her to do whatever she could to minimize the risks. Risks associated with advancing age were noted by two other participants who also indicated the possible interaction between their own disability status and the increased time and effort involved in raising a child with a disability.

This subject was also explored in one of the focus group discussions in response to a presented question. One woman with a genetically transmitted condition discussed the possible implications of having a child who would inherit her disability.

> With the issue of genetics, I would likely pass it on to my child and I have a feeling that my nephew already has it although he hasn't been tested yet. To me it's not really an issue because it's no guarantee that I'm going to pass it on, there's just a likelihood...but even if I do I think my child would have a very fulfilling life, regardless of whether my disability got passed on or whether they have another disability...That would still be my child that I would love and I would hope that they would have a fulfilling life...

Later on in the discussion, this participant was more ambivalent about this issue:

> ...Having those days when you're so angry about being disabled and the frustration of always having to prove to other people that I can do things...and having to see that in my child...seeing my child

> suffer through the same things that I suffered through...even if I can share my experience, I can't help the child go through it, he has to go through it himself...it would probably hurt me.

Despite the consideration of potential hardships, she ultimately did not consider the risk of disability as a major deterring factor for her. Furthermore, the hardships she discussed were predominantly associated with oppressive attitudes and perceptions rather than with the actual physical condition.

Relationship with partner

Several women noted the interplay between mothering and relationships with spouses or partners. One woman who was in a committed relationship at the time of the study, felt that she was now able to consider motherhood as a more feasible option. Whereas she felt a desire to have children at various stages of her life, she put it "on the back burner" as she did not consider mothering without a partner. Another participant also indicated her preference to parent in partnership but noted that having a partner was not a necessary condition for her as far as mothering was concerned.

Reflecting on some of her earlier thoughts about mothering, one woman noted that given the severe nature of her mobility impairment, she knew that having children would be feasible only with a partner who would take on major child-care tasks. Similar sentiments were expressed by another woman who described herself as highly ambivalent about having children. She noted that although she sometimes thought she would like to have children, it is something that her partner would also have to be highly committed to as he would have to do most of the physical care-taking during the initial stages of a child's life:

> I would like it (to have children), but I know he would have to do a lot of the work...I would not be able to care independently for an infant. He would have to be the main one who is taking care of the child and I can't see him wanting a baby enough to do these things...he really has to want this a lot.

Although she was quite confident that her partner would concede if it was really important to her, this participant emphasized that she would only consider having a child if it was something that her partner also strongly desires. Otherwise, she envisioned a major drain on the relationship.

Another participant expressed a concern as to how a child might impact the division of labor between herself and her spouse. She noted the different homes and backgrounds that she and her partner were from as a backdrop to their differing expectations about child-rearing and role division within the home. Her main concern was that her partner, who came from a very traditional family where the mother stayed home to raise the children, might have similar expectations if they were to have children of their own. Given her partner's higher earning bracket coupled with his belief that infants should be cared for at home by a parent, she reasoned that she would be the one to carry out most child-care and household responsibilities. This participant noted that some of her concerns were probably no different than those of non-disabled women who were contemplating motherhood, as she was physically independent and capable of carrying out many household tasks. The disability merely accentuates these concerns, as many tasks are far more onerous and time-consuming than they would be for a non-disabled person.

This section on role division and relationship with spouses suggests an interesting interaction between gender and disability. It seems that like their non-disabled peers, some women with disabilities expect to carry out more child-care and household duties than their spouses, whether by choice or by default. Women as a group perform a lot more child-care and household duties than men. Given this state of affairs, parenting in the context of a physical disability may be perceived as more challenging and problematic when the parent with the disability is a woman.

Physical caretaking

The issue of physically caring for a child was raised by every participant who was considering motherhood. Whereas some participants were married, or in long-term relationships, others were single, and had to consider raising a child as a single parent. Several women indicated that they simply didn't know whether they would be able to carry out certain child-care tasks, especially infant care:

> I am not informed...as far as my own ability or inability to look after a baby...I am lacking the experience so I really don't know...I am not saying that I can't, maybe I can, I don't know.

Two other women echoed similar concerns regarding lack of experience and basic knowledge about child development. Their reported lack of experience with infants may reflect a discomfort that some parents might have around allowing a person with a disability to handle their infant. One participant noted that while her newborn nephews were placed in her arms for her to hold, she always sensed the reluctance of the mother who was never more than a few steps away.

Despite the reported lack of experience of some study participant, all were cognisant of the time and energy that is entailed in caring for a child. At least two women noted their decreased energy level as a factor that they would have to consider:

> The older I get the less energy I have...there's no way I have the energy that I used to have five or ten years ago...in the last couple of years I've been with my friends who've had kids...I was really struck by the idea that it is a lot of work...the one person feeding them, the other trying to get the bottle ready...

Such concerns were mostly focused on the infancy stage. One woman discussed the possibility of adopting an older child so as to bypass this care-intensive period of a child's life. She felt a lot more comfortable thinking about a child who was past the "lifting stage" and could respond to verbal instructions and directions. Another woman, who wondered how she would feed an infant due to a limited control over arm movements, also envisioned less hurdles with an older child.

These participants made a clear distinction between the ability to independently meet children's physical needs and the ability to provide a nurturing and supportive home environment for children. One participant who was not properly mothered in her own childhood admitted that she sometimes worried that she may inadvertently "turn into her mother." However, she referred to this as an irrational fear that she could quickly put to rest, rather than a valid concern that had a significant bearing on her decision. She expressed a confidence in her ability to be very good mother in the social-emotional sense:

> I think emotionally and in terms of bringing a child up with values and feeling good about themselves and all...I think I could do all that really well.

Another participant also made a clear distinction between the physical and emotional components:

> As far as being emotionally there for the child I think I could do that...it's the actual physical caretaking that I'd be apprehensive about.

These quotes vividly demonstrate Lloyd's assertion that "the caring role is not synonymous with the caring function" (Lloyd, 2001, p. 723). However, the ability to fulfill a caring role is, in some cases, contingent upon assistance with some of the caring functions. The issue, then, becomes one of securing services and supports toward that end.

Availability of resources and supports

Virtually all study participants made reference to the insufficient resources and supports for parents with disabilities. The participant who was concerned that her spouse would have to carry out most child-care duties indicated at our second interview that she would consider motherhood as a more viable option if she had access to funded assistance – someone who would help her perform child-care duties. Being able to access funded assistance would provide her with an increased sense of options and control, regardless of what she ultimately chose to do.

Another participant was even more vocal about the importance of funded child-care assistance. She reflected on her recent decision to utilize attendant services for some of her own personal care needs, something that she has resisted in the past:

> It's an adjustment in thinking but I'm now seeing it as OK...if somebody can take care of that...if somebody can help me do the things that I have to do everyday that take a lot of energy from me now, then I have more energy to put into the things that are important... I've got more to give to me and to other people and certainly that would work in a mothering situation...if someone can help me there and it makes me feel safe, that will enable me to be there for my child.

Ironically, the fact that this woman had already been approved for (publicly funded) attendant services may work in her favor if she does have a child. In certain jurisdictions, people who rely on attendant services for self care have a greater chance of receiving additional hours to help them care for their children. A situation whereby no assistance is required for self-care but is fundamental for providing infant care is not recognized for accessing funded supports.

Although a number of participants expressed the need for a wider range of services, their projections were that it was highly unlikely that more funding will be forthcoming in light of budgetary cuts to social services in general and to people with disabilities in particular. They noted recent cuts to attendant projects and alternative transportation as indications of more cuts to follow. Given the sociopolitical climate at the time of the study, they were not hopeful about the prospects of increased resources for parents with disabilities. One participant further speculated that the current climate of cuts might even spurn a lower level of tolerance towards parents with disabilities by reinforcing the sentiment that people should not have children if they are not able to provide independent physical care.

Living with ambivalence

Study participants who are still undecided about motherhood were highly reflexive and introspective about their decision-making process, the responsibility that is entailed in parenting, and the motivation behind it. One participant referred to the fulfillment of raising children:

> I think it would be an incredible experience to be able to be part of someone's life and watch them grow...be there when they are learning things.

At the same time, she grappled with the implications of motherhood and the magnitude of the responsibility:

> Can I invest enough time and enough of myself to be the kind of parent that I want to be? It would mean for me to completely let go of a lot of those other commitments that I have...there's no way I could be out every night doing my committee work, seeing my friends which for me keeps me really connected. If I had a child I would want to be able to focus my energy but then what am I losing? Will I end up becoming more isolated?

Whatever decision this woman ultimately makes, will undoubtedly involve a great deal of self-reflection:

> I know that it would be a huge change for me...and a huge responsibility...I don't want to make that decision lightly and I think that I need to...if I ever go that route, to think about what is my motivation around that...is it because I don't want to be lonely? Is it because I want to leave a legacy?

Another participant put both motherhood and non-motherhood on the balance and critically explored the motivation for either one:

> I've always said that I wouldn't want to have them (children) for the wrong reasons and I wouldn't want not to have them for the wrong reasons...the wrong reasons not to have them are a lack of confidence...and some irrational thoughts. The wrong reasons to have them are because you want someone to carry on the name or you're doing it because society expects it of you...you know, so if I'm going to do it I want to do it for the right reasons.

At the same time, she noted that while she does not currently have a burning desire for a child, she wonders about what she would be missing by remaining childless. She also made reference to a comment she had recently heard from a woman at work after the birth of her child:

> This is a very successful career woman and she said without any hesitation whatsoever, "the most important thing that I have done to date is to have that child". That just made me think, I thought God, that's a very powerful statement and to think that I would be missing out on that experience.

She further noted the close relationship that she and her husband have with their parents and the possibility that she could one day have a similarly close relationship with adult children.

Ambivalence about motherhood was a common thread across interviews and was also articulated by some focus group participants. Interestingly, even the participant who indicated her partner's reluctance as the main barrier to parenting thought that she may herself "pull back" if he were to have a sudden change of heart. She was frank about her ambivalence, noting that some days she really wanted to have a child and other days she didn't. She further speculated that making the decision to remain childless might be easier for her as a woman with a disability:

> Maybe my disability is an easy "out"...otherwise I would feel guilty about being selfish, about not having a child even though I am in a stable relationship...that maybe I should want to give more of myself.

The freedom to choose a non-traditional lifestyle was noted by several other participants who indicated that they just never envisioned themselves as mothers as they were growing up. Speaking directly to this issue, one woman explained:

> I never felt like I had to follow anybody's path. I've always done my own thing...the traditional path wasn't set out for me and this allowed me not to go on that route...and probably in the last ten years I've consciously welcomed that.

Earlier I discussed some of the oppressive and restrictive elements associated with invalidating messages about sexuality and motherhood. The above comments suggest a more complex discourse on mothering and disability. Despite the undoubtedly negative impact of impediments to mothering that many women with disabilities face, it may have created a space for them to forge an identity apart from motherhood.

Exploring life with and without children: separating motherhood from female identity

Of the five childless women who participated in the in-depth interviews, all but one are still weighing their options, although most have indicated that they will likely remain childless. In addition to the in-depth interviews, this section draws heavily on two focus groups: one group was attended by women with disabilities who identified themselves as considering motherhood, whereas the latter was attended by those identifying themselves as unlikely to become mothers. These are women that are no longer vacillating between mothering and non-mothering and for whom childlessness is a permanent and stable aspect of their identities. Taken together, the two focus groups and the in-depth interviews with five participants provide the basis for this section on women without children.

A woman and not a mother

Study participants explored their lives and meaning-making as women without children. One woman indicated that she considered becoming a parent at a time when she longed for change and renewal in her life.

> There was so much growth in my 20s...I went from being a very naive kid who had been institutionalized for years to being a married woman with a good job, a degree, and my driver's license...there was

such a period of growth there and then in the last five years...the last big thing that happened was we got this house.

The need for renewal, however, can take many forms; this woman spoke about wanting to travel and become involved in disability issues on an international level. Other women also discussed the freedom to pursue different interests and activities, a freedom they would be less likely to have if they had children:

> I knew even as a young teenager that having a child changes your life and to love and nurture that child you have to make sacrifices and changes...my desire to have a child, I'm not even sure if it was there at all, but it certainly wasn't strong enough to override my desire for time for myself.

Women who participated in the focus group "Not Every Woman Is A Mother" also explored and even celebrated their lives as women without children. They lived as independent women, with and without partners and pets, and had friends and careers that kept them busy and challenged. One woman who liked to travel noted:

> I leave my cat with a bowl of food and water and go away for a week...she'll be fine when I get back...but you can't do that with kids.

Along with numerous stories of partners and pets, group participants shared some of the issues they faced as women without children. They discussed the pressure they felt, or have felt in the past, to have children:

> My concern is that society kind of says that a woman should be a mother and puts a lot of pressure on them to feel...that if we don't have children we are not fulfilled as women.

Some women indicated that they are getting the message that having children means "being normal," like other women. One participant noted:

> It feels like for some of us there is that pressure...that you are given more validity if you can attain that (become a mother)...you are seen as more "normal" and attain more status if you fulfil those sorts of roles.

Some perceive these pressures as coming from various sources, including the disabled community:

> You go up in status if you have children and that's the problem even in the disabled community...it's kind of a status thing for disabled women to have children.

Women who participated in this focus group were highly critical of the privileged status that is afforded to mothers and mothering in society. Some also shared a feeling of being marginalized at the conference on mothering and disability; they felt that the conference was a celebration of mothering for women with disabilities that left little room or space for childless women. They appreciated the opportunity to discuss their issues and priorities with other women who do not have children and felt that their voices need to be included in research on women with disabilities and motherhood.

Living in connection

Women without children who partook in the study underscored the value they place on living relational and connected lives. An article on women's development states that "for women, the primary experience of self is relational, that is, the self is organized and developed in the context of important relationships" (Surrey, 1991, p. 52). Study participants exemplified the centrality of this concept to their lives and meaning making. In interviews and in focus groups, a lot of emphasis was placed on relationships, especially with children and with other women.

All those who partook in the in-depth interviews as well as some of the focus group participants talked about having children in their lives. One woman noted:

> I've always had kids in my life...that has always been a big part of my life. My friend's kids. I mean I was there in the hospital when they were born...and I have nieces and nephews that I'm very close to...I was part of their growing up.

Another participant who was still undecided about mothering indicated that many of her friends were now having children, "so I'll have all these kids to play with". For a third woman, fond childhood memories of the relationship she had with her grandparents trigger thoughts of having similar bonds with children:

> Although I have to admit that I never wanted to be a parent, I'm very sad that I won't be a grandparent because I had wonderful grandparents and they were a very important part of my life...but that's where you get your friends' kids and you make those bonds...At some point in my life I would like to have a bond like that with a child but it doesn't have to be my child.

Participants also spoke about the central role that friendships played in their lives. One woman discussed the powerful connections she made with other women when she went through college. Others noted that some of the friendships they made in childhood and adolescence were still central to their lives today. While they had connection within and without the disabled community, they were especially connected to other women with disabilities with whom they shared similar past and present life experiences. Several women mentioned the strong bonds they had with their sisters; in one case, an older sister served the role of protector in childhood and a close friend and confidant in adulthood. Another participant whose parents were reluctant to acknowledge her relationship with men, always felt comfortable bringing her boyfriends to meet her sister.

Along with acknowledging the significance of existing relationships, study participants underscored the importance of creating opportunities to link with other women who were facing similar issues to their own. In the focus groups, several women noted how much they were looking forward to coming to a conference on motherhood and disability in order to share concerns and experiences with other women. I also interviewed several women who partook in an eight session mutual support group which focused on these issues. One participant emphasized the relevance of this experience:

> It's good to have the information and it's good to be able to talk to someone who has been through it...that's why I enjoyed the group so much because you realize that you're not alone in what you're feeling and thinking...we all seem to live in such isolation in a way that really these connections are hard to make...and you do make them in a wonderful situation like the group we had.

Focus group participants also emphasized the feelings of affirmation and connection that often develop in such contexts. They further expressed a need to form connections with women who had similar life trajectories. In response to a question of how the well-being of women with disabilities who do not have children can be enhanced, one participant emphasized the importance of forming connections with other women without children. Another participant noted the happiness she felt when she met another woman at the conference who, like herself, was not considering motherhood. While these women had friends who were mothers, as well as those who were considering motherhood, they also expressed a need for connection with other childless women.

The importance of choice

The importance of charting their own course with respect to mothering was an overarching theme in all of the interviews and focus groups. Regardless of where they were personally situated, participants underscored the importance of having control and agency over this aspect of their lives:

> I think that every individual, whether you're disabled or not, has the basic human right to make that choice. And nobody should tell you that because you have a disability, whether it be developmental, or physical, or whatever it may be, that you cannot become a mother or be a parent because of how society perceives you...society or anyone else should not make that decision for you...women have the right to choose not to be a mother as well...but the choice should be clearly our own and not determined by someone else, or even by my parents' attitude...I mean, they have concerns, I have concerns. But ultimately, it is my decision, my responsibility, my life.

Along with her ardent belief in self-determination, this participant was very frank about the challenges that she might face as a mother and concluded that it may in fact not be a possibility for her. Nonetheless, she emphasized her right to make this important decision in her life. Although she had always wanted to be a mother and still hoped to fulfill this dream, she envisioned herself as fully capable of leading a full and productive life apart from motherhood. Another participant, who attended a support group for women with disabilities, discussed the impact it had on her as far as validating her choices:

> The group showed me that I'm not alone, I'm not the only one who is facing this...it showed me that it is possible (to become a mother),

that I have choices...and that's empowering. It's up to my husband and I to decide – not friends, doctor, or family members. If my doctor would be shocked – I would go to another one.

Participants also expressed their disdain with societal assumptions and expectations that it is only natural that they would not have children as women with disabilities. Two participants got messages to that effect, one, from a stranger who struck a conversation with her at the shopping mall, and the other, at a recent family wedding. Interestingly, the former was a woman who had never seriously considered motherhood, whereas the latter was still considering her options, but was leaning towards remaining childless. Although both women described themselves as comfortable and fulfilled as women without children, it was important for them to articulate that this was a conscious decision on their part, rather than an inevitable reality.

A third participant referred to this phenomenon in the focus group:

I think...for women with disabilities, if they consciously decide they don't want to be a mother, people automatically assume that it's not your decision...that you're not going to become a parent...then if you don't become a parent then you're just...you're a self-fulfilling prophecy.

The right to choose not to become a mother was discussed at some length in the focus group "Not every woman is a mother". For the most part, group participants applauded the message of choice that pervaded the conference on motherhood and disability. However, some were concerned that women with disabilities who were once precluded from mothering may in fact experience pressure to exercise their reproductive freedom and choose motherhood. One participant was especially vocal with what she perceived as pressure from within the disabled community for women to become mothers. Another participant added that non-disabled women who chose not to have children were perceived as strong career women, whereas women with disabilities were devalued for similar choices. Group participants felt that wider options for girls and young women with disabilities should include the option to choose a life without children. This point was also made at one of the interviews:

I think that a message that young women with disabilities also need to have is that just because the majority says "It's OK, now you have a choice over your body...some may feel pressured to have a child...I mean some women really do want their own children and can and should have them but other women might think that they should just because they can".

Earlier I noted that the negative impact of restrictive messages notwithstanding, they may have catapulted participants' ability to forge a female identity apart from motherhood. As such, it is important that the changing perceptions on mothering with a disability do not "leave in the cold" women who are not mothers. As one participant noted:

> We went from a place where women with disabilities weren't allowed to become mothers and now we know that we can...but now we have to go a step further...there are going to be some women who choose to be mothers and need support, and then there are some who choose not to be and they also need support...so it's finding that balance.

Concluding comments

Women with disabilities have long argued that their similarities with nondisabled women are greater than their differences. Like their nondisabled counterparts, some women with disabilities wish to become mothers. Others, like some of the participants interviewed for this study, do not. Most participants who are still weighing their reproductive options, noted that becoming a mother is not at the top of their priority list. Some indicated that the quest for motherhood played a greater role in their younger days. However, analyzing their lives from within a feminist lens enabled them to reflect critically on these issues. One interview participant expressed a clear wish to become a mother. This, however, did not prevent her from envisioning a fulfilling and satisfying life for herself as a woman without children. Another participant noted that the expectation that she would not become a mother had in fact been instrumental in building her identity as a childless woman. Regardless of the decision they would ultimately make, these women were highly successful at forming a female identity apart from motherhood.

Study participants were passionate about their right to make choices and the need for these choices to be recognized and respected. Although they articulated numerous barriers and were particularly critical of the inadequacy of resources and supports for mothers with disabilities, most participants did not acknowledge that these barriers may limit their choices, or even make motherhood altogether unfeasible. Possibly, making such an explicit connection is counter-indicated with the need to feel in control of one's life and destiny, especially for those who have had to fight for self-determination.

This idea gains further credence from one of the focus group discussions where a number of participants made a point of emphasizing that it was their independent choice to remain childless. From the discussion that ensued, however, it was clear that there were in fact a number of barriers and impediments that at best constricted these choices. Possibly, talking about how barriers constrict choices at the personal level would be an acknowledgement of the limits to self-determination. A history of having one's self-determination denied or undermined may in fact precipitate a need to feel and present an inflated sense of control. Ironically, this could be counter-productive if it shifts attention away from providing resources and supports that could enhance choices. The importance of attitudinal changes notwithstanding, they cannot replace the need for more equitable policies and increased resources that would truly enhance choice and self-determination.

7
A Ramp to Mothering

The inspiration for the title "A ramp to mothering" comes from a 1992 court hearing on discrimination against parents with disabilities. In her testimony, Leigh Campbell-Earl, the disabled mother of a non-disabled infant, equated assistance with child-care for parents with disabilities to a ramp. She noted: "Just as a ramp (to the court house) enables me to exercise my civic rights today, I need a ramp to parenting – a ramp to enable me to exercise my human rights and to fulfill the responsibilities that go along with parenting" (Disability Rag & Resource, 1993, p. 11).

In this chapter I focus on the experiences and life stories of mothers with disabilities. It is based on 16 in-depth interviews, with eight participants, who have children ranging from infancy to adulthood. All but one, are mothers with young and school aged children. Two focus group discussions, one for disabled mothers with young children and the other for disabled mothers with older children, are also incorporated in the data.

In interviews and focus groups, participants shared a host of issues and experiences relating to mothering children at different phases of development. I heard rich, fascinating, and at times painful life stories relating to different facets of mothering. The nature of the relationship between mothers with disabilities and their children, and their consistent striving to enhance their children's well-being, will be covered in the next chapter. This chapter focuses on participants' pregnancy and early parenting experiences; the division of labour within families and access to informal support systems; and the impact of funded resources and their allocation on the lives of mothers and families. The chapter highlights the lived experience of mothering with a disability with its concomitant highs and lows, joys and tribulations.

The very beginning

Great expectations: reactions, perceptions, and experiences

Study participants discussed their own reactions to their pregnancies as well as the responses of family members, friends, and health-care professionals. One participant described the sense of elation she felt throughout her pregnancy:

> I was so thrilled...I never thought that I would have it. I was really excited to be pregnant and my husband was so supportive...food nauseated me, I hated cooking...he was always there making something to eat, saying "this baby is yours as much as mine and you're going to have to eat properly"...he was there coaching me through my childbirth classes...we were just thrilled, and his family and my family were both thrilled.

Throughout her childhood and adolescence, this woman was told that marriage and motherhood were not options for her. Nonetheless, her parents were overjoyed when she found a partner, married him, and became pregnant. For this participant, pregnancy and childbirth were not perceived to be risky; neither was her particular impairment expected to significantly hinder her ability to provide physical care. Rather, discouraging messages about motherhood resulted from the parents' belief that their daughter was unlikely to be successful in the social-sexual arena.

Another participant who conceived very easily described a sense of satisfaction that this part of her anatomy functioned so well:

> I do conceive really easily...that's the one part of my body that seems to work...my eyes and my uterus...I always figure, everything else is going to disappoint me, nothing else is completely reliable, but these two work well...it feels great.

Two participants, who had unexpectedly found themselves pregnant, had very different initial reactions to their pregnancies. One knew from the onset that she wished to continue with the pregnancy. Her goal was twofold: Gathering information about potential interactions between the pregnancy and the impairment, and doing all that she could to ensure a smooth transition to motherhood. The other participant led a care-free life prior to her pregnancy and had no desire to become a mother. Although she was initially upset when she learned about her pregnancy, this feeling was soon replaced with a clear conviction to continue the pregnancy and keep her baby. She was told that her unborn baby could be at risk due to medication she was taking before she learned about the pregnancy. Given her initial negative reaction coupled with the perceived risk to the foetus, several health-care professionals suggested that the pregnancy be terminated:

> A number of people said that to me...I was having nurses coming in and out because I was having my blood taken...it would be like...maybe say you have a cough, maybe you should have cough medicine...that's how casually they were saying it, "maybe you should have an abortion, maybe it would be for the best"...they thought his life wasn't important...I was on this medication and there was a strong possibility that something would be wrong with him (due to the medication) so I guess they thought that maybe if he was born with some kind of disability maybe I wouldn't want him and I'd be thinking: "My God, I wish I had that abortion"...But...I don't know about you, but I loved him from the start...He's my baby, if something's wrong with him, I'll deal with it...What really bugged me was that sometimes the same nurse would say it again to me you know, and finally I had to be sort of like a bitch you know, make it clear to them that I'm not going to give up my kid.

The pressure placed on this disabled woman to abort her possibly disabled foetus should be considered within the context of the eugenic ideology discussed earlier. As an unmarried woman with a physical disability, health-care professionals may have questioned her ability to care for an infant. As the carrier of a foetus at risk for birth defects, they may have questioned her desire or perhaps even her right to produce another "defective" individual. Her initial reaction to the pregnancy may have provided the legitimization for continuing to broach the subject with her. It seems highly unlikely that a non-disabled woman with a low risk pregnancy would be subjected to on-going suggestions that her pregnancy be terminated. Rather, the anti-disability sentiments that often underlie prenatal testing and selective abortions were probably at play in this case. According to these sentiments, no life at all is perceived to be better than life with a disability.

This mother-to-be hoped for a healthy child and did her best to take care of herself throughout the pregnancy. This included staying clean of drugs and alcohol, habits that she found difficult to kick in the past:

> I was thinking "this kid has enough strikes against him already", and I did stop, as soon as I found out about the pregnancy.

At the same time, she felt strongly about having and loving her child, irrespective of health status. Another participant who has a hereditary impairment, declined her physician's suggestion that she undergo amniocentesis:

> From my point of view if my kids inherited my disability, it wouldn't be an issue for me...because I have a disability, having a child take after me is sort of like being a musician and having a child take after you with their musical abilities...I think I'm the only human being in the continent that feels that way.

This participant reflected on the various contributions of people with disabilities to society. Further to my probing, she conceded that having an impairment may indeed result in greater hardship. However, she pointed to attitudinal and structural barriers as the true culprits:

> My kids have said to me "mommy, aren't you upset if you go some-where and it's not accessible and you can't go there? Don't you wish you could walk?" And I would say "no, I wish they had a ramp"...that's my perspective...it's the environment that's making it inaccessible not the disability that's making it inaccessible.

For a number of participants, close family members responded to their announced pregnancy with obvious concern. One woman noted that her mother's subtle messages ·were that she had a lot on her plate already and should not take on motherhood. As a result,

> I didn't tell her I was pregnant until I was so sick that I didn't want to hide it from her...and she was really worried.

The participant quoted above described a range of reactions, ranging from thrill and excitement by her co-workers, to nervousness and concern by family and friends, to clear dissatisfaction on the part of the attendants she worked with at the time. Her family and friends were mainly concerned about the impact of the pregnancy on her health, whereas the attendants were not used to dealing with her as a married, pregnant woman. Contrary to the range of responses in reaction to her first pregnancy, she got consistently positive responses when she announced her second pregnancy. By that time she had moved to another residence with a more open and receptive staff:

> By the time I was having the second one the staff were all excited about it, they thought this was great. A lot of them had kids of their own as well. My family had already been through it the first time and knew I was going to live so they were okay…They had also seen that Geoff stuck around for the first one…because I think that was another fear. They weren't sure if he would stick around…"there's no way a man's going to stick around to change a diaper…he'll be out of there". But they just didn't know Geoff and stick around he has.

Study participants had varied and diverse experiences in their dealings with the health- care system during the course of their pregnancies. A theme that came up in several interviews was the shortcoming of the health-care system in dealing with the dual factors of pregnancy and disability. One participant was hospitalized during her pregnancy for a non-pregnancy related health issue. When her blood pressure became highly elevated, the medical team did not entertain the possibility that it was pregnancy-related and planned to release her from the hospital. When she persisted to express a concern about this, a blood sample was taken and she was diagnosed as having toxaemia and was immediately transferred to the maternity ward. Her son was born several days later, a month before his due date. Given that pregnancy and disability are rarely considered in combination, this woman's status as disabled may have overshadowed her status as a pregnant woman. Indeed, stereotypes can seem more real than an actual woman in advanced stages of pregnancy.

Two other participants had the antithetical experience of having their disability ignored or under emphasized. One woman was uncomfortable with her General Practitioner's casual attitude towards the possible implications of her pregnancy. Although he had no direct experience or even knowledge about pregnancy and childbirth for women with her impairment, he did not consider her to be at risk or feel that any special measures need to be taken. She subsequently switched to another physician who was responsive to the pregnancy, the impairment, and their potential interaction. Another participant also found that her impairment was overlooked by her treating physicians. Being very young and inexperienced at the time, she was characteristically passive and compliant in her interaction with physicians:

> I had no experience and I got pregnant right away...the pregnancy was difficult...I don't know why, but the doctors didn't hone into my (disability). They should have...they should have really honed into it...Other doctors after that did the same thing (in subsequent pregnancies) and of course I thought you know, the disability, maybe it doesn't matter...but boy did it matter...by the time I had the fourth child I had trouble standing...and the pain was unbearable.

Whereas this participant's submissiveness could be attributed to her young age at the time and to traditional deference to authority figures, another mother reflected on her attempts to be proactive in preparation for the birth of her second child. Following a bad experience with her first pregnancy, she was determined to do all that she could in order to retain a greater measure of control. However, as she found out during her second pregnancy, this was easier said than done:

> It's not that easy...I had a meeting with the anaesthetist when I was about three and a half months pregnant...I didn't like her right from the beginning...it was just one of these clashes of wills...she was saying that I would have to have an epidural...and I wanted to know if I could have one where I could continue to move around... "Why would you want to do that?" "Because I want to do that"...but it wasn't like she was prepared to discuss this with me...and it's so frustrating...when the health-care professional doesn't want to discuss it with you...like they're not going to tell you why you can or can't do that... so even though I said that I wouldn't give up control again, it's not so easy to do.

It is important to indicate that some of the experiences of study participants in their contacts with the health care system are not dissimilar to those of non-disabled women. Women have traditionally been alienated from the process of pregnancy and childbirth, which used to be seen as the exclusive domain of physicians. Women with disabilities, however, are likely to have more frequent contacts with the health care system over the course of their pregnancies, a system that has traditionally compartmentalized and labelled them as deviating from the norm. Furthermore, while the medical system has a long history of managing illness and disability, it is still in its infancy when it comes to dealing with the reproductive issues of women with disabilities. Consequently, women with disabilities are often "groping in the dark" as they attempt to gain information about pregnancy in the context of disability.

A baby is born

A number of women discussed the experience of giving birth as well as their stay in the maternity ward. One woman had to convince the staff in the delivery room that she was about to give birth; she was told that she could not possibly be feeling the labour pains she reported given the level of her injury. This further attests to the privileged status typically afforded to medical diagnosis over a woman's experience of her own body. Another participant recounted her experiences in the hospital with the birth of her first baby:

> Every shift there was a new nurse and I was grilled as to how I was going to bathe my baby, how I was going to take care of her...every single shift, a new nurse would ask me how I would manage...they grilled me, like "how are you going to bathe, have you thought about that?" "Yes, I'm going to get in the bathtub with this baby and I'll put her between my legs and I'll bath her."

Fortunately, her unpleasant experiences were balanced with more positive ones. She singled out one nurse who was most supportive in helping her to overcome difficulties with breast-feeding:

> She was working alone that night, although it may have been two of them in the ward...she took the time, she got all the pillows propped up and she set the baby down where I could nurse her, and she said "you tell me when you're ready for the other side"...she was just wonderful.

Nurses on the maternity ward were singled out by another participant for their attempts to facilitate her breastfeeding with different aides and devices. A third woman who gave birth less than a year ago also recounted a positive hospital experience all around. She was told by a hospital social worker that parenting with a disability was becoming more and more common and felt a genuine interest on the part of the social worker to become more knowledgeable about this topic. Her obstetrician gave her delivery choices:

> I was thinking that maybe I can push the baby, that was a big thing for me throughout my pregnancy...the doctor said, "it's your decision, I'll support you with whatever decision you make...you can try to push...we really have no way of knowing what strength you have."

Her appreciation for the physician's flexibility and support notwithstanding, this participant indicated that it would have been great to have access to information about the birthing experience of another woman with a similar impairment. Given the current interest in parenting and reproductive issues for persons with disabilities, it is hoped that women and their doctors will have more resources to draw upon in the near future.

Another participant described a negative hospital experience during the birth of her first child:

> Well I don't remember much...I just remember them constantly coming in...people from the hospital's social service department... and I was feeling really bad...this was before and after the birth... and I guess it must have been the toxemia but I had also attributed it to the steroids...I just felt icky and headachy and lethargic...not really in control...I felt they were sort of undermining me by coming...I don't remember much of it because I was feeling so out of it, I just remember this feeling of real intrusion, you know, and even when I'd be like trying to nap they'd come in and ask me questions...it felt very very nosey.

This participant was a highly articulate professional woman who usually had very strong self-presentation. Being as ill as she was at that time did not allow her to make use of the internal resources that were typically at her disposal:

> I was really sick, I hadn't washed my hair for days...you know, those little things that you do to make yourself respectable...I was tired and swollen and had a really bad headache...so I imagine that they took one look at me...and put me in that "box" (of not coping well).

Having since given birth to her second child, she had a very positive experience this time around. She did not suffer from any complications and was able to negotiate her stay in the hospital without any hurdles. For this woman, the ability to present herself as a competent and responsible adult was somewhat compromised during her first pregnancy due to the effects of severe toxemia. Although hospital personnel were probably accustomed to the side effects of toxemia, they may have been overly vigilant given that this new mother was physically disabled.

Most participants noted the great care they had taken to plan and organize for the baby's arrival. From renting a crane that would facilitate their own care in the hospital, to devising a baby bassinet that they could access more readily than the one provided in the hospital, to ensuring that supports were in place once they arrived home, few stones were left unturned. Hospital workers are likely to feel confident discharging a disabled mother who is so well "put together." However, a different dynamic is likely in operation when, in addition to her disability, the new mother does not present as a model of efficiency and competence. Under these circumstances, a disabled woman is likely be scrutinized to a much greater extent than her non-disabled counterpart with a similar presentation. The participant quoted above referred to a recent case where hospital officials called Child Protection Services following the birth of a baby to a blind couple:

I really felt for that blind couple...her transgression apparently was that she had trouble breastfeeding...everybody has trouble breastfeeding...and she pushed the baby away and said "take her away" or something like that. And this was interpreted by the hospital staff as a mother who can't cope...the hospital called CAS who basically set conditions for the parents to be able to take their baby home.

Bringing baby home

For families in general, bringing a newborn baby home from the hospital involves major adjustments in routines and priorities. Further adjustments and accommodations often need to be made when the new parent also has a physical disability. A number of participants recounted their early parenting experiences, emphasizing the negotiation of roles within the family, the formal supports that they utilized, as well as their internal experiences as mothers of newborns.

The participant who felt undermined in the hospital by constant visits from social service personnel, also felt intruded upon when she returned home:

> Somehow through one of these visits they set up a therapist to come visit me at home. She was just awful...she would come in and she would have no suggestions that were of any assistance to me...She had no imagination at all in terms of equipment or assistive devices. I had really bad postpartum anxiety, I was really hyper anxious...the baby was losing weight, my milk supply was down and it was one of these self-cycling things...I thought that I can't protect him and stuff like that...you know, I think many new mothers go through that in varying degrees...and here I am under the magnifying glass of this person...I just hated having her around. It'd be a whole hour and I can remember sitting there and hearing the clock tick while she was there.

This new mother felt that she had no choice but to endure these visits if she were to continue getting home-care assistance several times per week. As far as she was concerned, the visiting therapist was a gate-keeper to needed services, and as such, she had to put up with the visits. She also noted that some of the home-makers who came in to clean the house attempted to engage her in unwanted conversations. This mother was clearly in need of instrumental support versus social-emotional support. She had a wide network of friends and probably wished for uninterrupted time with her new baby. The workers' attempts to engage her in conversations were thus perceived as an imposition.

Another participant experienced a sense of relief when she took her baby home from the hospital:

> I had trouble breast-feeding him at first...and in the hospital, I was getting different advice from all these different nurses...one would tell me one thing and then the other nurse would say "I can't believe she told you that, that's not good"...they were all giving me different things...finally I just told them all to go away and I thought "okay I'll just deal with it"...so me and him figured it out ourselves.

Going home allowed her the time and the space to get to know her baby and find a method that would work for them both. Having her mother there for the first little while gave her the confidence she needed to later proceed on her own. Although this participant is close to her mother and appreciated the help she got from her, she was also relieved when her mother left several weeks after the baby was born. She was especially pleased with her mother's comment that she was leaving sooner than expected given the daughter's ability to handle her new born baby.

Several participants described the various adaptations they made, either to equipment or to procedures, in order to be able to care for their babies. One noted that her babies also learned to adapt to her:

> When I would pick them up I would use my right side a lot and they'd lean on my right side. And then as babies they almost automatically knew to reach for my right side, they would tend to lean in that direction.

Two other participants experimented with different methods of lifting their infants, noting that the children did not seem to mind being lifted in non-conventional methods:

> I had to get him out of his stroller one day and I just grabbed his sleeper and picked him up...I just picked him up a little bit because he was wearing a diaper so it wasn't like it was hurting him...so I lifted him up just a little bit to see if he'd whine but he didn't complain, so I thought OK, he's fine...I lifted him a little bit higher and he was still fine, so finally I just picked him up and he just gave me a dirty look because I woke him up when I did it. But he was fine.

This new mother learned an alternatively safe and comfortable way of lifting her infant. The above quote reflects the gentle and gradual manner in which she conducted this "experiment" checking the baby's safety and comfort every step of the way. Another participant, who also found it easier to lift her child by his clothes, discovered that dressing her baby in sturdy over-alls allowed her to continue to lift him in this fashion beyond infancy.

Having described various accommodations to conventional practices, I find it important to emphasize that not all disabled mothers can simply find alternative methods of caring for their infants unassisted.

One participant described the frustration associated with being unable to hold her infant or care for her without assistance:

> I never really felt disabled until I had a kid...because there are times you want to go in the middle of the night and pick them up and you can't...and that's the first time it would hit me square between the eyes like hey, you've got limits here, there are things that you just can't do...when you've got a little kid howling for something and you literally can't do it and (husband) has gone down to the store for milk and you know there's nothing you can do... "the baby's napping, I'm just going to go for a few minutes, I won't be long"...and of course the minute he'd be gone she'd wake up and you know you can't do anything...you know she's okay, she just wants some comfort...and she probably thought "Hey, you're there, why aren't you doing anything"...nothing helps in these situations, you really have to grit your teeth and bare it...I'd just try to sit by her or play with her and distract her...if there was anybody I could call I would call them.

The situation described above, as frustrating as it may be, spanned no more than several minutes. By having other people around to carry out child care duties, this mother ensured that her infant never had to wait long to have her needs met. Since the birth of their first child, her husband had been the main care provider while she had been the main breadwinner. When her daughter was still an infant, she was also successful in securing funding for an assistant who would work under her direction in order to facilitate her mothering. The role of this assistant will be described later in this chapter.

Negotiating roles within the family: informal support systems

The word family usually conjures images of loving bonds, common goals, nurturance, and support. Another aspect of family life that tends to receive less attention is the massive amount of work involved in meeting the needs of its members. In this section I focus on the division of labour within families and the use of informal supportive networks by mothers with disabilities. I describe participants' accounts of varying degrees of familial support, ranging from substantial support to insufficient or non-existent support.

Division of labour and availability of family support

Another participant also required considerable assistance with child-care duties. Although she did not need attendant services for her own self care, she was virtually unable to independently care for an infant. As noted earlier, receiving funded assistance can be a lot more difficult under such circumstances. She described the division of labor within her family, which included regular and consistent help from her mother and some help from her sister:

> The three of us (herself, husband and infant son) all sleep in the same room. It's a pretty big room...he's got his crib in the corner. Sometimes the baby wakes up before me and wakes me up...Danny will pick him up and bring him to the bed where I change his diaper and get ready for work. My mother, because she lives at home, she'll hear me around and she'll knock on the door and she'll pick him up.

Although this couple and their baby resided with extended family, they preferred to eat dinner on their own. Help was also available when this mother returned from work and began dinner preparations. Given that she came home before her husband, I asked her how she managed these tasks:

> It would be difficult if it would be just me by myself. Because my mom's there, somebody is available all the time. So if I'm making dinner I'll just leave him with somebody because my sister also lives at home...somebody will be watching him or they'll bring him down for me and put him in the high chair and I'll talk to him while I'm cooking. That works out...I don't know how I could do it without that, you know.

Having someone on hand also enabled her to change the baby's diaper, something that she enjoyed doing herself. The baby's father gave him a bath and attended to him when he woke up at night. Despite the input by all family members, this participant singled out her mother whose constant presence and support was a testament to her dedication. She further stated that although her husband was appreciative of the help they were getting, she wondered at times if he was really aware of all the work that her mother did:

> I think he realizes that. But because he's never experienced not having my mom in the house I sometimes wonder if he knows how

much help we're really getting, you know. Because I say to him, "you know, if my mother wasn't there it'd be a totally different situation". And he says "I know, I know"...but like I think that I think about it a bit more than he does.

Another woman whose parents live in another city, described how wonderful it was for her when she took her infant son to visit her parents:

I didn't do anything. My mother would take care of him and she'd feed him his pablum in the morning. When he was hungry (for breast feeding) they would give him to me. It was like I could have a vacation from him but didn't have to be away from him. It was perfect.

At the time of the interview, this participant was eagerly awaiting her mother's visit, indicating that it would enable her to get many things done. She jokingly commented on her mother's attempt to spend as much time as possible with the baby:

She warned me in advance, she said "I'm just going to totally monopolize your kid when I'm here"...and that's good...I have a lot of stuff to do, I'm really behind. Now that he's bigger, it's really difficult because I have to plan everything to the point of having to plan when I can go pee. When my mom will be here it'll be fun because I get to spend time with him still but she'll do everything...I know she will.

Although this woman was no longer romantically involved with the baby's non-disabled father, he continued to co-habit with them and was reportedly involved in the baby's care. She referred to him as a good father, while acknowledging frequent fighting and an often tense home atmosphere. Whatever level of involvement this father had, it did not appear to match the assistance that this participant received from her own mother.

A third participant spoke fondly of her committed mother-in-law and sister-in-law, both of who live in close proximity:

They (mother and sister-in-law) have been super in helping and being around...whatever they can do. There have been times when one lives out of town or one is busy with work, or whatever, but when they're around they're like 110%...When (husband) first started working on Saturdays they (kids) were still young and there would be times when someone would want juice and there wouldn't be juice. I had a booking, an attendant would be coming to help me with lunch at 12:00 so at 12:00 I could make them juice, but not at 11:00 when they were screaming about it...It's like "do you think you could wait an hour?" and they'd say "no", and I'd say "well you know, let me call grandma. If grandma's there then you can have juice. Otherwise you're just going to have to wait"...and she would trot right over and do it.

The father being the main care provider in addition to the support of a funded assistant meant that this family did not depend on informal supports for the day-to-day functioning of the family. Nonetheless, it was reassuring and affirming to know that this familial network was willing and able to help when the need arose.

All of the participants quoted thus far, in addition to several others, discussed the sharing of family responsibilities between themselves and their spouses. One participant noted:

Phil has always done...not the bulk of child-care, but certainly child entertaining. Like he's much better at playing blocks with him and lego and all those things. Like he'll do that for hours whereas I get really bored after a while. So they spend more time together.

This trend was beginning to change somewhat as this participant's son was getting older and was beginning to enjoy card games and other activities that required thinking and concentration. These were the types of activities that the mother enjoyed doing with him. In this case, the division of roles in terms of child entertainment were based more on personal preferences. The dedication of this father notwithstanding, this woman noted that it was she, rather than her husband, who carried the bulk of the domestic responsibilities, despite her having a demanding career.

Another participant commented on the disparity between her current family situation where work was shared between herself and her husband, and the culture in which she was raised where women did all of the care-taking:

My husband spends so much time with the kids...like they are involved in hockey and baseball and their dad is always there with them. It's really nice to see, where in my culture it isn't something that men would do. Men didn't change diapers, men didn't make meals. It was the woman's job. It could be that from that perception... I may not have been able to cope with the standards of motherhood of that particular culture.

She spoke with great fondness about her husband's commitment to the family and the sharing of duties at home:

The disability in some ways has allowed for more equality to take place in our relationship.

However, when I asked for a more detailed breakdown, it appeared that she still carried out a larger portion of the workload.

Another woman who had a husband and two teenagers emphasized the value she attributed to carrying out whatever tasks she was realistically able to perform. This was despite the effects of extreme fatigue and her need for rest periods throughout the day.

Sometimes I get asked, "Why do you do that? Why don't you have the kids do that and then you will have energy to do something else that you want to do instead of doing the cooking"...Robin (her neighbour), I am sure she can see me sitting at the sink peeling potatoes thinking: Why doesn't Jodi (daughter) do that? Robin, she's often said: "the kids really don't help you much, do they?" But there are a lot of things I don't mind doing...I mean I can sit there and peel potatoes, you know, I look at it as something I can still do. When my hands start shaking then I won't be able to do it any more.

She also noted that this was something that her husband appreciated:

I don't go grocery shopping anymore but I still do the shopping list because I do all the cooking...Craig likes that whole idea that I can still get dinner ready. He doesn't have to do that when he gets home.

Notwithstanding her attempts to hang on to tasks that she could still perform, she acknowledged that this did come with a price:

Having people over is not a regular occurrence because it tires me out...I (conserve my energy) so I can make dinner at night and sort

of be half awake when the kids get home. It's mostly my family that
I'm dealing with.

This participant emphasized the many things that her husband did
for the family, noting that she would probably be in a far worse
physical shape if it wasn't for his help. She shared with me her belief
that unlike her husband, many men would not stand by a wife with
a disability:

when I think of a lot of men I know, they'd just say "bye bye, see
you..." and just leave.

Insufficient or lack of informal support

The experiences presented above reflect varying levels of informal
supports for mothers with disabilities. Rather than being a dichotomous construct, informal support lies on a continuum, with some
having more than others at different phases of their lives. In this
section I present the voices of participants who fall on the low
end of the continuum as far as informal supportive networks
are concerned. I first present situations where supportive networks
were either totally absent or minimal and far outstripped by the
number of stressors. Reference will also be made to situations where
some needs were met by informal supports while others were
neglected.

One participant described a particularly difficult time in her life after
the birth of her youngest child when her yet undiagnosed illness was
playing havoc with her body. She noted a sense of relief following her
diagnosis as it provided a rationale for some of her symptoms. The
diagnosis did not, however, result in the mobilization of informal
supports:

To me it (the diagnosis) came as a relief. To everyone else it was
like "Oh, my goodness, we should have recognized that maybe
something was going on here...we really feel bad about it..." and
they still pulled away. I'm talking about existing friends at that
time and family from both sides. I would ask for help but there
was very little that was given...I did ask and it didn't make a
difference. When there's such an overwhelming amount of
work, one little thing doesn't make a big difference but it does
help.

This woman's newly diagnosed disability, coupled with the health problems of her new born infant, precipitated the breakdown of her marriage:

> As it progressed (the disability), it very definitely was a factor. All these things (stressors) kept piling up and piling up, and more and more responsibilities were being demanded of both of us. I was going down hill, and he wasn't understanding any of it...nor could he cope with me being labeled with the illness, nor could he cope with the youngest having so many problems. So you see, all those things are just so intertwined...it's enormously overwhelming, the whole picture...not having supports in place, not knowing what this other world is like from the other side of the fence, you know.

Another participant who is now the mother of adult children, had to be hospitalized for extended periods of time when her children were young. She reflected on some of the hardships she encountered as she tried to raise her children almost single-handedly:

> He was a very hard man to live with, he wasn't any help. Whenever I was ill or had to go to the hospital he would run. When I was pregnant and I needed him to be around he would run. He was always running when there was something wrong like an illness...I was so worn out...it was so difficult because (even when he was home) he was not much of a help...and I had all these little kids...I had to bathe them, put them to bed. He was out in the back yard with the guys fooling around with cars instead of being a father where he'd be in there helping me. He wasn't that type of a father.

This young mother knew that her husband could not be trusted with the children and that the full responsibility for their health and well-being rested with her. When her youngest son was six months old, she had to go into hospital for a series of operations that spanned several years:

> I couldn't leave them with him, God knows what would have happened to them. So when I had to go into the hospital I had to make a big decision. I called the Children's Aid...and they took the

children into care while I was in the hospital because I was there sometimes 6 to 8 months (at a time). My kids spent practically their whole childhood going in and out of the Children's Aid.

This young disabled mother of five felt that she had no other option but to put her children into care. I asked her where her extended family was in all of this:

> They (sisters) were all busy with their own families. Mind you, my mother did take my daughter when she was younger. But my mother was in her 60's and 70's so she couldn't take all the kids. She tried my son once but he was too much for her. I can understand... 5 kids are a lot, you know. But no...my mother-in-law wouldn't say "I'll take one or two kids" or my sisters say "I'll take a kid", no...they were busy with their own lives...they weren't interested.

Of the eight mothers I interviewed, this participant had the most heart-wrenching stories to tell of her plight as a young disabled mother devoid of all informal sources of support. Along with the participant quoted before her, her situation exemplifies extreme gaps between stressors and informal supports. Other participants, who were higher on the continuum of informal support, may have nonetheless felt isolated and/or unsupported in certain domains. One who was no longer romantically involved with the father of her infant son, continued to co-habit with him for the sake of the baby:

> Tony (baby's father) is so miserable all the time...he's totally different than he used to be...We get along sometimes but a lot of the times we don't...probably more times it's just fighting or not talking to each other or yelling at each other...it's like a sitcom, you know, two people who don't go out anymore, fight a lot but are still together for the kid.

She also expressed frustration over the clutter in their small apartment that made it difficult for her to get around and find things that she needed. Almost every waking moment was consumed with meeting the baby's needs, leaving her with little time for herself. It appears that despite the physical presence of the non-disabled father, the brunt of child-care and household management fell on this mother's shoulders. Furthermore, the frequent fighting and tension she reported could further drain her resources and thus constitute a risk factor.

Another woman, who described the many things that her husband did for the family, also expressed some negative sentiments. She indicated that she occasionally felt undermined by her husband who at times disregarded her wishes and made parenting decisions single-handedly. She noted with disapproval the big weekly allowance that her teenage daughter received. I asked her who made these decisions:

> Well, my husband and I do but I can say "I wouldn't give her that much"... "Here, take it", he says to her...you know, he can say that just right in front of me. He knows I disagree but he goes ahead and gives it to her anyway.

It is important to indicate that this was one of the few critical comments made about a spouse who was generally described in very positive terms. It seems, however, that while this participant received a high level of instrumental support from her spouse, she did not feel that she had equal power as a partner and a co-parent. This cold be further perpetuated by her reported tendency to keep things to herself rather than communicate her frustration.

A ramp to mothering: formal support systems

In this section I present participant accounts of the ramps that facilitated their ability to care for their children. I begin by describing situations where such ramps were either not available or were ill-equipped to meet the needs. I then describe situations where formal supports do a good job of facilitating mothering activities and are thus worthy of the title "ramps to parenting."

Mothering: an unramped territory

The young mother who phoned Children's Aid when she had to be hospitalized felt that she had no other avenues of keeping her children fed and cared for. She described the first time her children went into care, the youngest being only six months old:

> When they first went into care, oh, I cried...I cried to see my little baby going. They came and got him. Oh God, it was such a traumatic time. And he was crying, he didn't want to go, and oh, my God...my daughter was crying because she was losing her little brother because they promised they'd put them together but they didn't...they separated them which was especially difficult for the

youngest and the oldest...she was sort of trying to watch over him because he was so small...it was very traumatic for both of them to be torn apart...These are scars that they're going to have for the rest of their lives.

This mother's lengthy stays in hospital, coupled with the total absence of informal support systems, provided the context for the intervention of social services. The children were in care as long as this mother was in hospital while her husband was having affairs with other women. Although she initially contacted Children's Aid on her own initiative, she later experienced their involvement as a hindrance rather than a support. Other than having conditions placed on getting the children back, she received no assistance with re-integrating her family:

Children's Aid basically took the children into care and kept them there while I was sick. But they didn't try working with me after to try and help out...You know, it was really traumatic coming home...and I didn't get the kids back right away because they were going to make sure that I could do things. And like I said, if my husband wouldn't have been there, I wouldn't have gotten the kids back because they would have felt I wasn't capable of taking care of them.

Ironically, this mother felt that her ticket to getting her children back after hospitalizations was to get back with the children's father; the same father who could not or would not look after his own children in her absence. This gives further credence to the finding by Nosek et al. (2001) that mothers with disabilities are more likely to remain in dysfunctional relationships due to fears that they will lose their children. This was a significant consideration for this mother, given the total absence of resources in the 1960s and 1970s when she was raising her children:

In those days there was no home care, there was no long-term care, there was nothing...I'm really thankful now that they've got all this in place, I think it's fantastic. But in those days, it was stay in the hospital, go to a convalescent home...you know, like they didn't take the family into consideration.

The formal supports that this mother received amounted to her children being taken into care over the course of her hospitalizations.

Upon their return home from care, it was increasingly difficult for her to assert authority over her growing children. With no professional assistance to help her re-integrate her family, she was faced with challenges that appeared insurmountable at times. In her plight to get the children back from care in the early years, and manage their behaviour when they got older, she continued the cycle of resuming a relationship with their father. The "system" clearly failed this young mother, leaving her to parent in a hostile and unramped territory.

Whereas this participant received no formal supports besides having her children taken into care, another participant received home-making services shortly after the birth of her daughter:

> We had a homemaker for a few years after Jodi was born. The doctor arranged it...but I think that really screwed her up. It was through the Visiting Homemakers...but they kept changing. Like every 2–3 months they'd send somebody new because they didn't want them to get attached. I was in bed most of the time and the home-maker was supposed to take care of the children.

Fatigue being the most problematic aspect of her disability, this mother found it exhausting to go through the routines time and time again, with each new homemaker. She also noted that the home-makers did not form a connection with the children. She described an incident that took place when her daughter was two years old:

> I remember when she was two years old, Daniel would have been four at the time...I was in the kitchen at the time, sitting down...and Jodi, she was two years old, marked a line with a chalk across the floor and she said to the home-maker "don't cross the line"...and that just threw me...because she just didn't get along with any of them. Well, the ones she did get along with, then, you know, all of a sudden they were gone.

Although this mother received home-making support that enabled her to rest, she did not perceive this service as helpful or supportive. A host of interacting factors resulted in this state of affairs. Her lack of involvement in arranging this support (it was arranged by her physician) and her reported lack of control over the frequent changes in homemakers was disruptive to the children and taxing for the mother. Furthermore, her own acknowledgment that she did not readily adjust to unfamiliar people and novel situations was consistent with her somewhat passive presentation over the course of the interviews. These factors, coupled with impairment-related fatigue, culminated in this mother's negative experiences with home support. Her conviction to terminate this arrangement as soon as she managed to curb the impact of her fatigue, attests to the overall failure of this formal support system to meet its target:

> After that I started taking this drug that made me feel less tired....I could finally stand up for more than a minute...I said to Craig: "the first thing we're doing is getting rid of all of them"...and I phoned them right away and said "don't send any more".

Formal supports as a ramp to mothering

Contrary to the above cases where formal supports were either unavailable or ill-equipped to meet the needs, two participants described formal supports that enhanced their roles as mothers. One described the backdrop to the inception of the role of a nurturing assistant:

> When Erin was an infant and I was going back to work, I would come home from work and would want to hold her for a while and play with her. But because she was so little and I don't have the strength, I was afraid to hold her, that if she squirmed that I would drop her. Geoff had been in that role all day...he wanted to have a break, you know, not to sit there beside me and help me hold the baby and play with her. So I thought "gee, if I'm going to have a relationship with my baby and not be part of the furniture"...like I want to be her mother in some sense of the word, I want to be a person she can have fun with. So when she was a few months old I started pushing for that.

She described how the nurturing assistant helped her interact with her infant:

> It took a little bit of figuring out, it has to be a person who under-stands that they are just an intermediary facilitator, the way a lan-guage interpreter would be...the first person we had, she was very sharp...she really understood what it was that I was trying to do...She'd pick up the baby's rattle for example, and shake it, and as soon as the baby's attention was on the rattle, she'd pass it to

me...so immediately the baby would shift her focus on me, and then she (the facilitator) was out of the picture.

The role of the assistant is to be of help in the background rather than to actively interact with the baby. She noted that in some cases that she was aware of, assistants perceived their role as providing direct nurturance to the baby:

> I know some people have had trouble where the assistant would come in and kiss the baby, and hug the baby, and play...and it's like, "no, no, no. You're here so that I can do that. The first thing you should do when you come in the door is pick up the baby and give the baby to me so that I can give them the big kiss because you're here, not you give them the big kiss because you're here"...you know, it's a very fine line.

Given that the funding she received covered a limited number of hours per week, it was important for this mother that the time be spent on helping her build a relationship with her baby. As the children got older, the role of the assistant also changed. She listed some of the activities that the assistant would help carry out beyond the infancy stage:

> Hold them, play with them, finger paint, organize closets, sew on buttons, take them out for walks, go to the park – like with me, not for me...it took a bit of figuring out...it needs to be the right kind of a person, someone who is secure enough to be just an intermediary facilitator, you know, the way a language interpreter would be in the middle.

In accordance with the children's developmental stage, the role description of the assistant changes while the philosophy behind the concept remains the same. The assistant works under the direction of the mother, enabling her mothering, rather than making independent decisions about the children:

> If one of the kids would say to an assistant "can I have a piece of baloney?" they'd say "well, if it's OK with your mom", or "you'd have to check with your mom." Like they'd just never take it upon themselves to decide that because they understand that's not their role. And then if it's "no," then they're (the kids) mad at me, they're

not mad at them. That's one of the things that tells me that it has achieved what I wanted it to achieve. Because they see me as the person who says "yes, you may, no you may not, or yes you may but later on"...I want them to see me as an authority figure and as someone whose opinion they have to respect.

The assistant can also help reinforce consequences that the mother has spelled out, such as taking the child to her room for a time-out period. This would all be discussed ahead of time to ensure that the nurturing assistant is indeed prepared to follow through on the mother's decisions:

We would have that all laid out so that there would be no surprises.

Having access to this assistance had facilitated a strong relationship between this mother and her children. As the children got older, the need for this assistance was diminishing, with a consequent reduction in hours that the mother was requesting:

I'm winding it down now because as Jamie gets older I just don't need it as much. There's still somebody here a couple of evenings a week. The next budget year I've already said that I'm giving up one of these nights...I decide when it's phasing down and I've been keeping my commitment on doing that because that was one of the selling points. It's not like my ongoing disability that I'll need help with for how ever long I live for. This is just something I needed for that span of time when they were very young.

Beyond meeting the needs of her own family, this mother has been instrumental in helping other parents obtain similar supports. Several years ago, she got a call from another province regarding a young single mother with a similar disability. Using her own experience as an example, she recommended that as a single mother with an infant, the young woman be given 24 hour support, more than what she herself received in a full week:

She got 24 hour nurturing assistance. The last I heard she was doing fantastic, you know. When the baby was two years old she sent me a Christmas card and some pictures. She found people in the building where she lives, she sort of organized it that they'd be on call and then she'd pay them when she called them. So they weren't like glued to her side all day. But she needed someone so she had to purchase a support circle because she didn't have one.

As this participant asserts, a formal support circle becomes critically important in cases where informal supports are inadequate or are unavailable. Another study participant described how formal supports have enabled her to continue to meet her children's needs as a single mother devoid of assistance from friends or extended family:

> It's a real roller coaster life because you don't know when you're going to be feeling OK and not OK with the energy level and everything...the children don't understand that at all...and to me, they shouldn't have to understand too much. They sort of get upset and angry that mom is not feeling well or mom has to lie down or whatever, but I feel it's very important to have people in place to pick up the pieces for that...good, supportive people. That's why I've advocated so much for parent-directed child care assistance, which is part of the attendant services that I get.

This participant, like the one above, described services that facilitated her role as the children's mother. However, as a single disabled mother who did not receive help from extended family, she required a much higher level of formal support. The fluctuating nature of her disability precluded her from providing independent care to her children on a consistent basis:

> With my energy level going up and down, well there are times when I just can't get out of bed and can't tell when that's going to be. Those days (spent mostly in bed) are few and far between because I don't allow them to happen until they're extreme...and then I call everybody and say "please come and help"...I've got three reliable part time attendants who come at different times of the day. I have a morning person, a mid-day person, and a night person...it's an excellent case scenario, a role modelling of how things should be done for families.

She emphasized her role in directing the care of the children even when she was resting and the assistants were in charge. Resting when an assistant was present allowed her to conserve her energy for the in-between time when she was alone with the children.

In describing the smooth operation of the system she had in place, this mother noted the importance of maintaining good communication and an amicable relationship with the assistants:

> There's excellent communication between all of the part time attendants that I have and myself...we all work together in unison. If one can't do something then someone else will try ...and they know that I'm the primary source to speak to. We have a really nice, family-like kind of communication and especially with the children it's really helpful because they feel that these are great people that help us.

The two participants whose formal support systems provided a ramp to mothering are highly involved in every aspect of the service provision. They lobbied for the services, trained the workers and are continuously managing and monitoring the supports. Their strong advocacy skills and their insistence on directing their own services are important contributing factors to their overall positive experiences.

Concluding comments

The narratives of mothers with disabilities provide us with a rich source of information on spousal relations, assistance from extended family members, and interaction with formal mechanisms of support. Based on data relating to informal support systems, two interconnected issues related to women and caring are highlighted: the division of labour within the nuclear family, and the availability of informal support beyond the nuclear family. The experiences of study participants point to a general similarity between caring tasks of disabled and non-disabled mothers. A number of examples were given which suggest that like their non-disabled counterparts, mothers with disabilities take prime responsibility for home and children. Their involvement in childcare and domestic labour seems to be more prominent than that of their spouses. Further to that, several of the accounts indicated a breakdown of the family system when the mother was not well enough to hold it together.

As to the issue of informal supports beyond the nuclear family, it is again mothers, and at times sisters, who provide this support. While referring to the gendered nature of extended family care-giving is stating the obvious, women's caregiving responsibilities across the lifespan were largely ignored in the past. The issue of women as caregivers to adult family members was all but absent from the feminist agenda of the 1960s and 1970s that focused instead on young women's issues (Hooyman & Goneya, 1995). Nonetheless, current feminist literature on family care emphasizes the point that "in most instances, family caregivers is a euphemism for one primary caregiver, typically female" (Hooyman & Goneya, 1995, p. 3). As a feminist researcher, I also fell into the trap of not questioning the supports provided by female family members. Upon hearing the heart-wrenching story of the young mother who had to place her children in care, it was her mother and sisters, not her father and brother, that I found myself angry with.

As Keith and Morris (1996) point out, professionals who assess the needs of citizens with disabilities typically assume the availability of unpaid family members. Given the limited budgets they have to work with and the numbers of those who require services, they can hardly be blamed for prioritizing those who are totally devoid of informal systems of support. Nonetheless, such practices come with a large price tag. Differences in individuals, family systems, and contexts notwithstanding, heavy reliance on informal supports due to lack of options run the risk of over-taxing, and possibly eroding even solid and supportive systems. Research on spousal relations denotes the risks associated with a stark imbalance in reciprocity. Reciprocal relationships should be defined broadly and people with disabilities can contribute to a relationship in multiple ways. Nonetheless, the exclusive performance of daily chores by non-disabled family members due to lack of choice, is undesirable. Researchers and practitioners who espouse both disability rights and feminist principles, are best equipped for the challenge of balancing the needs of adults in need of care, many of whom are women, with the needs of those who provide the care, almost all of who are women. Most importantly, such practitioners should be accountable to the people they are meant to serve and strive for consumer-directed services that can truly enhance self-determination.

One of the participants quoted above indicated that although she is getting a relatively high level of support, "it gets taken up really fast due to the amount of work that has to be done to run a family". A lot of her time is spent advocating for herself and for her children, ensuring that they continue to have access to resources and supports:

They are making me present my case every year now...the price is the amount of energy that's required to make it almost a legal argument, it's like writing a paper every time, like a legal case. I've been called a hysterical mother...but I believe that if we do a whole family profile, we're entitled to the services...each individual has the right to fight...if enough strong, vocal people in the community have the needs that I have (and express them), then people at the top would be forced by lobbyists like myself and they'll have to put more money into the pot...because it's only the loudest that get heard.

For some of the participants, their insistence on directing their own services coupled with their strong advocacy skills, are important contributing factors to their overall positive experiences. It is important to indicate that directing one's services need not necessarily be interpreted as being on hand to direct every single activity. During my second interview with the participant who had a negative experience with homemakers, I asked her whether having more control might have resulted in a better outcome. Her answer was that directing services was very tiring for her; "I would find it tiring to have to instruct the person in what to do...I would be thinking: I may as well do it myself." She made reference to a more recent experience with a homemaker where the latter wanted every activity to be consumer directed. This really defeated the purpose of homemaking support for this participant who suffered from extreme fatigue and required a more hands-off approach.

Another participant also noted that some service providers do not allow an attendant to shop independently for a consumer, as the service has to be consumer driven. In her case, it is much easier to send the attendant with a shopping list and conserve her own energy for her children, rather than having to come along on a shopping trip. These experiences attest to the need for an open-minded and flexible approach to the definition of consumer driven services. While directing one's personal care or the care of one's children is of ultimate importance, having a say in how the chicken will be cooked for dinner may be more involvement than some consumers wish to have. Clear and open communication between a consumer and a service provider should serve to alleviate many such barriers.

8
Promoting Our Children's Wellness

Parenting is largely about the creation of a nurturing and caring atmosphere where children's physical and emotional growth can take place. This entails facilitating the expression of feelings, maintaining open lines of communication, and ensuring that children feel loved and protected. It also involves providing a structured and predictable environment, setting behavioural limits, and fostering cooperative, pro-social behaviour. The pregnancy and early parenting experiences of study participants and their varied experiences with formal and informal supports were explicated in the previous chapter. This chapter focuses on (a) participants' attempts to ensure the physical and psychological well-being of their children; (b) their child-rearing philosophies and practices; and (c) the overall nature of the parent-child relationship.

Promoting growth and enhancing well-being in children

Promoting their children's growth and enhancing their well-being was a central theme in most of the interviews and focus groups. At the most basic level this included measures to ensure that children were safe and out of harm's way. One mother noted that when her children were old enough to sit on the footrest of her wheelchair she'd take them out for a walk on her own. Although it was satisfying to be able to take them out unassisted she had some concerns about safety issues; she knew that she couldn't physically defend a small child if someone decided to grab her and run. Her solution was to be highly vigilant about who was around and to always leave information as to where she was going and when she expected to return. As her children got a little older she relied on verbal instructions to keep her children safe:

> From a young age I taught them that if they listen to me I can keep them safe...I explain to them that if they listen to me then I can do things. Like if a fire alarm goes, if they just listen to what I tell them they'll be safe you know, they're not going to burn to death. I think it's very important for children to feel safe. I don't want them to feel anxious like if they're home alone with me that there's more of a threat to their security than if they're home alone with their dad. Because even though there are things that I can't do, they still see that I get it done somehow. Like I know who to call or what to do or I can teach them to do things themselves.

Keeping her children safe meant that this mother was never alone with them for more than a few minutes when they were babies and could not respond to verbal instructions.

Another participant could not always be available herself to meet her children's needs due to the nature of her impairment. Nonetheless, she ensured that the children were well cared for irrespective of her health status:

> I want to be such a mother and always wanted to be a mother and parent these children. I miss the physical part (of parenting)...I can give them love and nurturance, but with bad headaches and bladder pains, I often have to lie still and be quiet and they don't understand that. But no matter how bad I feel I manage to come through...or have someone else who I know is there for the children.

As a single mother who did not have an informal support system that she could consistently rely on, this participant had assertively negotiated with a host of agencies and providers in order to ensure that the children had access to growth-enhancing resources. Her strong advocacy skills were apparent in her description of her involvement in her son's academic programming:

> You have to be labelled disabled before you're taken seriously. I've had to fight so hard for my rights and his rights because we're not severely disabled. Right now we're dealing with that because he's not up to par. And they (educators) want to push him into

grade 1. And I was like "no, you're not doing that." So I'm taking the time now to make sure that all the assessments are done properly to see if we have to hold him back just so that he is developed mentally and socially. Because if you put him in an ordinary grade 1 he's going to be trampled on. I've seen that happening with my oldest one so I won't allow it to happen now. I'm going to fight for my kids.

Another participant also described her dealings with the school system. She initiated contact with her son's teacher when he was having some difficulties and began to refer to himself in derogatory terms:

My son was having difficulties at school. He was coming home crying, saying that he is stupid. But we weren't going to let anyone categorize our son... The teacher wasn't going to refer him for resource support but we insisted. We also involved him so that he didn't feel that we were talking about him in the third person. He was part of the process. This year we're working with him to help him understand his difficulties. That he needs a bit more time and he needs a quiet environment where there's little distraction... I don't want people underestimating him just like I didn't want people underestimating my potential (as a child). I don't want him frustrated because people don't expect him to do well.

A theme that ran across a number of interviews and focus group discussions was the attempt to shield children from any burden related to the maternal disability. A number of participants emphasized that they did not want their disability to become a source of hardship for their children. One mother noted that although she encouraged her children to help out, she didn't want them to feel that they need to look after her:

They are developing skills to be a little more independent. But I don't want them to be adultified children. Even the thought of taking care of mommy...I don't want my children to take care of mommy. To be kind and respectful and to listen and to be responsible for their actions and to do simple things sometimes – that's great. To me, that's teaching morals and values of life. But for my children to take care of me I think is wrong. I think children should not be taking care of their parents.

Almost identical sentiments were expressed by another participant:

> I don't want my children to take on or have a sense that they have to take care of me. I am their parent. I think that a child has to be able to feel that they can be kids. And I guess you need to be able to say to yourself I'm going to take care of myself if it means getting the resources out there to help me take care of myself but to set a limit on what you expect of your children.

A third participant who relied on attendant services for personal care, emphasized how important it was to her that hired service providers, rather than her spouse and children, assisted her in personal care. She expressed a concern that attendant services that were now publicly funded may be targeted for cuts in the future:

> I wouldn't want to rely on my husband to do my attendant care. And I wouldn't want to rely on the kids to help do that because I didn't have them to do that. Some people think I had them so they could help me out but I didn't have kids for that reason. That's why I live in a setting where there is attendant care available so that I can just be doing what I would be doing as a member of the family, regardless of the disability. I'm independent for that (self care). Like there are times when they might help out with different things but we help each other out and that's normal, right?

As of lately she had gotten her older child to help out with the laundry. However this was instituted with the goal of promoting the youngster's independence and sense of self-efficacy rather than as a necessity related to the mother's disability.

A related topic that came up in one of the focus groups was the attempt to protect children from the burden of worry. Interestingly, several women noted that the "super mom" role model that their own mothers provided as they were growing up, made it difficult for them as mothers with disabilities:

> When I was growing up the image that my mother portrayed is that you have to let your kids think that everything is fine...to constantly portray the image that everything is O.K. even though you feel like shit...That was the image that I grew up with and that was the image I also felt I had to continue with my own kids and I think

that caused a really severe depression because I couldn't do it...I couldn't be that super mom.

Focus group participants struggled with how much they should share about their disability and how that might affect their children. These issues could be more complicated in cases where the impairment was progressive or had an unpredictable course and thus had changing implications for the mother and the family. One focus group participant made eloquent connections between women's reflections on their own mothers on the one hand, and their attempts to protect their children from burden on the other hand:

> We talk about our parents who looked as if they are so strong and everything is just fine and then behind it we realize that we try to do that too sometimes with our own kids simply because we don't want to burden them with the worry. We're there to make their life better, that's how we see ourselves and we don't want to get that stuff that we hear about "you're treating your child as a parent, you're overburdening them with all your feelings" and those kinds of things.

I would like to complete this section by presenting the words of yet another study participant, this time a mother of an infant. Throughout the three interviews that I had with this mother she reflected on what she could do to foster her son's growth and enhance his well-being.

Holding her unplanned but much loved baby, she talked about how she would respond to a question that he may pose in future as to whether he was planned or not:

> You know, I was thinking, if he ever asks if he was planned or not...I was thinking, I always watch the show Roseanne. I love that show. Anyway, one of her kids asked: "Was I a mistake?" and she said, I can't even remember what words she used, but she said: "mistakes are things that happen that you think back and you say oh, I wish it would never have happened...you weren't planned for but we're happy we had you and we would never have changed anything. We would never hope that you weren't around." And I was thinking that's the kind of thing I would say to him.

Throughout our interviews this mother gave a number of examples of how she would like to handle various situations that may arise in the process of raising her son. From current issues of striving to reduce the high level of stress in her life so that it doesn't negatively impact the baby, to future scenarios of how she would talk to him about alcohol and drugs, this mother emphasized her commitment to the well-being of her child. As a low-income single mother, she dreamed about moving to a safer neighbourhood, getting her son involved in wholesome activities, putting money aside for his future education. Her unfaltering love and commitment notwithstanding, she struggled with multiple and unabating stressors that compounded her difficulties as a mother with a disability. Alongside declarations of love and commitment and the visibly strong bond that she had with her infant, this mother shared the difficulties associated with accessibility problems, lack of money, and constant demands on her time, just to mention a few. She noted, for example, that her child was so demanding these days that she even had to plan when she could go to the bathroom. The stressors she enumerated could indeed present a risk factor to growth and well-being, unless they are mitigated by various resources and supports.

The challenge of setting boundaries and managing children's behaviour

The subject of discipline and behaviour management is one of the most widely discussed parenting issues. The scores of books, videotapes, workshops and presentations are testament to the ongoing interest in this topic. Nurturing a caring relationship goes hand in hand with managing behaviour in a constructive way. Discipline and control are not ends in themselves; they are part of fostering congenial and harmonious relationships with youngsters. Parenting in the context of a physical disability may have specific implications for discipline and behaviour management. Some parents with disabilities may not be able to catch a toddler who is trying to get away or pick up a child in the midst of a temper tantrum. Furthermore, the ongoing demands of parenting that are energy-taxing for most parents, may be especially challenging for those who deal with fatigue on a regular basis.

Some participants discussed the disciplinary challenges they had come across as parents as well as the strategies and techniques used to overcome them. One mother noted the difficulties she came across when her children were very young:

> When they were little toddlers and they wouldn't dress or whatever, my husband was always there to help out with that...and at that

point we also had to sit down and sort out disciplinary procedures because I couldn't chase after them, and when they ran off when I was trying to dress them, I couldn't always do it. My husband could pick up and spank but that wasn't going to work for me so we needed to come to some kind of a compromise and some con-sistency...because how he dealt with it had implications for how I could deal with it.

Taking a parenting course helped these parents come up with disciplinary measures that would work for both of them. They began using a system of contracts and consequences, giving as many choices as possible in accordance with the children's level of maturity and development.

Another participant who had some funded assistance, occasionally used this support to implement consequences such as taking a young child to her room. This would all be discussed ahead of time to ensure that the support person is indeed prepared to follow through on the mother's decision: "we would have all that laid out so that there would be no surprises". Whilst physically taking a young child to time-out is sometimes a necessity, this mother dealt with misbehaviour on a verbal level whenever possible:

I'm much more of an explainer and I try to reason with them even when they're quite little. I always wanted them to be able to deal with me on that verbal level.

Now that the children are older it is increasingly easier to rely on verbal explanations and logical consequences as demonstrated by the following scenario:

Close by there is a big open pool and they like to go swimming...I don't get in the water with them. I'm there to watch what's going on and if anyone gets in trouble, call a life guard's attention to it. But then of course they never want to come out of the pool and come home. Right from the outset I've said to them: "I'm here and I've got the time and I'm willing to take you. But it means you've got to come out as soon as I say it's time to come out. If you don't do that I just won't be able to take you on my own. You're going to have to wait until your dad feels like taking you" and that's like once a week not once a day...like he can just pull them out and there you go, whereas I've got to talk...can you imagine talking a kid out of a pool in July? Like the last thing they want to do is leave the water. But you know, they do, because the first time one of them wouldn't come when I called, then the next day it's like "I'm not taking you swimming today and this is why." I have to be (consistent). It's the kiss of death if I'm not. And they go "Oh, we'll be good today, we'll go out" and I say "no, that's what you said yesterday so today you won't go swimming. Tomorrow I'll give you another chance."

This participant gave various other examples that attested not only to her consistent parenting style but also to her attempts to accentuate the positive and reinforce desirable behaviour wherever possible. Her strong parenting skills notwithstanding, she jokingly noted:

Believe me, I don't do it as perfectly as it might sound that I do...(sometimes) it just all falls apart and I scream at them.

Another participant who also relied on verbal communication and logical consequences encouraged her two young children to solve problems with words:

It's a totally non-violent atmosphere that I have here. You have an anger problem, let's sit down and talk about it. I'll actually get them together and I'll say: "OK, you sit here and you sit there and I'll sit here. Now what is it that you're upset about? How can we make this better?"... the other day, the seven year old says "mom, you sound like a judge."

In addition to her solid parenting skills, this mother's ability to deal with conflicts and misbehaviour in an effective manner was probably enhanced by the funded assistance she was able to secure as a single disabled mother. She conserved her energy by having someone else carry out household tasks as well as provide direct care when she was in need of rest. Being able to get the rest she required to replenish her strength allowed her to be a more effective and compassionate parent. This point is further accentuated by a comment made by another mother who participated in a focus group for mothers with disabilities. Reflecting on the years when she raised her son as a single mother, this participant noted:

Around the discipline issue, there are two things. One is the energy level, again depending on what your situation is. I couldn't be consistent to follow through on stuff because I was just wiped out. I felt that if I asked for help around that stuff I was giving up my child and in fact on one occasion someone did suggest the Children's Aide. I had wonderful help but not enough of it. Part of it was that it's not out there automatically and part of it was that I was afraid to disclose the need.

Contrary to some of the above examples, the mother whose children were in care during her hospitalizations experienced major obstacles around discipline. I asked her what it was like when her children returned home from care:

It was very hard when they came back. Of course, whoever they were staying with had rules and regulations and things that they did and then I would have to try to get them to do what I wanted. It was really difficult. And then you had a man there that did a lot of yelling and spanking.

This mother spoke about the negative impact of frequent changes, an unstable family environment, and harsh and inconsistent disciplinary measures by the children's father. Consequently, she felt that her children were often out of control as adolescents.

The mother who had a frequent change of homemakers when her children were young, and little involvement in the day-to-day running of the house, also experienced behavioural challenges, this time with a pre-schooler:

She'd come home at lunch and she'd walk through the door and start screaming...just screaming about stuff. That went on for two or three years...it got to the point where I didn't talk to her hardly because it didn't matter what I said, it made her mad... I can remember thinking: "I'm not surprised some children get the shit kicked out of them by their parents", you know, because I can think of two or three times where I was just ready to strangle her.

Most parents who are honest with themselves can relate to this candid description of a highly intense situation where emotions run amok. Such scenarios are by no means unique to families of disabled parents, nor can they be said to characterize them. Nonetheless, this quote demonstrates that a wide discrepancy between stressors and supports can constitute a significant risk factor. The combined experience of study participants suggests that having access to appropriate resources and supports can have a facilitative impact on discipline and behaviour management. Mothers who are low on supports are likely to experience their disability as an impediment to their ability to provide proper parenting and manage their children's behaviour. On the other hand, mothers who have access to formal and informal supports are better equipped to set boundaries, follow through, and promote cooperative behaviour.

Relationship with children

The preceding sections on enhancing children's well-being and providing structure and guidelines for behaviour provide a backdrop for the types of relationships that study participants have with their children. The participant who was successful in securing funded assistance noted that it enabled her to play a more significant role in her children's life. Consequently, she felt that she had a solid connection with her children that could be separated from the father's relationship with them:

> It's been good in that sense because I do feel that I have my own relationship with them that's separate from, you know, (their dad's) relationship with them. I met a gentleman from out west...he wished that he had something like that because he found like his two year old did not relate to him very much. Everything was the mother. (The child) didn't know how to relate to him or sit with him. Like my kids at a very young age if they wanted me to read to them they knew they could either sit on my lap or beside me on the bed or if it was a heavy book they knew they'd have to help me hold it up. And they just did that quite spontaneously.

These adjustments that the children intuitively learned as toddlers were a lot easier to negotiate as they get older. Now that the relationship was based less and less on physical care-giving, this mother felt that she could play an even greater role in the children's lives. She jokingly referred to this period in their lives as the "golden years" when the children were no longer toddlers and had yet to enter the potentially rocky adolescent phase. When I asked her how she envisioned her life ten years from now, she reflected on future relationship with her children:

> I anticipate that the children will probably be doing well in school and that they'll have some tools and self-discipline to be able to do

that. I imagine that they'll have some friends and they'll be doing lots of stuff I'm not going to approve of with them. But I hope you know, that they maintain the trust. Like if they ever did get in any kind of trouble or if they were getting offers to get into trouble that you know, they'll still feel O.K. to come and talk to us about it and not that we're going to go through the roof and flip out, and so far we really don't. Calamity has happened and we don't flip out about stuff like that.

For a number of participants, the fulfilment derived from motherhood is particularly magnified given the barriers that may have prevented them from experiencing it. Having been told early in life that she would not become a mother, one woman reflected on the joy of motherhood:

I don't know if this is just a mother or whatever, you know, but when they go to their kindergarten classes and they do things that are so touching. You know, like I think I'm so lucky to be where I am at this date and time because I may not have ever had the opportunity to enjoy this.

In a focus group discussion, this mother also shared the joy she felt over the open display of affection from her now pre-adolescent children:

I really treasure it when my eight year old still, you know, when I'm sitting on the couch, will curl up on my lap and put his head on my shoulder. Or my eleven year old when we're walking down the street, will put his arm around me. You know, that kind of a thing.

The humorous response of another focus group participant that "it will break your heart when it stops," was well received by all group members who emphasized the more difficult and challenging adolescent years. Throughout the focus group discussion, many humorous references were made to "raging hormone syndrome" and "wonderful adolescent roller coaster ride."

The young mother who resisted pressures to undergo an abortion, gave a number of examples of the strong bond and intimacy that she had with her baby and the sense of "oneness" that new mothers often described:

I always think that it's too good to be true. I love him so much...and I feel so protective of him. I know what he needs, I know when he's complaining. I always know what he wants. I know exactly what he wants.

She talked about the type of relationship she would like to have with her son when he gets older:

I'd like to be his friend, I don't want him to just think of me as his mom. I want him to come home from school and sit down and tell me what he has learned...I'd like to have a relationship like that. And when he gets older he can tell me his girl problems.

Recognizing the dynamic nature of a mother-child relationship, she reflected on what it may be like years from now, when her infant son grows up:

You know what I think? I wonder if his friends will make fun of me. I wonder about that and I wonder if it'll be hard for him having a mom who is in a wheelchair. I wonder if he'll be embarrassed. But then I think, maybe he'll stick up for me.

The issue of how children respond to a mother's disability came up in a number of interviews and focus groups and is relevant to the discussion of parent-child relationships. Several participants noted that their children were quite comfortable with disabilities in general and were not embarrassed about their mother's disability. One group participant noted that her disability was not an issue for her now adult children:

I never went through the stage of my children being embarrassed of me. I developed polio when I was 18 months old so my children didn't know any different. I never seemed to get any negative feedback and if they did hear things at school they never repeated it to me, so I don't think they did. I'm pretty sure they would have come back and said something.

Another woman related a conversation she overheard just the other day as she came to pick up her son from day-care:

He said something yesterday. I went to pick him up from day care. I was just watching him play with other kids in the sandbox and he was getting up to leave. One of the little girls whom I didn't recognize said: "Why is your mom in a wheelchair?" And he just said: "Oh, she broke her back as a kid." That's all he said. It was sort of like matter of fact. I was so proud of him the way he said that, you know, I thought: you couldn't give a better answer to another kid than that. It was just so matter of fact.

She noted the importance of mothers with disabilities being present at children's activities. Several other mothers who participated in focus group discussions also emphasized the benefits of being visible and involved in their children's schools and activities. Some came to their children's class to speak about disabilities. In one case an 11-year-old boy was teased by his classmates about his mother's disability. Things improved considerably after the mother came to speak with the class. While being involved in children's activities could foster tolerance and a good parent-child relationship, some locations are inaccessible, thereby restricting disabled parents from full participation in their children's lives. One mother noted that due to the inaccessibility of many facilities, her husband had been the more involved parent in extra-curricular programs and activities.

Contrary to the above indications of acceptance and comfort with a mother's disability, another participant shared that when her daughter was young she did not want to be out in public with her disabled mother:

I had the scooter then. She'd sit on my lap but she'd never go for a walk. You know, my husband could take her to the park but I couldn't. I think she was embarrassed even when she was 4 years old.

Interestingly and perhaps significantly, this is the same little girl who had frequent and unexpected changes in care-givers for the first few years of her life. It is a factor to which the mother attributed various difficulties that she had had with her daughter throughout the years. Being disagreeable and uncooperative as a young child, she became somewhat distant as a teenager, preferring to spend most of her time with her friends outside of the home. Although one cannot assume a definitive causal link between early experiences with homemakers and the distant mother-daughter relationship, such a connection is certainly plausible.

The young mother who had frequent surgeries over the course of her children's childhood felt that she had no choice but to place them in care so that they would be looked after in her absence. Whenever she returned home after one of her surgeries, she immediately set about getting the children back from care:

> It was very important (to get the kids back)...They were my kids and I wanted to take care of them...they were going into care because they would have better care than if they'd stayed home with their father...but it was very important that I get them back...that was the driving force. I never thought of ever you know, keeping them in care. It never crossed my mind.

Reflecting back on those years, this mother asserted that placing her children in care was the only option available to her. Nonetheless, she continued to feel guilty about the impact of this experience on her children. She further felt that her now adult children had continued to hold her responsible for what they had endured:

> Apparently there are foster homes that are very abusive and that. But I didn't know that then. You know, I always felt that my kids blamed me for what they went through...I still have that feeling. I did talk about it with all of them and explained it and I know they know what their father was like. They have no illusions what so ever about what their father was like but I think deep down they still blame me...I'm the one that had the operations so of course it's my fault. If I wouldn't have had the operations they wouldn't have had to go to Children's Aid.

This mother agreed with my comment that since the children's father was never available to begin with, you can't blame someone who you never expected anything from:

> That's it, right. And so when I wasn't there...I guess I was the force that kept things together and when I wasn't there everything fell apart. So I guess they blame me for making things fall apart.

She noted, with some degree of sadness, the somewhat distant nature of her relationship with her adult children and her sense that she couldn't really count on them in times of need:

> Because of me being so sick (when they were children) my daughter runs when you mention sick. She's scared to death of it. And the other

ones I think are about the same. They're kind of afraid of being...you know, of someone being sick. I can't count on them...They will call and ask how I feel. But if I need help I definitely won't pick up the phone and call my kids. This is where I phone my friends.

She also speculated about the parallel between the diminished connection she felt with her siblings as a young child and the relationship she has with her own children. Having spent a year and a half in hospital as a toddler, she never formed a close alliance with her siblings who were also significantly older than she was. Her frequent hospitalizations as a young mother provided a formidable barrier to the formation of a close alliance with her children:

The bonding that I was talking about when I went away to the hospital and I didn't bond with my siblings, I think the same thing pretty much happened with my kids, depending on which kid and what operation. Like my (oldest), I wasn't having operations so I bonded with her and I had her for a while before having (the others) so we sort of had time together so we bonded. But as time went on and I started having surgeries I wasn't bonding with the kids like I probably should have. And with them being pulled away all the time, I don't think they had a chance to bond with anybody either because they were going to different homes and everything. So we really both lost.

The mother who described relationship difficulties with her adolescent daughter may have also been affected by her reportedly limited contact with her daughter as an infant, the latter being cared for mostly by homemakers and by the father. In both cases the maternal disability was a precursor to some degree of inconsistency in the children's care.

Hence, it is not the impairment itself but the context in which it is embedded that can have a potentially adverse affect on the relationship between mothers with disabilities and their children. In situations where the contact with mother is stable and continuous and the children receive consistent and nurturing care when she is unavailable, the relationship has a greater chance of being a close and fulfilling one. Furthermore, it is important to emphasize the obviously complex and dynamic relationship between all parents and their children, regardless of disability status. By their very nature, relationships go through ebbs and flows, peaks and valleys. Even the closest of relationships experience periods of greater distance and lessened intimacy. Clearly, maternal disability is but one of many factors which could affect the relationship between mother and child.

The dynamic and changing nature of mother-child relationships is also reflected in the accounts of the two mothers noted above. For one mother, the difficulties she experienced with her daughter were somewhat tempered by the overall positive relationship she has had with her son over the years. Furthermore, she has recently noticed a positive change of attitude on the part of her daughter and an increased willingness and interest to spend more time at home, especially with mom. The participant that described the relationship with her adult children as somewhat distant, has made efforts over the years to talk with each one of them about what they all went through as a family. This has resulted in some degree of healing and a greater closeness with one son in particular. As some of these children are now parents themselves, their mother makes an effort to be an available grandparent and establish a loving relationship with her grandchildren.

Earlier I described the loving relationship between one participant and her infant son. This mother gave a number of examples that attested not only to her love but to her ability to be attuned to the needs of her baby. Alongside descriptions of the joyous moments of motherhood, this participant candidly described other, less harmonious scenarios. She noted the frustration associated with having almost no time for herself, living in cramped, unkempt quarters in a crime-infested neighbourhood, and having frequent conflicts with the baby's father:

> I have way too much stress in my life. A lot of the time he's gone (the father). I have a lot of money stress. I have a lot of stress about him getting bigger. I never feel sorry for myself about my disability but I do worry. I am stressed out, definitely. You see, I thought that babies, once they weren't newborns anymore, then everything gets easier. But now I'm getting to realize that that's really the easiest time... I get in a fight with Tony and we yell at each other and half the year I can't get around...You know, I just think I don't like being here. I'm not very happy here, you know.

She also admitted, with clear self-reproach, that the baby is often witness to the yelling that goes on and that she herself may be less than patient with him in the midst of a fight.

I chose the above quote not to undermine or cast a dark shadow over this mother's descriptions of the joys and rewards of mothering.

Rather, I see it as a candid reflection of the delicate co-existence of barriers and difficulties on the one hand, and joyous and rewarding moments on the other hand. By choosing to present them concurrently in this section, I also hope to underscore the role that context plays in relationships. Many factors impact and will continue to impact the relationship between this mother and her child. Her strong love and commitment notwithstanding, the number and magnitude of stressors in her life, if left unmitigated, can present a risk factor to the relationship with her child.

Concluding comments

Women who participated in this study provide us with a glimpse into the lived experience of parenting with a physical disability. As one would expect in any group of mothers, a range of parenting practices, experiences and relationships was reported. This diversity cannot be attributed to any specific factor pertaining to the nature, severity, or age of onset of the mother's disability. The variability of experiences notwithstanding, participants' life stories demonstrate a strong commitment to children, actions to ensure their care and well-being in different circumstances, and attempts to shield them from any burden related to the maternal disability. Whilst challenges and barriers were candidly reported, by and large, they do not overshadow the joy and fulfillment that these women derived from motherhood.

The issue of children caring for disabled parents (dubbed young carers) was noted in chapter three. The present study did not find any indication of this phenomenon amongst the children and families of participants. If anything, there were indications of participants' desire to shield their children from the burden of care. There were further indications of heightened sensitivity to this issue, with some mothers noting societal perceptions that maternal disability translates into provision of care by children.

The theme of shielding children from the effects of the disability can be better understood in the context of the institution of motherhood on the one hand, and the medical model of disability on the other hand. Motherhood as institution was predicated on romanticized notions of ever-present, all-giving, self-sacrificing mothers. Feminist critiques of these romanticized notions notwithstanding, mothers continue to be at risk for self-erasure in the process of caring for children. This risk may be exponentially higher for mothers with disabilities. In their relationship with children, they are "supposed" to be on the giving end and not on the receiving end of care. As people with disabilities, they have to fight stereotypical images of being dependent and in need of care. Narrative accounts of mothers with disabilities consistently point to their struggle to be perceived in a care-giving role. Lack of distinction between the ability to be a responsible, caring parent and the ability to carry out all child-rearing tasks or self-care tasks unassisted, can contribute to this disabling discourse.

Related to the topic of enhancing children's well-being is participants' accounts of the child-rearing practices they utilize and their overall relationship with their children. The emphasis on consistent parenting practices and reliance on verbal explanations and instructions was noted by a number of mothers. This is consistent with narrative accounts found in the literature suggesting that such children tend to respond to verbal instructions from an early age. I began to take my (now 16-year-old) son out on my own as soon as he was able to climb into the car seat on his own. Although he was assertive and strong willed from a young age and would frequently negotiate parental limits, I knew I could count on his following my verbal instructions even as a young child. Olkin (1999) recounts that her own children learned from a very young age to always remain within voice range as she could not chase after them. "Even when they tested every other limit they obeyed this one" (p. 129).

In my previous work as a counsellor I have often come across parents who have struggled with how to enforce limits with teenagers. Clearly, physical strength is irrelevant in getting older children to respond to limit setting. Solid and consistent parenting practices from a young age go a long way in preventing unmanageable situations and disregard for parental authority. Indeed, a number of participants showed a good deal of ingenuity in fostering an enjoyable yet manageable family atmosphere. These mothers can be a source of knowledge and inspiration to disabled and non-disabled mothers alike.

An important consideration is the relationship between child-rearing practices and the level of formal and informal supports. One woman noted the difficulty with being consistent and following through in the context of fatigue and limited supports. In other cases, insufficient, inadequate or nonexistent supports were implicated in adversely affecting the ability to handle behavioral issues. In extreme situations, this can have a lasting effect on the overall nature of the relationship between parents and children. Relationships are not formed and maintained in a vacuum, nor can they be nourished by good intentions alone. Although the people involved in the relationship enact the lived experience of being together, their behaviours are not just a reflection of personal intentions but of extraneous forces as well. Negative distal and proximal factors like economic deprivation, crowded housing, and insufficient formal and informal supports penetrate the interactions between otherwise loving individuals. These powerful influences can slowly erode ties created by much individual effort on the part of parents and children. Indeed, one particular case exemplified the lasting impact that these factors can have on the relationship between a mother and her children.

I believe that this study can advance our understanding of the relationship between parental disability and child well-being. The experience of study participants suggests that the welfare of children need not be compromised due to parental disability. Study participants gave numerous examples from their daily lives that described their attempts to ensure their children's welfare. They also described loving relationships and positive communication with the children, as well as their pride in children who were well adjusted, caring, and appreciative of human diversity.

Alongside these accounts, and sometimes intertwined with them, are indications of how stressors such as poverty and lack of support can compound difficulties related to the disability. It is safe to say that in the presence of internal and external resources and supports, parental disability in and of itself need not present a significant risk factor. On the other hand, the high rate of poverty, single-parenthood and attitudinal barriers that characterize the lives of many women with disabilities, may indeed, if unmitigated, present a risk to family well-being.

9
Conclusion: Striving for Wellness

In the past two decades, the psychological literature has evidenced a growing interest in wellness, resilience and protective factors. This approach can be seen as antithetical to the pathology-based tradition in psychology that focused on diagnosis and treatment of dysfunction and disease. Eminent scholars like Michael Rutter (1987, 1994), Norman Garmezy (1994) and the late Emory Cowen (1991, 1994, 1996), have pushed the mental health field to adopt a wellness orientation based on the concepts of strength and resilience. They maintained that the human capacity to overcome adversity has been overlooked in an incessant search for pathology; an argument revived recently by the new positive psychology movement (Seligman, 2002).

People faced with a number of life adversities have been shown not only to cope with stressors but to develop their capacities in fulfilling ways. Unfortunately, the burgeoning literature on children and adults who cope successfully with adverse life circumstances (and are thus considered resilient) has seldom been applied to study the lives of people with disabilities. This is despite the fact that the concept of resilience can be fruitfully applied to disability research and holds much promise for the lives of disabled individuals and their families. Nosek (1996) has contended that although resilience has been studied in reference to survivors of war and children who survive family violence, it is seldom applied to women with disabilities (p. 168). Women in my study showed me how unjust this gap in the literature really is. As I listened to participants' stories, I realized how important the concept of resilience is in understanding their meaning-making and life trajectories.

This gap in the literature has recently been addressed in such studies as those carried out by the Centre for Research on Women with

Disabilities (Howland & Rinalta, 2001; Nosek et al., 2001) and Through the Looking Glass' Research and Training Centre (RTC) on Families with Adults with Disabilities (Kirshbaum & Olkin, 2002; Toms Barker & Maralani, 1997). With wellness promotion as their focus, these centres have produced research results that are challenging previously held beliefs regarding the inevitability of distress and maladjustment in response to disability. I believe that the data that emerged from the current study on motherhood can both inform and be informed by a wellness framework and can contribute to this body of literature.

Given the lack of attention to resilience in the disability literature, and its tremendous potential to elucidate complex patterns of coping, I choose to discuss my findings in light of resilience and allied concepts such as risks and protective factors. I begin by providing a brief overview on resilience and wellness promotion and argue for the relevance of these concepts to disability research. I then utilize the concepts of resilience, risk and protective factors and wellness promotion, to my own research on women with disabilities.

Resilience and wellness promotion for people with disabilities

In an invited address to the American Psychological Association, the late Emory Cowen (1991) made reference to his failed efforts to find a dictionary meaning for the word wellness.

> Does the word wellness really exist? Who knows? It *should* exist! But whether or not it does, the functional point to stress is that allocations of our energies and resources must go increasingly toward building wellness rather than toward struggling, however compassionately, to contain troubles.   (Cowen, 1991, p. 404)

He further stated that the 21st century should be marked by significant movement toward wellness in both research and action.

In an effort to counteract the negative impact of deficit-oriented medical models, Cowen promoted the concept of wellness (1991, 1994, 1996). Inspired by the health-promotion movement and by a more inclusive definition of health by the World Health Organization (1986), Cowen offered concepts as well as interventions to strengthen health-enhancing mechanisms, not only for people at risk, but for the population at large. He believed that the time was overdue for shifting the reigning paradigm in mental health from one that emphasizes pathology to one that fosters well-being. Wellness may be conceptualized as a favourable state of affairs, brought about by the balanced satisfaction of personal, relational, and collective needs; needs that are met by psychological, physical, and material resources (Prilleltensky, 2004b). Cowen (1991, 1994) identified several key constructs that can synergistically guide potential health-enhancing interventions. In his 1994 article he describes five pathways to wellness promotion: "(a) forming wholesome early attachments; (b) acquiring age-appropriate competencies; (c) exposure to settings that favour wellness outcomes; (d) having the (empowering) sense of being in control of one's fate, and (e) coping effectively with stress" (p. 158). Cowen emphasizes the interactive nature of wellness promotion. These five pathways complement each other and should work in tandem in order to achieve wellness. They are rooted in the four key wellness constructs identified by Cowen in his 1991 Distinguished Contribution to Psychology in the Public Interest Address: competence, empowerment, social system modification, and resilience.

The concept of competence implies the ability to meet life's challenges effectively. These challenges are multifaceted in nature and include the successful negotiation of physical, academic, affective, and social tasks. Experiencing a sense of mastery early and throughout life enhances the ability to cope effectively with stressful situations and circumstances (Garmezy, 1994; Gore & Eckenrode, 1994; Haggerty, Sherrod, Garmezy & Rutter, 1994; Rutter, 1987).

Empowerment, the second building block for wellness, refers to interventions and social policies designed to enhance people's control over their lives. This concept has been particularly useful to the plight of marginalized and powerless groups, as their suffering is marked by a profound lack of power and control over their fate (Nelson & Prilleltensky, 2004; Prilleltensky & Nelson, 2002). This is not to say that these groups lack the ability to direct their lives, but rather that oppressive conditions and ideologies restrict their access to power (Cowen, 1991, 1994; Lord & Hutchison, 1993). As has been amply documented, restoring a measure of empowerment has salutary psychological and material effects at the individual and community levels (Serrano-Garcia & Bond, 1994; Zimmerman & Perkins, 1995).

Social system modification, another important contributor to wellness, highlights the need to change social structures inimical to the fulfilment of human needs. Numerous are the organizations and social barriers that interfere with the promotion of wellness. "Whereas some institutions act coincidentally to enhance wellness, others, oblivious to incidental outcomes effects, may pose unintended obstacles to wellness" (Cowen, 1991, p. 407). Schools, hospitals, social agencies and worksites are all examples of social institutions bearing on the well-being of the population.

Resilience is the fourth pillar of wellness identified by Cowen (1991). It refers to the ability evidenced by some people for adaptive and healthy outcomes despite exposure to extreme adversity (Consortium, 1994; Cowen, 1991, 1994, 1996; Garmezy, 1994; Prilleltensky, Nelson & Peirson, 2001; Rutter, 1987). Studies documenting the life course of individuals exposed to risk at a young age, reveal that a significant proportion of them develop in adaptive ways. Much can be learned from these individuals and the ecological climate surrounding their development for the promotion of psychological well-being. These are individuals who overcome the odds and manage to stay afloat when all indicators would have predicted that they would sink (Cowen, 1991).

Resilience is the outcome of dynamic interactions among risk and protective factors. Risks may be defined as personal characteristics, events, or circumstances which enhance the likelihood of a negative outcome. Conversely, protective factors are personal characteristics, events or circumstances which enhance the likelihood of positive mental health outcomes (Haggerty et al., 1994; Nelson, Prilleltensky & Peters, 2003). Risks and protective factors can operate at the personal, familial, and societal levels. Individual risk factors include organic vulnerabilities, low intelligence, and genetic predispositions to mental illness. At the family level, some common risk factors include marital discord, divorce, and parental mental illness. Societal risk factors known to affect psychological well-being include poverty, urban violence, exposure to drugs and alcohol, and discrimination.

Like risk factors, protective factors may be clustered in the following categories: attributes of the individual (high intelligence, good temperament, good problem-solving abilities, positive social orientation, competence and self-efficacy, etc.); attributes of the family (bonding with parents, family cohesion, supportive relationships, adequate parental supervision, etc.); and attributes of the environment (supportive networks, schools that encourage mastery and competence, social safety net, responsive social agencies, lack of prejudice and discrimination) (Consortium, 1994).

It is important to realize that single risk or protective factors can have different meanings in different contexts (Shinn & Toohey, 2003). For example, while the death of a parent is always a stressful event, the outcome for the child is contingent upon the particular context surrounding the loss. In situations where adequate financial and emotional supports are available to the child and the loss does not result in inadequate care, he or she would likely overcome this tragic event. On the other hand, when such supports are unavailable to the grieving child, the negative impact of the death will be much more pronounced. Another example of the importance of context in interpreting the meaning of risk and protective factors is the case of parental divorce. For years, mental health professionals have warned against the negative repercussions of parental divorce. While divorce is always a stressful event for a child, it does not necessarily lead to negative outcomes. Moreover, the lack of parental separation may result in exposure to high degrees of discord and/or domestic violence, the outcomes of which can be more damaging than the divorce itself. A child's exposure to divorce may be more or less damaging depending on events and circumstances that precede and follow it (Gore & Eckenrode, 1994; Rutter, 1994).

Cowan's four wellness constructs of competence, empowerment, social system modification, and resilience, are highly relevant to some of the challenges faced by people with disabilities. Competence, an important ingredient in the promotion of wellness, is contingent upon exposure to learning opportunities. Unfortunately, many people with disabilities have been denied such opportunities due to prejudice and diminished expectations. Traditionally, people with disabilities have been viewed as eternally dependent and in need of care and thus, in little need for competency training.

The relevance of empowerment for the promotion of wellness in people with disabilities is made crystal clear by Fawcett and colleagues (Fawcett et al., 1994). They claim that

> When people with disabilities, ethnic minorities, older adults, women, and others lack power, they usually experience adverse conditions disproportionate to other members of society. Empowerment – the process by which people gain some control over valued events, outcomes, and resources – is an important construct for understanding and improving the lives of people of marginal status.   (p. 471)

Empowerment is a process that can have beneficial effects for people with disabilities at the personal, communal, and societal levels (Fawcett et al., 1994; Lord & Hutchison, 1993). Whereas most attempts to promote empowerment have targeted the individual level, Cowen (1991) states that "a primary goal for empowerment theorists is to promote policies and conditions that enable people to gain control over their lives, on the assumption that doing so will reduce problems in living and enhance wellness" (p. 407).

Social system modification applies to the lives of people with disabilities in multiple ways. Whereas architectural barriers that restrict full participation in public life are being gradually removed, attitudinal barriers are more resistant to change. Although significant gains have been made in recent years in both physical and sociological conditions, much remains to be done to facilitate full participation by people with disabilities in society. Furthermore, many adults with disabilities have been subjected to oppressive institutional practices in their early contacts with educational, health, and social services. As the literature suggests, and participants in this research attest, improved accessibility and appreciation for disabled people's contributions have increased the quality of life for disabled people in significant ways.

The importance of context in the interplay between risks and protective factors discussed earlier in relation to resilience, has important implications for understanding stress and coping in the lives of women with disabilities For example, parental disability has traditionally been considered a major risk factor to children's well-being. However, as research on risks and protective factors demonstrates, "a focus on isolated life events is not the most appropriate way of viewing most stressors" (Rutter, 1994, p. 355). When parental disability is accompanied by sufficient formal and informal supports and adequate resources, children may be at no higher risk than children of non-disabled parents. Moreover, the particular challenges associated with parental disability can have a steeling effect so long as the situational demands do not exceed children's capacities. This is supported by literature which suggests that exposure to mild stressors and challenges can in fact enhance children's sense of self-efficacy (Garmezy, 1994; Rutter, 1987, 1994).

In order to fill the gap in the literature concerning an analysis of risks and protective factors in the lives of women with disabilities, I present below a summary of my research and its implications for wellness promotion. I present three tables describing risks and protective factors for girls with disabilities, young women with disabilities and those who do not have children, and mothers with disabilities and their families. This conceptual framework will provide the basis for formulating recommendations for wellness promotion in the three groups. The discussion of risks, protective factors, and interventions in each group will be divided into three levels of analysis: micro, meso, and macro levels. By micro level I refer to personal, interpersonal, and familial factors. The meso context includes mid-level organizational structures such as schools, hospitals, social services, and community agencies. The macro level of analysis pertains to social policies and cultural norms that determine the ideological climate of society and the allocation of resources in the community.

This conceptual framework should be regarded as flexible and permeable and not as a rigid grid. Overlap among the various levels is natural and expected. The purpose of dividing interventions into three distinct levels is to avoid perpetuating the problem of focusing exclusively on person-centered strategies and interventions. As Prilleltensky and Nelson have pointed out, most therapeutic and preventive interventions in the field of mental health tend to focus on the individual at the expense of crucial changes needed at both the meso and macro levels (Nelson & Prilleltensky, 2004; Prilleltensky & Nelson, 1997; 2002). The main advantage of identifying clearly the three levels of intervention is that policies and interventions can be formulated at multiple points of entry. Parallel interventions at the three levels are typically needed in order to achieve enduring changes. Micro level changes aimed at enhancing personal competency must be accompanied by transformations in the realm of social policy. Likewise, social systems change cannot be effective without a sense of personal efficacy and control. In essence, the three levels of intervention complement one another and each one of them should be given due consideration.

I will discuss in the text only a few examples from the data pertaining to risks, protective factors, and possible interventions. The purpose of this discussion and accompanying tables is not to provide an exhaustive coverage of these issues, but rather to illustrate the potential utilization of this conceptual framework.

Girls with disabilities: risks, protective factors, and possible interventions

The life stories of all participants who grew up with disabilities suggest the presence of some risk factors at the micro level of analysis (see Table 9.1). At the familial level, a common theme was a lack of any reference to a disabled daughter's sexuality and sexual identity. One set of parents sheltered their daughter to the point that no opportunities were afforded for developing self-help skills and competencies. In another case a disabled daughter was openly rejected by her mother. Most participants had no role models of adults with disabilities in their

Table 9.1 Girls with disabilities: risks, protective factors, and possible interventions

	Risks	Protective factors	Possible interventions
Micro Level	* parental rejection * parental over-protection * parental reticence to acknowledge girl's sexuality * inaccessible house * lack of role models of adults with disabilities * rejection/exclusion by non-disabled peers * poor social skills * poor self-esteem * internalized oppression	* parental nurturance and support * parental promotion of competence and independence * exposure to disabled adults via sports * strong ties with peers with disabilities * links with non-disabled peers in the community * high intelligence * competence and independence * recognizing oppression and fighting for control and self-determination	* foster the development of self-help, academic, and practical skills at home and at school * provide experiences of mastery and control at home and at school * encourage the development of a healthy sexual identity * provide ample opportunities to interact and develop friendships with peers with and without disabilities
Meso Level	* professionals who engendered pessimism in parents * being placed in an institution * sexuality not acknowledged in segregated settings * violations of privacy during medical exams * academics under-emphasized in special schools * being labelled in regular schools * powerlessness in institutional and medical settings * a focus on deficit and disease that characterized the above settings	* teacher who set high academic expectations * respectful and supportive medical personnel * professionals (Occupational therapist and Counsellor) who encouraged exploration of sexuality * recreational counsellor who facilitated involvement in disabled sports * satellite program (independent living) for physically independent teens at an institution	* foster optimism and hope in parents of newborns with disabilities; connect parents with other families of children and adults with disabilities * carry out medical examinations in a respectful manner where privacy and personal agency are upheld * set high academic expectations at home and school * foster a general climate of tolerance and diversity in schools * expose disabled and non-disabled students to competent role-models of adults with disabilities

Table 9.1   Girls with disabilities: risks, protective factors, and possible interventions – continued

	Risks	Protective factors	Possible interventions
Macro Level	* parents not having resources to fund wheelchair * lack of resources to provide respite from care to parents * policy that enabled school to reject a severely disabled child * oppressive societal attitudes about disability which impact families, institutions, and communities.	* wheelchair and other needs funded in an institutional setting (but not while living at home) * enhanced awareness of how oppressive factors frame the personal experience of disability * a change in policy that allowed a greater measure of control for young adults with disabilities	* provide funded respite to parents of children with disabilities * work toward the preservation of existing programs for disabled children and families * insist on a more just allocation of societal resources

homes, schools, or communities. Some suffered rejection and/or exclusion by non-disabled peers. Several women recounted having poor self esteem in their childhood.

The impact of these risk factors can be moderated by the presence of micro level protective factors. Stories were told of nurturing and supportive parents whose love and commitment were unfaltering. Some parents actively promoted the development of competencies in social, academic and practical domains. Beyond the parental home, links with disabled and non-disabled peers in school and the community provided friendship, affirmation, and social support. Personal attributes such as high intelligence and independence were highly protective in some situations. Another important attribute mentioned by several participants is their ability as children to recognize the oppressive factors and ideologies that framed their experiences. Anger over the injustice in their lives mobilized some girls to fight for self-determination.

Beyond global lists of micro level risks and protective factors, it is important to attend to the specific contexts and circumstances that surround them. For example, the girl who was openly rejected by her mother was the same one who was later introduced to disabled sports and thus came in contact with adults with disabilities who served as positive role-models. Another girl whose severe disability and poor prognosis could have resulted in extreme dependency, had a mother who pushed her to attain as much control and independence as her condition would allow. The early training for independence in conjunction with her obviously strong intellectual abilities were important protective factors for this youngster who suffered multiple adversities at all three levels of analysis. Conversely, the childhood stories of another participant reveal minimal exposure to risks and maximal exposure to health-enhancing protective factors.

Risk factors can also be found at the meso level of analysis in the lives of girls with disabilities. The pessimism engendered in families by professionals is an important backdrop to the familial interactions and dynamics reported above. Some parents were told that their daughters would die, others were counselled to place them in institutions, and yet others were advised to expect little in the way of normal development. Girls were also impacted directly by iatrogenic practices in medical, educational, and institutional settings. Violations of privacy during medical exams accentuated the risks to a healthy sexual identity posed by parental reticence to acknowledge sexuality. In segregated settings, a greater emphasis was accorded to physical therapy often at the expense of imparting academic skills and competencies. This lax approach to skill-building can severely limit future opportunities and thus pose a significant risk factor. In one case, the reluctance to provide adequate study space at an institution amounted to clear suppression of academic talents. This participant's strong will and self-determination ultimately gained her satisfactory conditions for studying.

The above example of a girl's struggle for her right to proper learning space illustrates the interaction between different levels of risks and protective factors. In this situation, as in several others, micro level strengths (high intelligence, determination, self-advocacy skills) were protective in fending off meso level risks (being denied learning opportunities). Furthermore, strengths at the micro level were probably instrumental in eliciting protective factors at the meso level of analysis. In an institutional setting otherwise described by this participant as oppressive and disempowering, there was a teacher who recognized her strong academic abilities and pushed her to excel. The woman whose childhood involvement in disabled sports provided an important turning point in her life, singled out a recreational counsellor who facilitated this involvement. Like in the previous example, this girl had a number of micro-level strengths that probably served to activate protective factors at the meso level. As she herself indicated, "I've always been able to kind of find what I needed along the way". These examples support claims made in the literature regarding the tendency of protective factors to co-occur. Other meso level protective factors include professionals (an occupational therapist, a counsellor) who encouraged the development of a healthy sexuality and a physician who fostered hope for achieving stage-appropriate milestones in personal and professional domains. Sadly, all examples of meso level protective factors pertain to single individuals who stood out in otherwise disempowering institutions.

The inter-connection between various levels of risks and protective factors can also be illustrated at the macro level. A policy that enabled a school to reject a severely disabled child could have significantly and irreversibly restricted her social and academic development and her ability to develop future competencies. Likewise, the one case of parental rejection occurred in a family that was exposed to other societal stressors. It could well be that having formal respite from care may have served to buffer the stress of a disabled child in an already stressed family situation. The inadequate level of resources and supports extended to families of disabled children mirror the discriminatory practices of dominant societal institutions at the time.

As can be expected, the data is rather scant with respect to macro level protective factors in the lives of girls with disabilities. Several women made reference to the process of conscientization that they went through in adolescence. Conscientization refers to the process whereby people attain an increased level of awareness concerning the deleterious impact of societal ideologies and conditions on their lives (Freire, 1970; I. Prilleltensky, 1994). One participant noted the ameliorative impact of this process as she, along with other peers with disabilities, became aware of the systemic oppression that they were subjected to at school. In another case, conscientization motivated a girl who had been institutionalized throughout her childhood to fight for her right to live independently in the community. Along with her peers, she successfully lobbied for consumer-directed attendant services which facilitated independent living for young adults with disabilities. Efforts such as these pave the way for other macro level changes which enhance the self-determination and well-being of marginalized groups.

The interplay of risks and protective factors are helpful in elucidating possible interventions at the three levels of analysis. Beginning with the micro level, a number of themes emerge from the data as particularly germane for wellness enhancement. Competency and self-efficacy are important protective factors for all children. In the case of girls with disabilities, it is crucial to develop self-help, academic, and practical skills to compensate for physical challenges associated with the disability. In order to gain as much control over their lives as possible, homes and schools have the responsibility and the opportunity to provide girls with experiences of mastery and control. Imparting cognitive and problem solving skills lays the foundation for future experiences of success at school and at work. As reported in the literature and demonstrated by the current study, the educational system has traditionally been remiss in affording children with disabilities opportunities for growth and autonomy. In the context of teaching self-help skills, it is imperative to adapt existing programs to the unique profile of the child. Fostering independence does not necessarily mean meeting all of one's physical needs unassisted. A child whose disability requires her to obtain help with personal care should be helped to articulate her needs and wishes and negotiate for proper services.

Interventions in the social and affective domains might include exposure at a young age to peers with and without disabilities. Several participants emphasized the value of having peers with disabilities as they were growing up. One woman referred to this as the main benefit she derived from a segregated setting. In the current context of integrated settings, the importance of connecting with other children with disabilities should not be undermined. The family and the school can play an important role in facilitating contact with other children with disabilities as well as in building friendships with peers without disabilities in the school and in the community. Most study participants experienced some difficulties in their interaction with non-disabled peers. For some, this resulted in social isolation in Junior High School, a time when social support is especially critical for adolescent girls (Gore & Eckenrode, 1994). Along with early exposure to peers, girls with disabilities can be helped to explore ways of initiating and maintaining meaningful friendships. The many existing programs designed to enhance social skills can be adapted to the particular needs and challenges of girls with disabilities.

Another major theme that has direct implications for intervention is the need to foster a healthy sexual identity. Most participants described experiences at home, at school and in the community that pose a significant risk to a healthy sexuality. Conveying positive messages about a disabled girl's changing body and her wishes to form intimate relationships, can be affirming and health-enhancing. In attempts to foster a healthy sexual identity, parents and educators may help disabled girls to explore the impact of negative societal messages pertaining to sexuality and disability. This process of conscientization can result in de-blaming and may also lay the foundation for taking a stand against oppression.

In keeping with the interventions suggested at the micro level, institutions such as hospitals, schools, and social service agencies must work to eliminate discriminatory and unjust practices that place vulnerable individuals at risk. Such meso level changes are already occurring as suggested by some of the current literature on disability. For example, the outcry of people with disabilities against powerlessness and violations of privacy in medical settings, have resulted in changes to hospitals and clinics. In addition to protesting against oppressive practices, people with disabilities have taken an active role in training service providers to better serve individuals with a range of disabilities (Odette, 1994; Saxton, 1996).

Educational reforms have also occurred since the time that study participants attended school 20–30 years ago. However, while segregated settings are probably the exception rather than the norm, the education of children with disabilities may still be compromised if active steps are not taken to enhance their sense of efficacy and control. Furthermore, schools also have a major role to play in fostering a climate of tolerance and diversity where children with different challenges and abilities can feel at home. Exposing disabled and non-disabled children to competent professionals with disabilities be they teachers, clinicians, or individuals in the community, can also serve to dispel myths and promote tolerance.

Macro level changes are needed that can enhance micro and meso level interventions. Parents who raise children with disabilities need resources and supports that will enhance their parenting efforts. A more just allocation of societal resources will result in less stress for such families. In the current economic climate of cutbacks to social programs, there is a serious risk of reducing already scarce resources available to such families. Therefore, disability rights organizations and independent living movements have an important advocacy role to play in preserving programs. These organizations serve as the conscience of the public and strive to hold governments accountable to the needs of marginalized populations.

Women who are not mothers: risks, protective factors, and possible interventions

A number of micro level risk factors have been identified in the data for young women with physical disabilities and for those who are not mothers (see Table 9.2). Although my particular focus is on women without children regardless of their age, I also make references to risks and protective factors faced by young adult women with disabilities. Women who experienced a lack of sexual acknowledgment in childhood were susceptible to similarly devaluing messages in their adult lives.

Some families actively discouraged disabled daughters from pursuing an intimate relationship. Others avoided the subject altogether, probably out of concern that a disabled woman is likely to experience sexual rejection. A closely related risk factor is a lack of acknowledgment that women with disabilities have the same right to reproductive freedom as women without disabilities. An undermining of their reproductive options sometimes resulted in women having limited information about the choices that were available to them, including their ability to safely carry a child and to care for a baby following its birth.

The ability to separate motherhood from their identity as women is the most salient protective factor at the micro level of analysis. Most study participants demonstrated a strong sense of self as women without children. Their criticism and rejection of traditional ideologies

Table 9.2 Women who are not mothers: risks, protective factors, and possible interventions

	Risks	Protective factors	Possible interventions
Micro Level	* sexuality not acknowledged by family members * experiences of sexual rejection and devaluation by men * being discouraged from choosing motherhood * choices not being acknowledged and respected * concerns about division of labour within the family (i.e. will partner be an active participant in child care?) * concerns about social isolation * not knowing how the disability might impact own ability to carry out child care duties	* families that recognize sexuality and respect choices * affirming messages from friends * strong sense of self as a childless woman (separating motherhood from female identity) * strong bonds with friends, some of whom are also women with disabilities without children * having rewarding relationships with children (nieces, nephews, friends' kids)	* form connections with other women, including women with disabilities who do not have children * affirm the right to reproductive self-determination in contacts with family, friends, and the community at large * obtain information on motherhood in the context of disability, including available resources and supports that may be accessed
Meso level	* being discouraged from having children by health-care professionals * not getting sufficient information that could expand choices * concerns that negotiating for formal supports with child care will be difficult and perhaps futile	* an information and support group organized by a women's health organization * a mothering conference which provided opportunities for information and networking	* in medical settings, convey positive messages to women and families re: reproductive choices and the right to self-determination * furnish women with information that can serve to expand their options * keep up-to-date on the most recent literature on parenting with a disability

Table 9.2 Women who are not mothers: risks, protective factors, and possible interventions – *continued*

	Risks	Protective factors	Possible interventions
Macro level	* societal messages that women with disabilities are undesirable as sexual partners * societal messages that such women are in need of care and cannot provide care * insufficient and inconsistent allocation of resources that could facilitate parenting tasks	* active participation in feminist and disability consumer groups that strive to expand images of womanhood and motherhood	* resist and strive to change restrictive and oppressive images of female sexuality and attractiveness * resist and strive to change restrictive images of motherhood

helped them forge a positive female identity apart from motherhood. One woman explicitly referred to this when she noted that she always knew that she didn't have to be a mother to be a worthwhile person. Having strong bonds with other women and being active in careers, grassroots organizations, and leisure activities, were also important protective factors. Receiving positive and affirming messages about their right to reproductive self determination was also conducive to well-being. The interplay between micro level risks and protective factors can be illustrated in the relationship between one participant and her parents. Although these parents were reluctant to acknowledge their daughter's sexuality in childhood and were ambivalent about her being in relationships as a young adult, they were described by the daughter as very loving and supportive. Now a mature woman, this participant attributes her parents' attitude to discriminatory and oppressive societal norms regarding sexuality and disability. Her love for her parents notwithstanding, she further asserted her right to choose her own course in life.

Risk factors at the meso level of analysis include a lack of information about reproductive options in the context of a particular disability. I include this as a meso level risk as it speaks to the void in information made available to women by physicians and other health-care professionals. In some cases, health-care professionals actively discouraged women from considering motherhood. An example in point is the physician who was eager to schedule an appointment for a tubal ligation for a young patient who was merely inquiring about her options. The disparity in knowledge about the reproductive health of disabled versus non-disabled women was noted in chapter 3 and can be detrimental to the well-being of women with disabilities. Participants were also uninformed as to what formal supports might be available to help them carry out childcare responsibilities. More importantly, they were pessimistic about their ability to receive this assistance in the current political climate of competition for scarce resources.

As I indicated in the previous section, risks at the meso level can often be counteracted or buffered by micro level protective factors. Women were critical of institutions and professionals who undermined their right to make choices. Some also demonstrated their intent to fight discriminatory practices, should they choose to pursue motherhood. One very specific meso level protective factor was a support group initiated by a women's health organization. The intent of this group was to provide an opportunity for women with disabilities to explore mothering-related issues in a supportive environment. Despite the initial intent that this group would serve women with and without children, it was attended by a small group of women who were interested in exploring motherhood. This eight-session information and support group covered various areas of interest such as childbirth options, assistance with child care, and behaviour management for parents with disabilities. Two participants who attended this group made reference to its positive impact on their lives and meaning-making. They especially noted the salutary effect of sharing stories and experiences with women who face similar issues. Involvement in feminist and disability grass-roots organizations can also serve an important protective function.

At the macro level, risk factors pertain to both cultural perceptions and allocation of resources. Images of women portrayed in print and electronic media, leave no doubt as to what is considered desirable in a woman. Images of women with disabilities rarely fit that picture. The prevailing culture of sexuality makes no room for the inclusion of women who do not fit the prototypical image. Experiences of rejection conveyed by study participants are reflective of the restrictive concept of the desirable woman. A poignant example of this was given by two participants in almost identical stories. Both recounted how men they met at nightclubs were interested in them so long as their disability was not apparent. The men promptly took their leave when the disability became obvious.

Societal portrayals of the ideal mother are similarly constricting. Almost without exception, mothers are portrayed as young, vibrant and with an unlimited reservoir of energy and strength. The invisibility of mothers with disabilities in the public eye is reflected in the meagre supply of resources available to them. The impact of scarce resources is felt in the relationship between women with disabilities and their families. Restrictive messages from parents reported by some participants, may well relate to the former's concern about the lack of practical and financial assistance accorded to parents with disabilities. In the absence of such resources, parents may envision themselves as having to provide such supports. This is an example whereby a risk at the micro level is exacerbated by dynamics operating at the macro level. Expanding images of motherhood to include women with disabilities, and expanding images of femininity to include women without children, may prove to be an important macro level protective factor.

The risk and protective factors outlined above can guide strategies and interventions at the three levels. The importance of connections with other women suggests that this is a worthy investment for women with disabilities. The definition of a family need not be restricted to spouse and children or even to blood relatives. Strong and lasting friendships often take on family-like characteristics and can be conducive to wellness. Affirming the right to reproductive self-determination is another important micro level strategy. Several participants gave examples of educating others within their families and communities about these issues. This awareness promotion can have a positive effect not only for the women themselves but also for future generations of women with disabilities. Beyond affirming their right to reproductive self-determination, disabled women without children should avail themselves to information pertaining to motherhood in the context of disability. For some participants, the decision to refrain from motherhood was intertwined with the scarcity of information available to them. Information can be a source of strength and should serve as the backdrop to whatever reproductive choice women ultimately make.

Meso level strategies and interventions are contingent upon empowering and respectful attitudes of health care and other professionals. Professionals who come in contact with parents of children with disabilities can convey positive messages about future prospects. In the case of girls with disabilities, this should include visions of mature women making informed choices about relationships and reproductive options. The potential that this can have in enhancing the self-determination of adult women was alluded to by two focus group participants. One woman lamented that within her own family and ethnic community, "It's difficult to get it into their heads that women with disabilities can become mothers". The other participant added: "My family needs some awareness...of the possibility of me having a child". Professionals can play an important role in facilitating this awareness. The importance of empowering messages notwithstanding, furnishing women with information that will expand their choices is within the purview and the responsibility of health care professionals. In the literature review I mentioned the recent interest and surge of information on reproductive issues for people with disabilities. It is imperative that information on research being conducted in large medical and rehabilitation centres be disseminated to and accessed by service providers.

Macro level protective factors have clear implications for macro level interventions. Changing restrictive and oppressive concepts of female sexuality and attractiveness must take place at a variety of settings such as schools, hospitals, and grass roots movements. Hegemonic notions of sexuality that permeate these institutions should be resisted and deconstructed. The same strategy of resistance should be applied to restrictive images of motherhood. Narrow conceptions of motherhood limit the scope of available resources. Different types of mothering require different types of resources. An expanded notion of motherhood would naturally lead to a wider definition of acceptable resources. This would give more meaning to the notion of reproductive choice for women with disabilities. "Choosing" to remain childless due to lack of appropriate supports might well be considered a contradiction in terms.

Mothers with disabilities and their families: risks, protective factors, and possible interventions

Data pertaining to mothers supports claims is made in the literature regarding the scarcity of information on pregnancy and disability (see Table 9.3). This was a micro level risk factor for some of the mothers who participated in the study. One woman noted how she longed to speak to another pregnant woman with a similar disability. Another pregnant participant had difficulty getting information even after contacting the umbrella organization associated with her disability. The birth of a baby precipitates other stressors for mothers. At the micro level, these stressors pertain to insufficient or inadequate supports from partners and others and to a generally weak informal support system. One mother described her daily routine whereby all of her time and energy was expended on meeting the needs of her baby. Another mother recounted the difficult period following her diagnosis. Having a toddler, an infant, and a recently diagnosed disability, support was not extended by her then-husband, family, or friends. Another micro level risk factor is the lack of communication between one young mother and the home makers who were contracted to help the family. I include this as a micro level risk due to the interpersonal nature of this variable. The inability to carry out certain activities with children was also noted by several participants and can be taxing for families.

The risk factors noted above notwithstanding, the data is rich with examples of micro level protective factors. At the personal level, these include creative alternatives for traditional methods of caring for babies, working with assistants while maintaining the role of primary care giver, and having strong communication and advocacy skills to obtain services for children. The interplay between micro level risk and protective factors is apparent in the case of the mother who found

Table 9.3 Mothers with disabilities and their families: risks, protective factors, and possible interventions

	Risks	Protective factors	Possible interventions
Micro Level	* having inadequate information on pregnancy and disability * insufficient or inadequate support from partners and others * expending all time and energy on meeting children's needs * inability to carry out certain activities with children * difficulties communicating with homemakers	* detailed planning for the baby's birth facilitated a smooth transition to motherhood * strong communication and self-advocacy skills * ability to find alternative methods of caring for baby or arranging for others to provide care * working with assistants while maintaining the role of mother contributing to the care and well-being of the children despite the limitations * having adequate support (mainly from partners and mothers) * having loving relationships with children * ability to communicate expectations, set boundaries and deal with behaviour problems	* strive to be an informed consumer of services and a proficient self-advocate * network with other mothers with disabilities for the sharing of information, expertise, and mutual support * develop effective parenting skills * seek and/or create alternative ways of caring for children, taking into consideration both the needs of the child and those of the mother
Meso Level	* pressure to terminate pregnancy * disability either under-emphasized or over-emphasized by physicians during pregnancy * unhelpful reactions/attitudes on	* professionals (nurses, physicians) who are encouraging, supportive, and focus on strengths * workers (such as nurturing assistants) who facilitate mothering	Disability consumer organizations should: * facilitate networking opportunities for mothers with disabilities and their families

Table 9.3 Mothers with disabilities and their families: risks, protective factors, and possible interventions – *continued*

	Risks	Protective factors	Possible interventions
	the maternity ward and by attendants * professional involvement (i.e. home makers, child protection workers) that is perceived as unhelpful by the mother * inaccessible schools and recreational facilities	* teachers who do not regard the parental disability as a detriment to the child * organizations and consumer groups that facilitate networking opportunities and help mothers become better consumer of services	* provide training opportunities that enhance mothers' abilities to be informed consumers of services * provide training opportunities for service providers and professionals that come in contact with mothers with disabilities and their families
Macro Level	* insufficient and inconsistent allocation of resources that could facilitate parenting tasks * professional and research literature which focuses on the risks of parental disability to children's well-being * societal attitudes which presume same as above * mother blaming in professional and research literature and in society at large	* having access to funded assistance with child care (as needed) * professional and research literature which focuses on conditions and contexts that promote wellness for mothers with disabilities and their families * changing trends in the professional literature in the above-mentioned direction * consequently, greater tolerance by the public for diverse ways of parenting and difference paths to wellness	* consumer organizations should strive to expand their mandate to include challenging unjust policies that have an adverse effect on mothers with disabilities and their families * feminist organizations should include mothers with disabilities in political and academic discourses on motherhood as well as actively lobby for resources that would meet the needs of these mothers and their families

herself newly diagnosed and devoid of informal supports. With an infant who was experiencing health problems in conjunction with her own failing health, this mother and her family were clearly at risk. Her ability to advocate and set in motion a host of health-enhancing formal supports was a crucial buffer in moderating a potentially overwhelming situation. This mother, and several others, emphasized their role in coordinating and directing the supports they were receiving. Hence, regardless of the extent of their disability or the activities with which they require assistance, they clearly function as parents. Other micro level protective factors include supportive spouses and assistance from extended family members, typically mothers.

The stories of mothers with disabilities are replete with examples of meso level risk factors. At the pregnancy phase, some physicians undermined the significance of the disability. One participant, now the mother of adult children, attributes the worsening of her condition to negligent physicians. As a very young and inexperienced recipient of health services, she did not think to question her physicians' judgment. Conversely, another participant switched physicians when she came across a similar attitude. A confident and mature woman and an informed consumer, this participant had the internal resources that served as a buffer against meso level risks. Another participant was advised and even pressured to "consider" an abortion by health-care professionals. Other meso level risk factors include negative experiences in the maternity ward and contacts with professionals (home makers, child protection workers) who were perceived as burdensome rather than supportive.

Meso level protective factors were also noted by participants. The same woman who encountered intrusive questioning in the maternity ward, also had positive experiences during her hospital stay. She spoke fondly of a nurse who facilitated her efforts to breast-feed and of a young doctor who expressed confidence in her ability to cope with the new situational demands. Another participant who faced multiple stressors, was encouraged by an affirming message from an occupational therapist. When she was feeling vulnerable and overwhelmed by the demands of motherhood, the therapist responded by pointing out how happy and well cared for the baby appeared. She further noted how impressed the professional team was with the mother's ability to cope. This affirming and empowering message had a positive impact which remained with this mother. Two mothers had funded assistants who helped them with child care. The assistants worked under the direction of the mothers in order to facilitate the latter's mothering tasks. Having had a number of such helpers over the years, both mothers reported consistently positive experiences. One mother who had a number of part time helpers, described a collaborative, family-like relationship between the assistants and the family.

The most pernicious and wide-ranging macro level risk factor is the insufficient and inconsistent allocation of resources. The presence or absence of financial and practical supports is determined by government priorities. Social policies set by elected officials shape the extent and quality of services available to citizens. Agencies operating at the meso level work within the financial parameters established by higher level officials. The political context within which workers make decisions affects their ability to render valuable services. Ultimately, what mothers with disabilities receive in the way of funded assistance, is directly related to the importance cabinet ministers ascribe to the well-being of this population. Therefore, one must examine the level of services available in light of prevailing social norms and resource allocation established by politicians and their helpers.

However removed from the public eye, offices where budget allocations are made have a direct and unrelenting impact on the lives of people experiencing vulnerability. As Prilleltensky has noted, when obscure legislative changes minimize benefits to disempowered groups, "we can't easily tell who is to blame, even though there is a definite human hand writing that legislation" (Prilleltensky, 1996, p. 315). Much like there is a human being producing these policies, there are real women and families suffering from their consequences. Two brief examples, one deriving from my research and the other from the experience of a community member, illustrate this notion. Both cases involve mothers who are independent as far as their own self care is concerned but are physically incapable of caring for young children unassisted. Both rely rather heavily on their personal support system in looking after their children. These mothers have been unsuccessful in their efforts to obtain funding for assistance with child care. Their goal was to secure some funding that would enable them to hire an assistant that would be at home with them rather than in their absence – much like the examples of the two participants who had such assistance. Ironically, having the ability to carry out their own self care unassisted, thwarts the likelihood that these mothers will receive the help they need in order to care for their children. One of the mothers had recently asked for short-term assistance with her toddler so that her husband could attend an out of town convention but was turned down. The other mother hoped to alleviate her heavy reliance on her own mother by getting some funded resources. Inability to access such resources runs the risk of eroding a rather solid informal support system by overtaxing it. A partner *should* be able to attend the occasional out of town convention and a grandmother should *not* be the sole source of help.

As can be expected, examples of macro level protective factors are few and far between. Two such examples are the families who had funded assistance which facilitated the mothers' caring tasks. While one mother received only a few hours of assistance a week, the other mother received supports that were significantly more extensive. Dissimilar contexts and family constellations likely account for this difference, as one mother had a wider informal network than the other. The allocation of services according to a global assessment of needs illustrates a constructive meso/macro level approach. It further illustrates the futility of making global assumptions about resources required by mothers with disabilities as a group. Rather, the need, and the consequent allocation of resources, should be determined by a multiplicity of factors. The mother's functional strengths and limitations and the availability of informal supports are but two examples of factors that need consideration.

Before shifting the focus to possible interventions, another macro level protective factor is briefly noted. In the literature review I critiqued professional and research writings that magnify the risks posed by parental disability, thereby perpetuating oppressive ideologies. Conversely, literature can be found which focuses on conditions and contexts that promote wellness for mothers with disabilities and their families. Just as the former can constitute a risk factor, the latter can have protective attributes. In addition to making a positive contribution to knowledge, such literature can foster tolerance by professionals and by the public at large for diverse ways of parenting and different paths to wellness.

The shrinking of the social safety net and fierce competition for dwindling resources has implication for strategies and interventions at all levels of analysis. Beginning with the micro level, mothers with disabilities who are in need of services and resources need to be strong self advocates. Examples from the research demonstrate the benefits of knowing how to advocate for oneself and one's family. The importance of being a persistent and determined consumer was articulated by one mother. In response to my question of what advice she would give to a disabled woman who wished to become a mother, this participant replied:

> You have to be strong in your commitment...you have to find out about resources and find people like myself who are willing to go the extra mile to help you...you have to fight for them (services) and not buy into other people's beliefs of you can't do this and you can't do that. Don't let other people's agenda be yours. Have your own agenda of what you want to do and stick to that even though many obstacles are put in your way. You have to find ways to overcome them. If I can't get in the front door I go in the side door. Or the back door. Or I create a door.

This forceful quote illustrates not only the importance of being a strong self advocate, but also the benefits that can be derived from collective action by people engaged in a same cause. Furthermore, networking with other mothers with disabilities can serve an important supportive function. Mothers can also learn from the experience of others who dealt with similar challenges and circumstances.

Another important micro level strength, and one which is related to advocacy, is the ability to clearly communicate needs and priorities. The participant who reported negative experiences with homemakers may have benefited from assistance in communicating with her helpers. Data gathered from this participant suggests a wide yet unarticulated rift between her conception of a homemaker and that of the assistant.

It is also important to pay attention to the development of effective parenting skills. Establishing clear communication and consistent boundaries with children from an early age facilitate a favourable and cohesive family climate. Several participants showed a good deal of ingenuity in fostering an enjoyable yet manageable family atmosphere. These mothers can be a source of knowledge and inspiration to disabled and non-disabled mothers alike. The benefit of mutual exchange of expertise underscores, once again, the need for networking and peer support.

Forming networks that connect mothers with disabilities is not a simple task. Meso level service organizations and consumer groups can do much to aid in the formation of such networks. Efforts of this nature have been launched with some success by consumer organizations like disabled women's organizations and centers for independent living. Some of their efforts include creating a registry for disabled parents and hosting support meetings in accessible locations. The unquestionable merit of such initiatives notwithstanding, these programs haven't always struck a responsive cord in their intended audience. It is quite likely that consumers expect from these groups more than what the organizations can provide in the current financial climate. Expectations of practical help by consumers, cannot always be satisfied by the agencies. An example in point is the unsuccessful attempts of some mothers to receive funded assistance with child care. Although consumer organizations can help such mothers manoeuvre their way through bureaucracies, there is little they can offer by way of material assistance. Once again we witness at the meso level, the impact of macro level cut-backs.

The limitations noted above notwithstanding, I have witnessed through my involvement with several consumer organizations how helpful some of their initiatives really are. In addition to the important role they play in helping people become more informed consumers of services, they also offer training to professionals in meso level organizations. In doing so, they reinforce the notion that change ought to take place not only within the recipient, but also within the provider of services. These initiatives should be continued and extended to meet the particular needs and challenges of parents with disabilities.

Consumer organizations have a mandate to develop and implement interventions at the micro and meso levels. Extending their mandate to macro level strategies may be a politically contentious issue. As macro level efforts may include challenging policies set by those who fund them, these organizations walk a delicate tight rope. The unquestionable desire to help consumers may be at odds with the limited mandates set by funders. Given the constraints experienced by these organizations, it is important that their efforts be supported by independent and progressive groups. Independence from governments affords social action bodies an opportunity to challenge unfair policies without apprehension of jeopardizing funding. Feminist organizations have a clear role to play in promoting the well being of women with disabilities and their families. Along with disability consumer groups, they must insist on the inclusion of mothers with disabilities in political and academic discourses on motherhood.

Concluding comments

The thrust of this discussion has been the promotion of wellness for women and girls with physical disabilities. As I bring this book to a close, I would like to switch the focus and remind the reader of the potential of this group of women to enhance the wellness of others. Beyond their ability to nurture children and families, women with disabilities make significant and valuable contributions to other marginalized groups and to society at large. I need only scan my data to find examples of such contributions. There is the trailblazer who advocated for supported living in the community and for nurturing assistance. Her efforts paved the road for other people with disabilities. There is the woman who knew that she had to leave home in order to protect her spirit. The plight she went through as a child was a driving force in choosing a helping profession: "I had made a promise to myself that some day I would get into something where I can help another person. Help another disabled child who was going through those struggles". There is the young mother who, in spite of the stressors in her own life, made time for volunteer work with teens at risk. And there is the mother of adult children who dedicates most of her time and energy to volunteer work: "I though that I've got to do something with my life…I just had to do something, I couldn't just waste away and not mean anything. Life has to mean something." Indeed, the stories of these women underscore how valuable their lives are, not only for themselves and their loved ones, but also for the rest of us.

These snippets of participants' lives and meaning-making give credence to the centrality of the concept of resilience discussed earlier. However, as one of the leading forces in resilience research reminds us, there is both great promise and danger in this concept (Garmezy, 1994). The danger lies in the sudden popularity of the concept of resilience. Risk has its base in epidemiology; resilience has its base in drama. The drama is that of the "American dream, the Horatio Alger legend – the mistaken view that any and all could succeed were they to work hard. These are myths that need rejection" (p. 13). The dramatic stories of courage and determination I was privileged to collect in the process of the research, should not lead us to romanticize the notion of resilience. Despite the inspirational value of these stories, Garmezy's caveat should not go unheeded. Our attention should not be diverted from the potentially deleterious consequences of sustained exposure to disempowering living conditions. The struggle of women with disabilities is intimately tied with the struggle for social justice. For as long as governments have their policies set by powerful interest groups concerned with economics more than with human needs, the welfare of people with disabilities and other vulnerable groups will continue to be at risk (Nelson & Prilleltensky, 2004; Prilleltensky & Nelson, 2002).

Striving for social justice for a marginalized group requires that its members be given a voice in the struggle. This research afforded a voice only to a segment of women with disabilities. For the most part, women who participated in my study are well-educated professional women who lead productive lives. None are members of a visible minority or belong to a lesbian community. Thus, the research is limited in its ability to explore the intersection of gender and disability with other social constructs such as race and sexual orientation. Also unexplored are the implications of this research to women who live with different types of disabilities. These limitations notwithstanding, the findings and framework for analysis and interventions articulated in the study may prove beneficial to future researchers.

References

Abberly, P. (1993). Disabled people and "normality". In J. Swain, V. Finkelstein, S. French & M. Oliver (eds), *Disabling barriers – enabling environments* (pp. 107–115). London: Sage.

Achilles, R. (1990). Desperately seeking babies: New technologies of hope and despair. In K. Arnup, A. Levesque & R. R. Pierson (eds), *Delivering motherhood: Maternal ideologies and practices in the 19th and 20th centuries* (pp. 284–312). London: Routledge.

Acker, J., Barry, K. & Esseveld, J. (1991). Objectivity and truth: Problems in doing feminist research. In M. M. Fonow & J. A. Cook (eds), *Beyond methodology: Feminist scholarship as lived research* (pp. 133–153). Indianapolis: Indiana University Press.

Aldridge, J. & Becker, S. (1993). Punishing children for caring. *Children and Society, 7*(4), 277–278.

Aldridge, J. & Becker, S. (1996). Disability rights and the denial of young carers: The dangers of zero-sum arguments. *Critical Social Policy, 48*(16), 55–76.

Alvesson, M. & Sköldberg, K. (2000). *Reflexive methodology: New vistas for qualitative research*. London: Sage.

American Psychologist (2003). Fundamental challenges in disability and rehabilitation (Special issue). *American Psychologist, 58*(4).

Amundson, R. (2000). Biological normality and the ADA. In L. Francis & A. Silvers (eds), *Americans with disabilities: Exploring implications of the law for individuals and institutions* (pp. 102–110). New York: Routledge.

Andrews, L. & Hibbert, M. (2000). Courts and wrongful births: Can disability itself be viewed as a legal wrong? In L. Francis & A. Silvers (eds), *Americans with disabilities: Exploring implications of the law for individuals and institutions* (pp. 283–292). New York: Routledge.

Armstrong, P. (1999). A remarkable woman. In M. Wates & R. Jade (eds), *Bigger than the sky: Disabled women on parenting* (pp. 164–165). London: The Women's Press.

Asch, A. (2000). Why I haven't changed my mind about prenatal diagnosis: Reflections and refinement. In E. Parens & A. Asch (eds), *Prenatal testing and disability rights* (pp. 234–258). Washington, D.C.: Georgetown University Press.

Asch, A. & Fine, M. (1988). Introduction: Beyond pedestals. In M. Fine & A. Asch (eds), *Women with disabilities: Essays in psychology, culture, and politics* (pp. 1–37). Philadelphia: Temple University Press.

Asch, A., Rousso, H. & Jefferies, T. (2001). Beyond pedestals: The lives of girls and women with disabilities. In H. Rousso & M. Wehmeyer (eds), *Double jeopardy: Addressing gender equity is special education* (pp. 13–48). Albany, NY: State University of New York Press.

Baily, M. A. (2000). Why I had amniocenteisis. In E. Parens & A. Asch (eds), *Prenatal testing and disability rights* (pp. 64–71). Washington, D.C.: Georgetown University Press.

Barnes, C., Mercer, M. & Shakespeare, T. (1999). *Exploring disability: A sociological introduction.* Cambridge: Polity Press.

Barnes, C. (1998). The social model of disability: A sociological phenomenon ignored by sociologists? In T. Shakespeare (ed.), *The disability reader: Social science perspectives* (pp. 65–78). London: Cassell.

Barton, L. (1996). Sociology and disability: Some emerging issues. In L. Barton (ed.), *Disability & society: Emerging issues and insights* (pp. 3–17). London: Longman.

Barton, L. (1998). Sociology, disability studies, and education: Some observations. In T. Shakespeare (ed.), *The disability reader: Social science perspectives* (pp. 53–64). London: Cassell.

Batavia, A. (2000). Ten years later: The ADA and the future of disability policy. In L. Francis & A. Silvers (eds), *Americans with disabilities: Exploring implications of the law for individuals and institutions* (pp. 283–292). New York: Routledge.

Begum, N. (1992). Disabled women and the feminist agenda. *Feminist Review, 40* (Spring), pp. 70–84.

Belohorec, A. & Kilcuchi, J. (1985, March). How do you mother when you are disabled? *The Canadian Nurse,* pp. 32–35.

Bergman, A. (1993, May/June). Yard work yes, child care no. *Disability Rag and Resource,* pp. 7–8.

Bertaux, D. (1981). From the life-history approach to the transformation of sociological practice. In D. Bertaux (ed.), *Biography and society: The life history approach in the social sciences.* Beverly Hills, CA: Sage.

Bhagwanji, Y., Thomas, D., Bennett, T., Stillwell, M. & Allison, A. (1998). *Relationships with parents with disabilities: Perceptions and training needs of Head Start staff.* QIC-D: University of Illinois.

Blackford, K. (1990). A different parent. *Healthsharing,* pp. 20–25.

Blackford, K. (1999). A child's growing up with a parent who has Multiple Sclerosis: Theories and experiences. *Disability & Society, 14*(5), 673–685.

Blumberg, L. (1994a, January/February). Eugenics vs. reproductive choice. *The Disability Rag and Resource,* pp. 3–11.

Blumberg, L. (1994b). The politics of prenatal testing and selective abortion. *Sexuality and Disability, 12*(2), 135–153.

Boston Women's Health Book Collective, 1998. *Our bodies, ourselves for the new century.* New York: Touchstone.

Brisenden, S. (1998). Independent living and the medical model of disability. In T. Shakespeare (ed.), *The disability reader: Social science perspectives* (pp. 20–27). London: Cassell.

Brown, L. S. (1994). *Subversive dialogues: Theory in feminist therapy.* New York: Basic Books.

Brydon-Miller, M. (2001). Education, research, and action: Theory and methods of participatory action research. In D. L. Tolman & M. Brydon-Miller (eds), *From subjects to subjectivities: A handbook of interpretive and participatory methods* (pp. 76–89). New York: New York University Press.

Buck, F. M. & Hohmann, G. W. (1981). Personality, behavior, values, and family relations of children of fathers with spinal cord injury. *Archives of Physical Medical Rehabilitation, 62,* 432–438.

Buck, F. M. & Hohmann, G. W. (1982). Child adjustment as related to severity of paternal disability. *Archives of Physical Medical Rehabilitation, 63,* 249–253.

Bury, M. (1997). *Health and illness in a changing society*. London: Routledge.

Campbell-Earl, L. (1993, May/June). A Ramp to parenting. *Disability Rag and Resource*, pp. 10–11.

Campbell, R. & Wasco, S. M. (2000). Feminist approaches to social science: Epistemological and methodological tenets. *American Journal of Community Psychology, 28*, 773–791.

Campion, M. J. (1995). *Who's fit to be a parent?* London: Routledge.

Clandinin, D. J. & Connelly, F. M. (1994). Personal experience methods. In N. Denzin & Y. Lincoln (eds), *Handbook of qualitative research* (pp. 1–27). Thousand Oaks, CA: Sage.

Cole, A. L. (1991). Interviewing for life history: A process of ongoing negotiation. In I. F. Goodson & J. M. Mangan (eds), *Qualitative educational research studies: Methodologies in transition* (pp. 185–208). London, Ontario: RUCCUS.

Cole, A. L. (1994). *Doing life history: In theory and in practice*. Paper presented at the Annual meeting of the American Educational Research Association, New Orleans, LA.

Cole, A. L. & Knowles, J. G. (1995). Methods and issues in a life history approach to self-study. In T. Russell & F. Korthagen (eds), *Teachers who teach teachers: Reflections on teacher education*. London: Falmer Press.

Cole, S. S. & Cole, T. M. (1993). Sexuality, disability, and reproductive issues through the lifespan. *Sexuality and Disability, 11*(3), 189–205.

Conine, T., Carty, E. & Wood-Johnson, F. (1987). Nature and source of information received by primiparas with rheumatoid arthritis on preventive maternal and child care. *Canadian Journal of Public Health, 78*(6), 393–397.

Conine, T., Carty, E. & Wood-Johnson, F. (1986). Provision of preventive maternal health care and childbirth education for disabled women. *Canadian Journal of Public Health, 77*, 123–127.

Connelly, F. M. & Clandinin, D. J. (1990). Stories of experience and narrative inquiry. *Educational Researcher, 19*(5), 2–14.

Consortium on the School-based promotion of social competence (1994). The school-based promotion of social competence: Theory, research, practice, and policy. In R. J. Haggerty, L. R. Sherrod, N. Garmezy & M. Rutter (eds), *Stress, risk, and resilience in children and adolescents* (pp. 268–316). New York: Cambridge University Press.

Contreras, A. 1999. Discussing sexuality with disabled girls. In M. Wates & R. Jade (eds), *Bigger than the sky: Disabled women on parenting* (pp. 23–24). London: The Women's Press.

Cowen, E. L. (1991). In pursuit of wellness. *American Psychologist, 46*, 404–408.

Cowen, E. L. (1994). The enhancement of psychological wellness: Challenges and opportunities. *American Journal of Community Psychology, 22*, 149–179.

Cowen, E. L. (1996). The ontogenesis of primary prevention: Lengthy strides and stubbed toes. *American Journal of Community Pyschology, 24*, 235–249.

Crewe, N. (1993). Spousal relationships and disability. In F. B. Haseltine, S. S. Cole & D. B. Grey (eds), *Reproductive issues for persons with physical disabilities* (pp. 142–151). Baltimore: Paul H. Brooks Publishing Co.

Crist, P. (1993). Contingent interaction during work and play tasks for mothers with Multiple Sclerosis and their daughters. *American Journal of Occupational Therapy, 47*(2), 121–131.

Crossley, M. L. (2000). *Introducing narrative psychology: Self, trauma and the construction of meaning.* Buckingham: Open University Press.

Crow, L. (1996). Including all of our lives: Renewing the social model of disability. In J. Morris (ed.), *Encounters with strangers: Feminism and disability* (pp. 206–226). London: The Women's Press.

Dally, J. (1999). In M. Wates & R. Jade (eds), *Bigger than the sky: Disabled women on parenting* (pp. 57–63). London: The Women's Press.

Daniluk, J. (1998). *Women's sexuality across the life span: Challenging myths, creating meanings.* New York: The Guilford Press.

Danziger, K. & Dzinas, K. (1997). How psychology got its variables. *Canadian Psychology, 38,* 43–48.

Davis, L. (2000). Go to the margins of the class: Hate crimes and disability. In L. Francis & A. Silvers (eds), *Americans with disabilities: Exploring implications of the law for individuals and institutions* (pp. 283–292). New York: Routledge.

Denzin, N. K. & Lincoln, Y. S. (1994). Introduction: Entering the field of qualitative research. In N. K. Denzin & Y. S. Lincoln (eds), *Handbook of qualitative research* (pp. 1–18). London: Sage.

Dick Gomez, S. (1999). Intervals. In M. Wates & R. Jade (eds), *Bigger than the sky: Disabled women on parenting* (pp. 171–175). London: The Women's Press.

Ducharme, S. (1993). From the editor. *Sexuality and Disability, 11*(3), 185–187.

Duffy, M. (1996). Making choices. In L. Keith (ed.), *"What happened to you?"* (p. 29). New York: The New Press.

Edwards, R. (1993). An education in interviewing: Placing the researcher and the researched. In C. M. Renzetti & R. M. Lee (eds), *Researching sensitive topics.* Newbury Park, CA: Sage.

Esten, G. & Willmott, L. (1993). Double bind messages: The effects of attitudes towards disability on therapy. *Women & Therapy, 14*(4), 29–41.

Ferguson, P. M., Gartner, A. & Lipsky, D. K. (2000). The experience of disability in families: A synthesis of research and parent narratives. In E. Parens & A. Asch (eds), *Prenatal testing and disability rights* (pp. 72–94). Washington, D.C.: Georgetown University Press.

Fawcett, B. (2000). *Feminist perspectives on disability.* London: Prentice Hall.

Fawcett, S. B., White, G. W., Balcazar, F. E., Suarez-Balcazar, Y., Mathews, R. M., Pain-Andrews, A., Sequins, T. & Smith, J. F. (1994). A contextual behavioral model of empowerment: Case studies involving people with disabilities. *American Journal of Community Psychology, 22,* 471–496.

Fine, M. (1992). *Disruptive voices: The possibilities of feminist research.* Ann Arbor: University of Michigan Press.

Fine, M. & Asch, A. (1988). Disabled women: Sexism without the pedestal. In M. Deegan & N. Brooks (eds), *Women and disability: The double handicap.* (pp. 6–22). New Brunswick, NJ: Transaction Books.

Finger, A. (1990). *Past due: A story of disability, pregnancy, and birth.* Seattle, WA: The Seal Press.

Finger, A. (1993). Mothers with disabilities. In F. B. Haseltine, S. S. Cole & D. B. Gray (eds), *Reproductive issues for persons with physical disabilities* (pp. 119–124). Baltimore: Paul H. Brooks Publishing Co.

Finkelstein, V. (1998). Emancipating disability studies. In T. Shakespeare (ed.), *The disability reader: Social science perspectives* (pp. 28–49). London: Cassell.

Flyvbjerg, B. (2001). *Making social science matter: Why social inquiry fails and how it can succeed again*. New York, NY: Cambridge University Press.

Francis & A. Silvers (eds), *Americans with disabilities: Exploring implications of the law for individuals and institutions* (pp. 331–341). New York: Routledge.

Francis, L. & Silvers, A. (2000). Achieving the right to live in the world: Americans with disabilities and the civil rights tradition. In L. Francis & A. Silvers (eds), *Americans with disabilities: Exploring implications of the law for individuals and institutions* (xiii–xxx). New York: Routledge.

Franzblau, S. H. (1996). Social Darwinian influences on conceptions of marriage, sex, and motherhood. *Journal of Primary Prevention, 17*(1), 47–73.

French, S. (1993). Disability, impairment or something in between? In J. Swain, V. Finkelstein, S. French & M. Oliver (eds), *Disabling barriers – enabling environments* (pp. 17–25). London: Sage Publications.

Freire, P. (1970). *Pedagogy of the oppressed*. New York: Continuum.

Garmezy, N. (1994). Reflections and commentary on risk, resilience, and development. In R. J. Haggerty, L. R. Sherrod, N. Garmezy & M. Rutter (eds), *Stress, risk, and resilience in children and adolescents* (pp. 1–18). New York: Cambridge University Press.

Gill, C. (1996a). Becoming visible: Personal health experiences of women with disabilities. In D. M. Krotoski, M. A. Nosek & M. A. Turk (eds), *Women with physical disabilities: Achieving and maintaining health and well-being* (pp. 5–15). Baltimore: Paul H. Brooks Publishing Co.

Gill, C. (1996b). Dating and relationship issues. *Sexuality and Disability, 14*(3), 183–190.

Gill, C., Kewman, D. & Brannon, R. (2003). Transforming psychological practice and society: Policies that reflect the new paradigm. *American Psychologist, 58*(4), 305–312.

Gillam, L. (1999). Prenatal diagnosis and discrimination against the disabled. *Journal of Medical Ethics, 25*(2), 163–171.

Gilligan, C. (1982). *In a different voice: psychological theory and women's development*. Cambridge, MA: Harvard University Press.

Glesne, C. & Peshkin, A. (1992). *Becoming qualitative researchers*. White Plains, NY: Longman.

Goodley, D. (1996). Tales of hidden lives: A critical examination of life history research with people who have learning difficulties. *Disability and Society, 11*(3), 333–348.

Goodman, M. (1994). *Mothers' pride and others' prejudice*. London, UK: Maternity Alliance.

Goodson, I. F. (1992). Studying teachers' lives: Problems and possibilities. In I. F. Goodson (eds), *Studying teachers' lives* (pp. 234–249). London, UK: Routledge.

Gore, S. & Eckenrode, J. (1994). Context and process in research on risk and resilience. In R. J. Haggerty, L. R. Sherrod, N. Garmezy & M. Rutter (eds), *Stress, risk, and resilience in children and adolescents* (pp. 19–63). New York: Sage.

Graves, W. H. (1993). Future directions in research and training in reproductive issues for persons with physical disabilities. In F. B. Haseltine, S. S. Cole & D. B. Grey (eds), *Reproductive issues for persons with physical disabilities* (pp. 333–338). Baltimore: Paul H. Brooks Publishing Co.

Greer, B. G. (1985). Children of physically disabled parents: Some thoughts, facts and hypotheses. In S. K. Thurman (ed.), *Children of handicapped parents: Research and clinical perspectives.* (pp. 131–143). Orlando, Fla: Academic Press.

Guba, E. G. & Lincoln, Y. S. (1994). Competing paradigms in qualitative research. In N. K. Denzin & Y. S. Lincoln (eds), *Handbook of qualitative research* (pp. 105–117). London: Sage.

Haggerty, R. J., Sherrod, L. R., Garmezy, N. & Rutter, M. (eds) (1994). *Stress, risk, and resilience in children and adolescents.* New York: Cambridge University Press.

Hammer Burns, L. & Covington, S. N. (1999). Psychology of Infertility. In L. Hammer Burns & S. N. Covington (eds), *Infertility counseling: A comprehensive handbook for clinicians* (pp. 3–25). New York: The Parthenon Publishing Group.

Harris, J. (2000). Is there a coherent social conception of disability? *Journal of Medical Ethics, 26*(2), 95–100.

Hird, M. J. & Abshoff, K. (2000). Women without children: A contradiction in terms? *Journal of Comparative Family Studies, 31*(3), 347–376.

Holland, J. & Ramazanoglu, C. (1994). Coming to conclusions: Power and interpretation in researching young women's sexuality. In M. Maynard & J. Purvis (eds), *Researching women's lives from a feminist perspective* (pp. 125–148). London, UK: Taylor & Francis.

Hooyman, N. R. & Goneya, J. (1995). *Feminist perspectives on family care: Policies for gender justice.* London: Sage.

Hough, E. E., Lewis, F. M. & Woods, N. F. (1991). Family response to mother's chronic illness: Case studies of well and poorly adjusted families. *Western Journal of Nursing Research, 13*(5), 568–596.

Howe, K. R. (1992). Getting over the quantitative-qualitative debate. *American Journal of Education*(February), 236–256.

Howland, C. & Rinalta, D. (2001). Dating behaviors of women with physical disabilities. *Sexuality and Disability, 19*(1), 41–70.

Hunt, D. (1992). *The renewal of personal energy.* Toronto: OISE Press.

Illingworth, P. & Parmet, W. (2000). Positively disabled: The relationship between the definition of disability and rights under the ADA. In L. Francis & A. Silvers (eds), *Americans with disabilities: Exploring implications of the law for individuals and institutions* (pp. 3–17). New York: Routledge.

Ireland, M. S. (1992). *Reconceiving women: Separating motherhood from female identity.* New York: Guilford Press.

Jones, R. K. & Brayfield, A. (1997). Life's greatest joy? European attitudes toward the centrality of children. *Social Forces, 75*(4), 1239–1270.

Kallianes, V. & Rubenfeld, P. (1997). Disabled women and reproductive rights. *Disability & Society, 12*(2), 203–221.

Keith, L. (1992). Who cares wins? Women, caring and disability. *Disability, Handicap & Society, 7*(2), 167–175.

Keith, L. (1996). Encounters with strangers: The public's response to disabled women and how this affects our sense of self. In J. Morris (ed.), *Encounters with strangers: Feminism and disability* (pp. 69–88). London: The Women's Press.

Keith, L. & Morris, J. (1996). Easy targets: A disability rights perspective on the "children as carers" debate. In J. Morris (ed.), *Encounters with strangers: Feminism and disability* (pp. 89–115). London: The Women's Press.

Kelley, S., Sikka, A. & Venkatesan, S. (1997). A review of research on parental disability: Implications for research and counselling. *Rehabilitation Counseling Bulletin*, 41(2), 105–116.

Kelly, L., Burton, S. & Regan, L. (1994). Researching women's lives or studying women's oppression? Reflections on what constitutes feminist research. In M. Maynard & J. Purvis (eds), *Researching women's lives from a feminist perspective* (pp. 27–48). London, UK: Taylor & Francis.

Kennedy, K. M. & Bush, D. F. (1979). Counselling the children of handicapped parents. *Personnel and Guidance Journal*, 58(4), 267–270.

Kent, D. (2000). Somewhere a mockingbird. In E. Parens & A. Asch (eds), *Prenatal testing and disability rights* (pp. 57–63). Washington, D.C.: Georgetown University Press.

Kewman, D., Warschausky, S., Engel, L. & Warzak, W. (1997). Sexual development of children and adolescents. In M. Sipski & C. Alexander (eds), *Sexual function in people with disability and chronic illness: A health professional's guide* (355–378). Gaithersburg, MD: Aspin Publishers.

Keye, W. R. (1999). Medical aspects of infertility for the counselor. In L. Hammer Burns & S. N. Covington (eds), *Infertility counseling: A comprehensive handbook for clinicians* (pp. 27–46). New York: The Parthenon Publishing Group.

Killoran, C. (1994). Women with disabilities having children: It's our right too. *Disability and Sexuality*, 12(2), 121–127.

Kincheloe, J. L. & McLaren, P. L. (1994). Rethinking critical theory and qualitative research. In N. K. Denzin & Y. S. Lincoln (eds), *Handbook of qualitative research* (pp. 138–157). London: Sage.

Kirshbaum, M. (1996). Mothers with physical disabilities. In D. M. Krotoski, M. A. Nosek & M. A. Turk (eds), *Women with physical disabilities: Achieving and maintaining health and well-being*. Baltimore: Paul Brooks Publishing.

Kirshbaum, M. & Olkin, R. (2002). Parents with physical, systemic, or visual disabilities. *Sexuality & Disability*, 20(1), 65–80.

Kocher, M. (1994). Mothers with disabilities. *Sexuality and Disability*, 12(2), 127–133.

Kopala, B. (1989). Mothers with impaired mobility speak out. *Topics in Clinical Nursing*, 14, 115–119.

Krotoski, D. M., Nosek, M. A. & Turk, M. A. (1996). *Women with physical disabilities: Achieving and maintaining health and well-being*. Baltimore: Paul Brooks Publishing.

Krueger, R. (1988). *Focus groups: A practical guide for applied research*. Newbury Park, CA: Sage.

Lather, P. (1986). Research: Between a rock and a soft place. *Interchange*, 17(4), 63–84.

Lather, P. (1991). *Getting smart: Feminist research and pedagogy with/in the postmodern*. New York: Routledge.

LeClere, F. B. & Kowalewski, B. M. (1994). Disability in the family: The effects on children's well-being. *Journal-of-Marriage-and-the-Family*, 56(2), 457–468.

Lemme, B. (2003). *Development in adulthood*. Boston: Allyn and Bacon.

Letherby, G. & Williams, C. (1999). Non-motherhood: Ambivalent autobiographies. Feminist Studies, 25(3), 719–728.

Lewis, F. M., Woods, N. F., Hough, E. E. & Bensley, L. S. (1989). The family's functioning with chronic illness in the mother: The spouse's perspective. *Social Science Medicine*, 29(11), 1261–1269.

Linton, S. (1998). *Claiming disability: Knowledge and identity.* New York: New York University Press.

Lipson, J. G. & Rogers, J. G. (2000). Pregnancy, birth, and disability: Women's health care experiences. *Health Care for Women International, 21*(1), 11–26.

Lisi, D. (1993). Found voices: Women, disability, and cultural transformation. *Women and Therapy, 14*(4), 195–209.

Lisle, L. (1996). *Without child.* New York: Ballantine Books.

Litwinowitcz, J. (1999). In my mind's eye: I. In M. Wates & R. Jade (eds), *Bigger than the sky: Disabled women on parenting* (pp. 29–33). London: The Women's Press.

Livneh, H. (2001). Psychosocial Adaptation to Chronic Illness and Disability: A conceptual framework. *Rehabilitation Counseling Bulletin, 44*(3): 151–160

Livneh, H. & Antonak, R. (1997). *Psychosocial adaptation to chronic illness and disability.* Maryland: Aspen Publishing.

Livneh, H. & Wilson, L. (2003). Coping strategies as predictors and mediators of disability-related variables and psychosocial adaptation: An exploratory investigation. *Rehabilitation Counseling Bulletin, 46*(4), 194–208.

Lloyd, M. (1992). Does she boil eggs? Towards a feminist model of disability. *Disability, Handicap and Society, 7*(3), 207–221.

Lloyd, M. (2001). The politics of disability and feminism: Discord or synthesis? *Sociology, 35*(3), 715–723.

Lonsdale, S. (1990). *Women and disability* (first ed.). New York: St. Martin's Press.

Lord, J. & Hutchison, P. (1993). The process of empowerment: Implications for theory and practice. *Canadian Journal of Community Mental Health, 12*(1), 5–22.

Magolda, P. M. & Robinson, B. M. (1993). *Doing harm: Unintended consequences of fieldwork.* Paper presented at the meeting of the American Educational Research Association, Atlanta, Georgia.

Marshall, C. & Rossman, G. B. (1989). *Designing qualitative research.* Newbury Park, CA: Sage.

Mason, M. (1999). Reclamation. In M. Wates & R. Jade (eds), *Bigger than the sky: Disabled women on parenting* (pp. 89–93). London: The Women's Press.

Mathews, J. (1992). *A mother's touch.* New York: Holt.

Marks, D. (1999). *Disability: Controversial debates and psychosocial perspectives.* New York: Routledge.

Maynard, M. (1994). Methods, practice and epistemology: The debate about feminism and research. In M. Maynard & J. Purvis (eds), *Researching women's lives from a feminist perspective* (pp. 10–26). London, UK: Taylor & Francis.

Maynard, M. & Purvis, J. (1994). Doing feminist research. In M. Maynard & J. Purvis (eds), *Researching women's lives from a feminist perspective* (pp. 1–8). London, UK: Taylor & Francis.

McEwan Carty, E., Conine, T. & Hall, L. (1990). Comprehensive health promotion for the pregnant woman who is disabled. *Journal of Nurse Midwifery, 35*(3), 133–142.

Meadow-Orlans, K. P. (2002). Parenting with a sensory or physical disability. In M. H. Bornstein (ed.), Handbook of Parenting, Volume IV. Social conditions and applied parenting. 7 New Jersey: Lawrence Erlbaum Associates Publishers.

Measor, L. (1985). Interviewing: A strategy in qualitative research. In R. Burgess (ed.), *Strategies of educational research* (pp. 55–77). London, UK: Falmer Press.

Melia, R., Pledger, C. & Wilson, R. (2003). Disability and rehabilitation research: Opportunities for participation, collaboration, and extramural funding for psychologists. *American Psychologist, 58*(4), 285–288.

Merriam, S. B. (1988). *Case study research in education*. San Francisco. Jossey-Bass.

Miller, B. (1999). Promoting healthy function and development in chronically ill children: A primary care approach. In R. Marinelli & A. Dell Orto (eds), *The psychological and social impact of disability* (pp. 67–85). New York: Springer Publishing.

Milligan, M. & Neufeldt, A. (2001). The myth of sexuality: A survey of social and empirical evidence. *Sexuality and Disability, 19*(2), 91–109.

Morgan, G. & Smircich, L. (1980). The case for qualitative research. *Academy of Management Review, 5*(4), 491–500.

Morris, J. (1991). *Pride against prejudice: Transforming attitudes to disability*. London: The Women's Press.

Morris, J. (1992). Personal and political: A feminist perspective on researching physical disability. *Disability, Handicap and Society, 7*(2), 157–166.

Morris, J. (1993). *Independent lives? Community care and disabled people*. London: Macmillan Press LTD.

Morris, J. (1996). Introduction. In J. Morris (ed.), *Encounters with strangers: Feminism and disability* (pp. 1–16). London: The Women's Press.

Morris, J. (2001). Impairment and Disability: Constructing an Ethics of Care That Promotes Human Rights. *Hypatia, 16*(4), pp. 1–16.

Moustakas, C. (1994). *Phenomenological research methods*. Thousand Oaks, CA: Sage.

Murray, M. & Chamberlin, K. (eds) (1999). *Qualitative health psychology: Theories and methods*. London: Sage.

Nelson, G. & Lord, J. (1996). *New paradigms, new partnerships: Research/action with people with disabilities*. Paper presented at the meeting of the American Psychological Association, Toronto, ON.

Nelson, G. & Prilleltensky, I. (2004). *Community psychology: In pursuit of liberation and well-being*. New York: Palgrave Macmillan.

Nelson, G., Prilleltensky, I. & Peters, R. DeV. (2003). Prevention and mental health promotion in the community. In W. L. Marshall & P. Firestone, *Abnormal psychology: Perspectives* (2nd ed.). Scarborough: Prentice Hall, Allyn and Bacon Canada.

New Mobility (www.newmobility.com)

Nosek, M. (1996a). Wellness among women with physical disabilities. *Sexuality and Disability, 14*(3), 165–181.

Nosek, M. (1996b). Sexuality and reproductive health. In D. M. Krotoski, M. A. Nosek & M. A. Turk (eds), *Women with physical disabilities: Achieving and maintaining health and well-being* (pp. 63–67). Baltimore: Paul H. Brooks Publishing Co.

Nosek, M. (1996c). Sexual abuse of women with physical disabilities. In D. M. Krotoski, M. A. Nosek & M. A. Turk (eds), *Women with physical disabilities: Achieving and maintaining health and well-being* (pp. 153–173). Baltimore: Paul H. Brooks Publishing Co.

Nosek, M., Howland, B., Rinalta, D., Young, M. & Chanpong, M. (2001). National study of women with physical disabilities: Final report. *Sexuality and Disability, 19*(1), 5–39.

Nosek, M. & Hughes, R. (2001). Psychosocial aspects of sense of self in women with physical disabilities. *Journal of Rehabilitation, 67*(1), 20–25.

Oakley, A. (1990). A case of maternity: Paradigms of women as maternity cases. In J. O'Barr, D. Pope & M. Wyer (eds), *Ties that bind: Essays on motherhood and patriarchy* (pp. 61–85). Chicago: University of Chicago Press.

O'Barr, J., Pope, D. & Wyer, M. (1990). Introduction. In J. O'Barr, D. Pope & M. Wyer (eds), *Ties that bind: Essays on mothering and patriarchy* (pp. 1–14). Chicago: University of Chicago Press.

Ochberg, R. L. (1994). Life stories and storied lives. *The Narrative Study of Lives, 2,* 113–144.

Odell, T. (1993). Disability and relationships. *Canadian Woman Studies, 13*(4), 56–58.

Odette, F. (1994). *Staying healthy in the nineties: Women with disabilities talk about health care.* DisAbled Women's Network (DAWN) Toronto.

Oliver, M. (1990). *The politics of disablement.* Basingstoke: Macmillan.

Oliver, M. (1992). Changing the social relations of research production. *Disability, Handicap and Society, 17*(2), 101–115.

Oliver, M. (1996). A sociology of disability or a disabled sociology? In L. Barton (ed.), *Disability & society: Emerging issues and insights* (pp. 18–42). London: Longman.

Oliver, M. & Barnes, C. (1998). *Disabled people and social policy: From exclusion to inclusion.* Edinburgh: Longman.

Olkin, R. (1999). *What therapists should know about disability.* New York: The Guilford Press.

Olkin, R. & Pledger, C. (2003). Can disability studies and psychology join hands? *American Psychologist, 58*(4), 296–304.

Olsen, R. (1996). Young carers: Challenging the facts and politics of research into children and caring. *Disability & Society, 11*(1), 41–54.

Olsen, R. & Parker, G. (1997). A response to Aldridge and Becker – "Disability rights and the denial of young carers: The dangers of zero-sum arguments". *Critical Social Policy, 50*(17), 125–133.

Olson, R. (1978). *Ethics.* New York: Random House.

Ornish, D. (1997). *Love and survival.* New York: Perennial.

O'Toole, C. (2002). Sex, disability and motherhood: Access to sexuality for disabled mothers. *Disability Studies Quarterly, 22*(4), 81–101.

Parens, E. & Asch, A. (2000). The disability rights critique of prenatal testing: Reflections and recommendations. In E. Parens & A. Asch (eds), *Prenatal testing and disability rights* (pp. 3–43). Washington, D.C.: Georgetown University Press.

Park, K. (2002). Stigma management among the voluntarily childless. *Sociological perspectives, 45*(1), 21–45.

Parker, G. (1993). Disability, caring and marriage: The experience of younger couples when a partner is disabled after marriage. *British Journal of Social Work, 23,* 565–580.

Peshkin, A. (1992). The goodness of qualitative research. *Educational Researcher, 22*(2), 24–30.

Peters, L. C. & Esses, L. M. (1985). Family environment as perceived by children with a chronically ill parent. *Journal of Chronic Diseases, 38*(4), 301–308.

Peters, S. (1996). The politics of disability identity. In L. Barton (ed.) Disability and society: Emerging issues and insights. Harlow: Longman.

Philip, M. (1996, May 11). Disabled taking on motherhood. *The Globe and Mail*, p. A12.

Phoenix, A. (1994). Practicing feminist research: The intersection of gender and race in the research process. In M. Maynard & J. Purvis (eds), *Researching women's lives from a feminist perspective* (pp. 49–71). London, UK: Taylor & Francis.

Pinder, R. (1997). A reply to Tom Shakespeare and Nicholas Watson, In L. Barton and M. Olver (eds), *Disability studies: Past present and future*. Leeds: The Disability Press.

Pledger, C. (2003). Discourse on disability and rehabilitation issues: Opportunities for psychology. *American Psychologist, 58*(4), 279–284.

Polkinghorne, D. E. (1989). Phenomenological research methods. In R. S. Valle & S. Halling (eds), *Existential-phenomenological perspectives in psychology: Exploring the breadth of human experience* (pp. 41–60). New York: Plenum Press.

Power, P. W. (1985). Family coping behaviors in chronic illness: A rehabilitation perspective. *Rehabilitation Literature, 46*(3–4), 78–82.

Prilleltensky, I. (1994). *The morals and politics of psychology: Psychological discourse and the status quo*. Albany, NY: State University of New York Press.

Prilleltensky, I. (1996). Human, moral and political values for an emancipatory psychology. *The Humanistic Psychologist, 24*, 307–324.

Prilleltensky, I. & Nelson, G. (1997). Community psychology: Reclaiming social justice. In D. Fox & I. Prilleltensky (eds), *Critical psychology: An introduction* (pp. 166–184). London: Sage.

Prilleltensky, I. & Nelson, G. (2002). *Doing psychology critically: Making a difference in diverse settings*. New York: Palgrave Macmillan.

Prilleltensky, I., Nelson, G. & Peirson, L. (eds) (2001). *Promoting family wellness and preventing child maltreatment: Fundamentals for thinking and action*. Toronto: University of Toronto Press.

Prilleltensky, O. (1995). Women with disabilities and mothering: A research project. In C. Collins, P. Israel & F. Odette (eds), *Women with disabilities and mothering: Sharing our stories, exploring our options*. Toronto: DAWN Ontario.

Prilleltensky, O. (2003). A ramp to motherhood: The experiences of mothers with physical disabilities. *Sexuality and Disability, 21*(1), 21–47.

Prilleltensky, O. (2004a). Abeism: A disability rights perspective. In G. Nelson & I. Prilleltensky (eds), *Community psychology: In pursuit of liberation and well-being*. New York: Palgrave Macmillan.

Prilleltensky, O. (2004b). My child is not my carer: Mothers with physical disabilities and the well-being of children. *Disability and Society, 19*(3).

Prilleltensky, O. & Odette, F. (1996). *Women with disabilities and motherhood: Researching in collaboration*. Paper presented at the meeting of the American Psychological Association, Toronto, ON.

Putnam, R. (2000). *Bowling alone: The decline and revival of American community*. New York: Simon & Schuster.

Reason, P. & Bradbury, H. (eds) (2001). *Handbook of action research: Participative inquiry and practice*. London: Sage.

Reid, D., Angus, J., McKeever, P. & Miller, K-L (2003). Home is where their wheels are: Experiences of women wheelchair users. *American Journal of Occupational Therapy, 57*, 186–195.

Reinelt, C. & Fried, M. (1993). "I am this child's mother": A feminist perspective on mothering with a disability. In M. Nagler (ed.), *Perspectives on disability* (2nd ed.) (pp. 195–202). Palo alto, CA: Health Markets Research.

Reinharz, S. (1992). *Feminist methods in social research*. Oxford: Oxford University Press.

Rich, A. (1976). *Of woman born: Motherhood as experience and institution*. New York: Norton & Company.

Riddell, S. (1989). Exploiting the exploited: The ethics of feminist educational research. In R. Burgess (ed.), *The ethics of educational research* (pp. 77–98). East Sussex, UK: Falmer Press.

Ridington, J. (1989). *The only parent in the neighbourhood: Mothering and women with disabilities* (Position paper No. 3). Disabled Women's Network Canada.

Rioux, M. (1996) Reproductive technology: A rights issue. *Entourage, 9*(2), 5–7.

Rogers, J. (1996). Pregnancy and physical disability. In D. M. Krotoski, M. A. Nosek & M. A. Turk (eds), *Women with physical disabilities: Achieving and maintaining health and well-being* (pp. 101–108). Baltimore: Paul H. Brooks Publishing Co.

Rogers, J. & Matsumura, M. (1990). *Mother to be: A guide to pregnancy and birth for women with disabilities*. New York: Demos.

Rousso, H. (1988). Daughters with disabilities: Defective women or minority women? In M. Fine & A. Asch (eds), *Women with disabilities: Essays in psychology, culture, and politics* (pp. 139–171). Philadelphia: Temple University Press.

Rousso, H. (1996). Sexuality and a positive sense of self. In D. M. Krotoski, M. A. Nosek & M. A. Turk (eds), *Women with physical disabilities: Achieving and maintaining health and well-being* (pp. 109–116). Baltimore: Paul H. Brooks Publishing.

Rousso, H. & Wehmeyer, M. (2001) (eds), *Double jeopardy: Addressing gender equity in special education*. Albany: State University of New York.

Rutter, M. (1987). Psychosocial resilience and protective mechanisms. *American Journal of Orthopsychiatry, 57*, 316–331.

Rutter, M. (1994). Stress research: Accomplishments and tasks ahead. In R. J. Haggerty, L. R. Sherrod, N. Garmezy & M. Rutter (eds), *Stress, risk, and resilience in children and adolescents* (pp. 354–385). New York: Cambridge University Press.

Sandelowski, M. J. (1990). Failures of volition: Female agency and infertility in historical perspective. In J. F. O'Barr, D. Pope & M. Wyer (eds), *Ties that bind: Essays on mothering and patriarchy* (pp. 35–59). Chicago: University of Chicago Press.

Saxton, M. (1994). Preface to the special issue on women with disabilities: Reproduction and motherhood. *Sexuality and Disability, 12*(2), 111–115.

Saxton, M. (1996). Teaching providers to become our allies. In D. M. Krotoski, M. A. Nosek & M. A. Turk (eds), *Women with physical disabilities: Achieving and maintaining health and well-being* (pp. 175–178). Toronto, ON: Brooks.

Saxton, M. (2000). Why members of the disability community oppose prenatal diagnosis and selective abortion. In E. Parens & A. Asch (eds), *Prenatal testing and disability rights* (pp. 147–164). Washington, D.C.: Georgetown University Press.

Seidman, I. E. (1991). *Interviewing as qualitative research*. New York: Teachers College Press.

Seligman, M. E. P. (2002). *Authentic happiness*. New York: The Free Press.

Serrano-Garcia, I. & Bond, M. A. (1994). Empowering the silent ranks: Introduction. *American Journal of Community Psychology, 22*, 433–446.

Shakespeare, T. (1994). Cultural representations of disabled people: Dustbins for disavowal. *Disability and society, 9*(3), 283–301.

Shakespeare, T. (1996). Power and prejudice: Issues of gender, sexuality, and disability. In L. Barton (ed.), *Disability and society: Emerging issues and insights* (pp. 191–214). Harlow: Longman.

Shinn, M. & Toohey, S. (2003). Community contexts of human welfare. *Annual Review of Psychology, 54,* 427–459.

Sidall, R. (1994). Lost Childhood. *Community Care,* 9–15 June, 14–15.

Silvers, A. (1998). *Disability, difference, discrimination: Perspectives on justice in bioethics and public policy.* Lanham, MD: Roman & Littlefield Publishers.

Sipski, M. & Alexander, C. (eds) (1997). *Sexual function in people with disability and chronic illness: A health professional's guide.* Gaithersburg, MD: Aspen Publishers.

Smith, J. (1983, March). Quantitative versus qualitative research: An attempt to clarify the issues. *Educational Researcher,* 6–13.

Smith, L. T. (1999). *Decolonizing methodologies: Research and indigenous peoples.* London: Zed Books and Dunedin: University of Otago Press.

Snitow, A. (1992). Feminism and motherhood: An American reading. *Feminist Review, 40* (Spring), 32–51.

Stammer, H., Wischmann, T. & Verres, V. (2002). Counseling and couple therapy for infertile couples. *Family Process, 41*(1), 111–121.

Steinbock, B. (2000). Disability, prenatal testing, and selective abortion. In E. Parens & A. Asch (eds), *Prenatal testing and disability rights* (pp. 108–123). Washington, D.C.: Georgetown University Press.

Stewart, C. (1996). Looking for perfection. *Entourage, 9*(2), p. 8.

Surrey, J. (1991). The self-in-relation: A theory of women's development. In J. V. Jordan, A. G. Kaplan, J. B. Miller, I. P. Steiner & J. L. Surrey (eds), *Women's growth in connection: Writings from the Stone Center* (pp. 51–66). New York: Guilford.

Tate, D. & Pledger, C. (2003). An integrative conceptual framework of disability: New directions for research. *American Psychologist, 58*(4), 289–295.

Thomas, C. (1997). The baby and the bath water: Disabled women and motherhood in social context. *Sociology of Health & Illness, 19*(5), 622–643.

Thomas, C. (1999). *Female forms: Experiencing and understanding disability.* Buckingham: Open University Press.

Thomson, R. (1997a). Feminist theory, the body, and the disabled figure. In L. Davis (ed.), *The disability studies reader* (pp. 279–292). New York: Routledge.

Thomson, R. (1997b). *Extraordinary bodies: Figuring physical disabilities in American culture and literature.* New York: Columbia University Press.

Thorne, S. E. (1991). Mothers with chronic illness: A predicament of social construction. *Health Care for Women International, 11,* 209–221.

Toms Barker, L. & Maralani, V. (1997). *Challenges and strategies of disabled parents: Findings from a national survey of parents with disabilities.* Oakland, CA: Berkely Planning Associates.

VanManen, M. (1990). *Researching lived experience: Human science for an action sensitive pedagogy.* NY/ONT: State University of New York/Althouse Press.

Wasserman, D. & Mahowald, M. (1998). *Disability, difference, discrimination.* Boston: Rowman & Littlefield Publishers.

Wates, M. (1997). *Disabled parents: Dispelling the myths.* Cambridge: National Childbirth Trust Publishing.

Wates, M. & Jade, R. (eds) 1999. *Bigger than the sky: Disabled women on parenting*. London: Women's Press.

Waxman, B. (1993). The politics of eugenics: The testimony of Barbara Faye Waxman. *The Disability Rag: Resource on parenting with a disability*, May/June, pp. 6–7.

Waxman, B. F. (1994). Up against eugenics: Disabled women's challenge to receive reproductive health services. *Sexuality and Disability*, 12(2), 155–171.

Waxman, B. F. (1996). Commentary on sexuality and reproductive health. In D. M. Krotoski, M. A. Nosek & M. A. Turk (eds), *Women with physical disabilities: Achieving and maintaining health and well-being* (pp. 179–187). Baltimore: Paul H. Brooks Publishing.

Wendell, S. (1996). *The rejected body: Feminist philosophical reflections on disability*. London: Routledge.

Wertz, D. (2000). Drawing lines: Notes for policymakers. In E. Parens & A. Asch (eds), *Prenatal testing and disability rights* (pp. 261–287). Washington, D.C.: Georgetown University Press.

Whipple, B., Richards, E., Tepper, M. & Komisaruk, B. (1996). Sexual response in women with complete spinal cord injury. In D. M. Krotoski, M. A. Nosek & M. A. Turk (eds), *Women with physical disabilities: Achieving and maintaining health and well-being* (pp. 69–80). Baltimore: Paul H. Brooks Publishing Co.

White, G. W. & White, N. L. (1993). The adoptive process: Challenges and opportunities for people with disabilities. *Sexuality and Disability*, 11(3), 211–219.

WHO (1980). *International classification of impairments, disabilities and handicaps*. Geneva: World Health Organization.

World Health Organization (1986). Ottawa charter for health promotion. *Canadian Journal of Public Health, 77*(6).

Widdershoven, G. A. M. (1993). The story of life: Hermeneutic perspectives on the relationship between narrative and life history. *The Narrative Study of Lives, 1*, 1–20.

Wikler, D. (1999). Can we learn from eugenics? *Journal of Medical Ethics, 25*(2), 183–194.

Willig, C. (2001). *Introducing qualitative research in psychology: Adventures in theory and method*. Buckingham, UK: Open University Press.

Willig Levy, C. (1999). Tehilah: Our answered prayer. In M. Wates & R. Jade (eds), *Bigger than the sky: Disabled women on parenting* (pp. 82–88). London: The Women's Press.

Woodill, G. (1992). *Independent living and participation in research: A critical analysis* (Discussion paper). Toronto, ON: Centre for Independent Living of Toronto (CILT).

www.disabledparents.net

Young Carers Research Project (2002). Final Report: A Carers Australia Project (www.carers.asn.au).

Yow, V. R. (1994). *Recording oral history: A practical guide for social scientists*. Thousand Oaks, CA: Sage.

Zarb, G. (1992). On the road to Damascus: First steps towards changing the relations of disability research production. *Disability, Handicap and Society, 7*(2), 125–138.

Zimmerman, M. A. & Perkins, D. D. (1995). Empowerment theory, research, and application [Special issue]. *American Journal of Community Psychology, 23*(5).

Index